Developmental Cognitive Behavioral Therapy with Adults

Developmental Cognitive Behavioral Therapy with Adults

Janet M. Zarb

Routledge
Taylor & Francis Group
New York   London

Routledge
Taylor & Francis Group
270 Madison Avenue
New York, NY 10016

Routledge
Taylor & Francis Group
2 Park Square
Milton Park, Abingdon
Oxon OX14 4RN

© 2007 by Taylor & Francis Group, LLC
Routledge is an imprint of Taylor & Francis Group, an Informa business

Printed in the United States of America on acid-free paper
10 9 8 7 6 5 4 3 2 1

International Standard Book Number-10: 0-415-95600-5 (Softcover)
International Standard Book Number-13: 978-0-415-95600-0 (Softcover)

Library of Congress Cataloging-in-Publication Data

Zarb, Janet M.
    Developmental cognitive behavioral therapy with adults / Janet Zarb.
        p. ; cm.
    ISBN-13: 978-0-415-95600-0 (pb : alk. paper)
    ISBN-10: 0-415-95600-5 (pb : alk. paper)
    1. Cognitive therapy. 2. Developmental disabilities. 3. Developmental psychology.
I. Title.
    [DNLM: 1. Cognitive Therapy--methods. 2. Adult--psychology. 3. Human
Development. 4. Psychopathology. WM 425.5.C6 Z36d 2007]

    RC489.C63Z37 2007
    616.89'14--dc22
                                          2006038314

Visit the Taylor & Francis Web site at
http://www.taylorandfrancis.com

and the Routledge Web site at
http://www.routledge-ny.com

DEDICATION

To George

CONTENTS

1

INTRODUCING THE DEVELOPMENTAL
COGNITIVE BEHAVIORAL THERAPY APPROACH

The aim of this book is to introduce a new psychotherapy approach that combines conventional cognitive therapy with a lifespan developmental psychopathology perspective. The major focus will be on treatment of adult role difficulties contributing to mental health problems. This approach examines the relationship between depression, anxiety, personality disorders, and other psychological problems and the client's difficulties in performing expected adult roles and tasks. It adopts a developmental psychopathology framework that considers behavioral and emotional problems in relation to normative sequences and achievements for particular ages and stages across the life cycle. This new approach will be referred to as *Developmental Cognitive Behavorial Therapy,* or *Developmental* CBT.

The initial phase of Developmental CBT adopts the most studied and commonly used CBT model developed by Aaron Beck and his colleagues and expanded by other therapists over the past forty years (e.g., Beck, 1976; Beck & Emery, 1985; Beck & Freeman, 1990; Beck et al., 1979; Beck, J., 1995; Meichenbaum, 1994; Padesky, 1994; Young, Beck, & Weinberger, 1993). This model is also frequently referred to as cognitive therapy (CT). The primary difference between the new Developmental CBT approach espoused in this book and traditional CBT approaches is the addition of a *developmental phase* of assessment and treatment that focuses on the client's inadequate resolution of normative psychosocial developmental tasks and transitions of earlier life stages. This approach evolved from a common observation by the author and other clinicians that a substantial proportion of people seeking therapy are experienc-

1

ing problems with adult life tasks and roles, such as leaving the parental home, coping with social or family relationships, or maintaining effective occupational status (Ruble & Seedman, 1996). Many psychotherapy clients are stuck at life transitions and have failed to resolve critical life-stage tasks in the past in occupational, interpersonal, partner, or family functioning areas.

In an attempt to address the client presenting problems and comorbid Axis I and II disorders, therapists may lose sight of the larger picture, namely the client's failure to resolve normative life tasks that may be maintaining the psychological disorders. For example, clients presenting with depression secondary to unemployment may have failed to develop sufficient self discipline in the early years for adequate job performance as adults. Similarly, they may have failed to attain educational prerequisites for a desired occupation or failed to develop sufficient independence from family of origin to establish a separate residence and viable career path.

THE EVOLUTION OF THE DEVELOPMENTAL CBT APPROACH

The integrated Developmental CBT approach outlined in this book evolved from years of clinical experience with both adolescent and adult clients manifesting developmental task difficulties at different age periods across the life span. It became clear that in addition to Axis I and II disorders and debilitating environmental stressors, many clients were also unable to perform what would be considered to be routine psychosocial tasks of various life stages, such as forming and maintaining satisfying interpersonal relationships with friends and colleagues or with intimate partners, leaving the parents' home and establishing an independent health-enhancing routine and career, or providing effective parenting. These developmental task difficulties often affect other areas of functioning as well, so that social, family, and work experiences may all be diminished in some cases. This fundamental observation suggested a need for developing new strategies specifically designed to address adult developmental task and role blocks. In this book, *psychosocial Developmental Task Difficulty* will be used to denote diminished psychological ability to negotiate normative life tasks, with roots dating back several years. These difficulties may also be referred to as developmental task blocks.

CHARACTERISTIC ROLE DIFFICULTIES OF
EARLY, MIDDLE, AND LATE ADULTHOOD

Particular role difficulties are characteristic of different life stages. During the early-adulthood years, clients tend to present with difficulties forming intimate partner relationships, difficulties initiating viable occupational paths, or difficulties leaving parents and establishing an independent adult life structure. There may be reluctance to make major commitments in areas of intimate partner relationships or occupational paths. Later on, during middle adulthood, clients may present with problems *maintaining* satisfying partner relationships or steady employment or problems functioning as effective parents. Some clients are unable to negotiate crucial life-course transitions such as terminating a destructive partner relationship or restructuring an unsuccessful initial career choice in order to pursue an alternative career with potential for sufficient economic remuneration or career satisfaction. Worries about being surpassed by younger colleagues may also surface at this stage. Mature adult clients may present with problems coming to terms with unfulfilled youthful occupational or relationship aspirations, so that they are unable to restructure goals and move on. A common complaint is that of being too old to rectify unfulfilled goals. Failure to resolve normative challenges not only increases a client's vulnerability to depression, anger, and anxiety disorders, but also decreases the person's ability to cope with unexpected stressful and tragic life events.

The Developmental CBT approach presented in this book combines standard cognitive-behavioral therapy techniques with new developmental assessment and therapy strategies and techniques that have been created and field tested by the author over several years for clients with a variety of developmental task difficulties. These new strategies, to be introduced in the next two chapters, have been designed to help clients identify psychosocial developmental blocks and to master steps necessary to resolve normative life-course transitions and roles to the extent that daily functioning and mental health begins to improve. The most challenging clients are those with coexisting personality disorders that render them highly resistant to altering their self-defeating developmental patterns. Often these dysfunctional patterns have helped them to cope with stressful situations and developmental challenges during childhood, adolescence, or earlier adult periods, but are no longer working for them and are delaying normal transitions.

LIFE SPAN DEVELOPMENTAL PERSPECTIVES ON NORMAL AND ABNORMAL PSYCHOSOCIAL DEVELOPMENT

A major concept of life span developmental perspectives is the notion of a life cycle composed of loosely defined developmental stages or phases. Life is a series of growth stages that the individual and family must successfully negotiate to avoid stagnation and chronic crisis. The concept of life stages provides a useful framework for identifying normative developmental tasks related to biological forces and to age-related social and cultural expectations that lead to changing roles. An underlying assumption is that an individual must master certain tasks at each developmental stage before successfully moving on to the next stage. Those who meet developmental challenges at a particular stage have developed skills that make them better equipped to meet successive new developmental challenges of later stages. Mastery of normative developmental tasks also increases the person's likelihood of successfully coping with nonnormative events or crises that may occur at any time in one's external environment, such as the death of a family member.

Social scientists in past decades have generally supported the notion of age-linked developmental periods for the *preadult years*. Children are viewed as going through an underlying sequence of common developmental periods of infancy, early childhood, middle childhood, pubescence, and adolescence, and psychologists have identified critical developmental tasks that must be mastered for a successful transition to adulthood (e.g., Conger, 1977). In recent decades developmental theorists have raised the possibility of identifying and documenting sequences of developmental periods and tasks of *adult years*, similar to those of childhood and adolescence. In spite of the common underlying sequence of developmental tasks, the diversity of different biological, psychological, and social conditions for each individual results in the uniqueness of each child. Child and adult developmental task literature influencing new developmental assessment instruments to be introduced in Chapter 2 includes the following: Bowlby, 1988; Carter & McGoldrick, 1989; Cohler & Boxer, 1991; Conger, 1977; Erikson, 1982; Featherman et al., 1994; Guidano, 1987; Havinghurst, 1972; Levinson, 1978, 1996; Okun, 1984; Vandenbos, 1998.

A life span developmental psychology perspective adopts the notion of normative developmental challenges or crises frequently occurring at transition periods between life stages, accompanied by increased vulnerability to stress. A *temporary* developmental crisis is considered within normal limits, and for most people it provides an opportunity for positive growth as the person resolves the crisis and moves on.

However, transitional challenges may prove to be ongoing unresolved crises, spanning months or even years, depending on the individual's coping style and external stress factors. Often basic skills for resolution of the normal developmental challenges are poorly developed.

A useful distinction has been made between developmental and nondevelopmental crises. *Developmental challenges or crises* are shaped by biological forces and age-related social and cultural expectations. They occur in response to the individual's attempts to cope with predictable, age-related challenges faced by most people, usually in relation to family, peer, and educational or occupational roles. Developmental challenges and crises emanate from tasks within the context of normal development and are frequently accompanied by symptoms of psychological distress. Mental health professionals may differ in their views of what constitutes a normal developmental challenge. For example, in light of the relatively high frequency of job loss and divorce in the present day, some may view these events as common developmental crises.

Nondevelopmental challenges or crises, such as accidents, physical problems, or abusive situations, occur in response to atypical, unpredictable challenges or external events that have no direct connection to age-linked periods. They are sometimes referred to as *situational crises*. Developmental and nondevelopmental crises may occur simultaneously, and sometimes a nondevelopmental crisis precipitates a developmental crisis. It is expected that situational crises will have the greatest negative and long-term impact when they interfere with resolution of major adult tasks and roles such as completing one's education, entering the work force, or forming a stable long-term partner relationship (Cohler, 1991).

A *transitional crisis* is a novel situation with new role demands. Therapy clients frequently experience difficulty meeting task demands because habitual problem-solving strategies and coping skills no longer work. From a cognitive-therapy perspective, the client may be having difficulty mastering the prerequisite cognitive interpretation and behavioral coping skills for successful task resolution and is therefore unable to come to a decision as to what to do. An important consideration is the degree to which the client had been able to successfully resolve similar normative transitions and novel role demands in the past.

Difficulties with normative developmental tasks and roles increase a person's vulnerability to external stressors and comorbid Axis I and II disorders. Mental health is seen in the context of the client's whole life cycle and the ability to successfully perform culturally expected roles, to resolve expected transitional crises, and to cope with disruptive adverse external life events and get back to adaptive daily functioning.

Healthy psychological development assumes client achievement of normative sequences and milestones for particular ages and stages (Cohler & Boxer, 1991).

Although authors vary somewhat in their designation of primary developmental tasks that children and adolescents must negotiate in order to develop in a healthy manner, most concur with the following five developmental tasks summarized by Young (1990): (1) *autonomy*, or the sense that one can function independently in the world; (2) *connectedness*, or the sense that one is connected to other people in a stable, enduring, trusting manner; (3) *worthiness*, or the sense that one is loveable, competent, acceptable, and desirable to others; (4) *reasonable expectations*, or the capacity to set realistic, achievable standards for oneself and others; and (5) *reasonable limits*, or the capacity to discipline oneself and to appropriately take the needs of others into account. Similarly, Levinson (1978) concludes on the basis of his adult life span research that psychological development in early adulthood may be considered healthy if the person has aspirations and establishes goals; forms satisfying relationships, makes commitments to persons and enterprises in family, work, and social spheres; strives with some enthusiasm and self-discipline toward attaining occupational goals; and develops competence in various adult social roles.

Mental health is also dependent on the individual's own perception of himself or herself as functioning normally. There is general agreement among people within particular age and cultural cohorts on the proper timetable for specific role transitions, such as leaving school, marriage, birth of first child, and securing a first entry-level job. People tend to use this timetable as a yardstick for evaluating their own lives and their own progress. Therefore, transitions may have a negative impact when they are developmentally off-time, off-sequence, or delayed.

CONCEPTS OF DEVELOPMENTAL PSYCHOPATHOLOGY: PSYCHOPATHOLOGY AS DEVELOPMENTAL DEVIATION

The term *developmental psychopathology* has been used to refer to a general approach to understanding relations between human development and its maladaptive deviations (Auchenbach, 1990; Cicchetti, 1990; Ciccetti & Cohen, 1995; Rutter & Stroufe, 2000). In recent decades, the emergence of developmental psychopathology has involved an integration of various disciplines. Normative changes that occur across the life cycle are taken into consideration, and behavioral and emotional problems are considered in terms of their relationship to normative sequences and achievements for particular ages and stages. A developmental psychopathology perspective does not prescribe particular theoretical explanations for psychological disorders but instead, provides a framework for organizing the study of psychopathology around milestones and sequences in physical, cognitive, social–emotional, and educational–vocational development. Consequently it is important to distinguish those developmental variations that are considered to be within normal limits from those that are more ominous, either because they disrupt development or because they reflect a pathological process that predicts a negative future prognosis for mental health.

If psychopathology is viewed as a distortion, disturbance, or degeneration of normal functioning, it follows that therapists who wish to understand pathology more fully must first understand the normal functioning against which psychopathology is compared (Cicchetti, 1984). To distinguish what is normal from what is potentially pathological at each stage, clinicians first need to be familiar with normative psychosocial developmental tasks for different adult periods. The academic basis of a developmental psychopathology perspective is longitudinal research on continuities and discontinuities of problems across developmental periods and identification of syndrome patterns requiring special help at each stage. Important contributions to the developmental psychopathology literature include studies of the relationship between early negative family, peer, and school experiences and subsequent adult task difficulties and mental health problems (e.g., Bagwell et al., 1998; Baldry & Farrington, 2000; Bedrosian & Bozicas, 1994; Deater-Deckard, 2001; Perris et al., 1994; Young, Klosko, & Weisharr, 2003). Developmental psychopathology focuses on specific skill deficits that function as mediators or links to areas of dysfunction. For example, mediators for inadequate peer relationships may be poorly developed social cognition skills or emotional regulation skills (Deater-Deckard, 2001). It is therefore up to therapists to devise ways to help clients address these mediators or skill deficits.

Investigations focusing on the negative impact of early dysfunctional parenting influences on adult psychopathology are particularly relevant to Developmental CBT (e.g., Bedrosian & Bozicas, 1994; Perris et al., 1994; Skinner & Wellborn, 1994; Young, 1990). For example, an underlying assumption of Skinner and Wellborn's theory of coping across the life span is that all people have basic needs for relatedness to others, for competence, and for autonomy or self-determination. On the basis of this assumption, it is possible to derive dimensions of universal stress, namely, events that threaten or damage these three basic psychological needs. Three universal stressors posited are *neglect*, because it threatens relatedness, *chaos*, because it undermines competence, and *coercion*, because it impinges on autonomy. *Coping* involves a person's endeavor to maintain, restore, replenish, and repair the fulfillment of basic psychological needs in the face of assaults on these needs. Close relationships are seen as critical to whether children develop the psychological resources needed to buffer threats to relatedness, competence, and autonomy. The way in which a child copes predicts whether he or she will engage or withdraw from future encounters with challenging situations (Skinner & Wellborn, 1994).

NEGATIVE EARLY INFLUENCES JEOPARDIZING NORMATIVE TASK RESOLUTION

It should not be surprising that many predictors of mental health problems are also predictors of adult developmental task difficulties. Early negative family, peer, and school influences have the potential to jeopardize adult resolution of normative developmental tasks. Children who grow up without sufficient support and encouragement provided by their home base are more likely to find intimate relationships difficult, to be vulnerable in conditions of adversity, and to have difficulties when it comes time to marry and have children of their own (e.g., Bowlby, 1988). Negative family influences may involve inadequate parental models, absence or loss of a parent through death or divorce, or dysfunctional childrearing methods. In addition to family dysfunction, negative peer and school experiences also increase the risk of subsequent role difficulties and related emotional disorders. Inadequate resolution of normative tasks from an early age may result from imitating dysfunctional parental models or from early traumatic loss or ongoing criticism received from peers or teachers (Peterson & Seligman, 1984).

Parenting styles, parental models, and habitual parent–child interaction patterns can significantly affect the child's potential for mastering effective life span coping skills. Long-term negative effects of early parenting and family dysfunction have been documented in the literature (e.g., Alymer, 1989; Bedrosian & Bozicas, 1994; Bowlby, 1973, 1988; Brewin et al., 1993; McClelland & Franz, 1992; Missildine, 1963; Perris et al., 1994; Rutter, 1985). Dysfunctional expectations, attitudes, and concepts about self and others and maladaptive relationships learned in the family of origin may exert powerful effects on an individual's coping styles in subsequent tasks involving intimate and social relationships and parenting styles with one's own children. This area of research has directly influenced the design of many of the new Developmental CBT assessment and therapy strategies.

DEVELOPMENTAL PATHWAYS,
COMPETENCE, AND RESILIENCE

The concept of developmental pathways to competence is also compatible with a Developmental CBT approach. This concept was adopted by Bowlby and others (Bowlby, 1973; Fischer et al., 1997). Pathology is viewed in terms of developmental deviation and therefore requires an understanding of normative development issues such as secure attachment, modulated impulse control, and effective entry into a peer group. Significant deviations in patterns of adaptation represent an increased probability of problems in negotiating subsequent developmental issues. Pathology involves a succession of deviations away from normative patterns. Change is possible at many points, and despite early deviation, changes in life circumstances or therapy interventions may lead the individual back toward a more serviceable pathway. However, change is constrained by prior adaptation, so that the longer a maladaptive pathway has been followed, the less likely it is that the person will reclaim positive adaptation (Bowlby, 1973).

The concept of *competence* encompasses a family of constructs related to the effectiveness of individual adaptation in the environment (Masten & Coatsworth, 1995). Life span developmental psychologists are interested in studying pathways to competence as well as pathways to deviance. Knowledge of these pathways contributes to theories of etiology, prevention, and treatment of psychopathology (Cicchetti, 1984, 1990; Sroufe, 1989). Definitions of mental disorders include the notion of impairment in adaptive functioning in some form. People diagnosed with mental disorders typically develop along distinctive pathways in which they build complex advanced skills. These pathways are often based on adaptation to trauma, such as maltreatment during early years, and do not fit normative developmental frameworks. Developmental psychopathology is concerned with processes by which patterns of dysfunction arise and may be prevented or ameliorated.

The construct of competence fostered the emergence of the study of *resilience* as a domain of inquiry in recent decades. *Resilience* refers to the emergence of good adaptation in the context of high risk or exposure to significant threats to development. Resilient children facing adversity do well, nonetheless, or they return to positive functioning following a short period of dysfunction (e.g., Masten & Coatsworth, 1995). Psychopathology is seen as an outcome of bio-psychosocial development, evolving through the successive adaptations of individuals in their environment. Key research initiatives within this framework center on the discovery of factors that place individuals on pathways probabilistically leading to later disturbances and factors and processes that deflect them from such pathways (Sroufe, 1997). Investigators are interested in identifying the processes by which effective adaptation in the environment develops among children from disadvantaged or threatening situations. The goal is to use this information to prevent or treat psychopathology and to foster competence in development (Fisher et al., 1997; Masten & Coatsworth, 1995).

Within a developmental psychopathology perspective, there is an interest in recognizing patterns of dysfunction that, while not properly considered disorders themselves, may be considered precursors of disorders. There is also an interest in conditions of risk that lie outside of the individual, in addition to the endogenous influences. Likewise, there is an ongoing interest in factors and processes that lead individuals away from disorder—a focus that goes beyond interest in management of symptoms.

The discussion so far has highlighted influences on Developmental CBT from the expanding theoretical and empirical literature in the area of life span developmental psychology and in the area of developmental psychopathology. The Developmental CBT approach also builds on the work of major contributors to the field of Cognitive Behavioral Therapy, especially Aaron Beck and his colleagues, cited above, and other CBT practitioners who have emphasized the importance of a historical analysis of psychopathology (e.g., Guidano, 1987). This approach has also been influenced by the work of Jeffrey Young and his Schema-Focused Therapy (SFT) model specifically developed to address long-standing cognitive patterns called early Maladaptive Schemas (EMS) associated with various personality disorders (Young et al., 1993; Young & Gluhoski, 1996; Young & Klosko, 1994; Young, et al., 2003). Young's work is particularly relevant since many of the early Maladaptive Schemas he identifies have also been observed by the author to play a major part in shaping and maintaining adult developmental task difficulties.

OVERVIEW OF THE DEVELOPMENTAL CBT APPROACH

As discussed above, Developmental CBT incorporates a developmental psychopathology perspective focusing on links between psychological distress and the client's difficulties resolving past and present normative psychosocial tasks. The aim of this book is to demonstrate methods for addressing a variety of typical client psychosocial task difficulties in peer, partner, occupational, and family functioning. The focus on skill deficits interfering with resolution of normative psychosocial tasks has led to the development of specialized techniques for assessing and altering maladaptive patterns maintaining a client's task blocks. The goal is to help clients sufficiently resolve normative life tasks such as those listed in Table 1.1 and thereby help them meet age-related cultural expectations for performance of major adult roles.

Developmental CBT adopts the following overlapping stages, suggested by the adult life span developmental literature:

- Childhood and adolescence (approximately birth to 19 years)
- Early adulthood (approximately ages 20 to 30/35 years)
- Middle adulthood (approximately ages 30/35 to 50 years)
- Mature adulthood (approximately ages 50 to 60/65 years)
- Late adulthood (approximately 65 years and older)

The relationship between the above stages and chronological age is necessarily flexible, given the degree of individual variation in major pursuits at any given age. The late adulthood stage after age 65 is beyond the scope of this book and will be left to a future volume.

Although the focus in this book is on *adult* psychosocial developmental tasks, the continuity of development across the life span is emphasized, so it is important to assess the client's past performance in resolving psychosocial tasks of childhood and adolescence. During childhood and adolescence, the youngster must continually rework relationships with parents, siblings, and authority figures, especially in school and community settings. At the same time, he or she must negotiate the inevitable anxieties and frustrations inherent in achieving inclusion in peer groups. During these early stages, the youngster will need to achieve a sense of belonging, friendship, and trust with same-sex peers as well as peers of the opposite sex.

Table 1.1 Major Adult Psychosocial Tasks

1. Separating from family of origin and establishing a viable independent adult life structure
2. Completing one's education and establishing and maintaining a viable occupation or career
3. Developing and maintaining satisfying friendships and adequate interpersonal skills for effective functioning in one's social and occupational milieu
4. Forming a stable long-term partner relationship or building a satisfying single-adult life structure
5. Effective parenting: providing adequate personal and economic support and effective socialization for children
6. Maintaining adaptive family of origin relationships
7. Maintaining a health-enhancing daily routine and home environment
8. Pursuing satisfying recreational activities

THE DEVELOPMENTAL CBT PROCESS

There are two basic phases of Developmental CBT. The initial *acute phase* aims to alleviate debilitating symptoms of client presenting problems interfering with daily functioning, especially symptoms of comorbid Axis I disorders such as depression and anxiety. It incorporates standard CBT therapy concepts and interventions and is essentially comparable to traditional CBT.

Once there is sufficient reduction in the severity of acute presenting problems and the client is stabilized, this initial phase overlaps with a second *Developmental Phase* that aims to guide the client through successive steps toward successful negotiation of age-appropriate developmental tasks. Through this process, the therapist will take into account the client's past difficulties in resolving normative developmental tasks of childhood, adolescence, and earlier adult stages. (In addition, the client's presenting problems and other symptoms of psychological distress may be considered within the framework of the client's developmental task resolution history). The developmental phase utilizes new developmental assessment instruments as well as new developmental change strategies to supplement standard CBT techniques.

DEVELOPMENTAL ASSESSMENT INSTRUMENTS

In carrying out the assessment, therapists must have a good understanding of normal functioning against which psychopathology is compared and utilize this knowledge in devising therapy interventions. Several new Developmental CBT assessment strategies have been designed to help client and therapist identify past, current, and potential future blocks to resolution of normative adult tasks. Over the course of therapy, clinicians seek to discover links between developmental task blocks and current presenting problems. These new developmental assessment strategies will be introduced in Chapter 2.

The new assessment strategies have been designed to ensure a comprehensive and methodical investigation of both positive and negative effects of the client's family, peer, school, and occupational experiences during earlier developmental stages. Basically, the assessment instruments have been designed to shed light on early influences shaping development of maladaptive pathways, factors, and processes that maintain maladaptive pathways, as well as factors and processes that have the potential to deflect people from their maladaptive pathways and to get them started on a more functional pathway. The goal is to help the client identify precursors of current task blocks and contributing factors and influences in the client's family, peer, or school experiences.

Further analysis enables identification of specific cognitive, behavioral, and affective patterns associated with various developmental task difficulties, which may then be designated as targets for change. Clinically based tables of characteristic themes underlying various categories of task difficulties are presented in Chapters 4 through 6 as a useful reference for therapists and clients. This is supplemented by descriptions of typical behavior patterns and early influences associated with specific adult task and role difficulties.

DEVELOPMENTAL CHANGE STRATEGIES

After identifying long-standing barriers to resolution of normative psychosocial tasks, the therapist then begins to utilize the new Developmental CBT change strategies for altering maladaptive developmental pathways. These developmental change strategies to be introduced in Chapter 3 have been specifically designed to weaken long-standing impediments to resolution of normative life tasks, and to teach necessary skills that clients lack for performance of major adult roles of current and future developmental periods. This necessarily involves altering maladaptive core schemas and behavior patterns that maintain developmental task difficulties. The therapist will seek to build new functional task-enhancing patterns to fill gaps in essential life skills. The client will need these new skills not only to resolve blocked tasks from earlier periods, but also to negotiate current adult developmental tasks and transitions.

THE COURSE OF THERAPY

Acute problems will be identified and addressed during initial sessions to stabilize the client. Cognitive, behavioral, and developmental data will be collected for each of the client's identified presenting problems and comorbid Axis I and Axis II disorders. The initial sessions rely primarily on standard CBT strategies for relieving acute aspects of presenting problems and Axis I symptoms. Afterwards, the emphasis of the individual sessions will change over time from a focus on presenting problems and related comorbid Axis I and II symptoms, to an emphasis on weakening core schemas and behavior patterns associated with blocked psychosocial developmental tasks. Moving into the Developmental Phase, the therapist will become increasingly aware of the overall picture of the client's development from childhood to the present. In the process of treating symptoms of the client's presenting problems and maladaptive core beliefs, the therapist will begin to form hypotheses about past psychosocial developmental task delays or difficulties that have had negative residual effects on the client's current functioning. The client will be helped to understand that while initial CBT interventions may have provided temporary relief from acute presenting problems, unsuccessful resolution of major life tasks will need to be addressed for purposes of future relapse prevention.

Over the course of therapy, the target areas and goals identified by the client will remain a priority, but the therapist will also raise problematic developmental issues that the client may not have mentioned. For example, if a client's presenting problem is friction with a boss or colleagues at work, the first phase of Developmental CBT might concentrate on problem-solving strategies and anger-control techniques for ameliorating stressful situations at work to ensure job continuity.

Following this, the focus of therapy sessions would gradually shift to the client's difficulties in establishing or maintaining a viable career path over the years. Further analysis may reveal a pattern of conflict with authority figures in school and later in work settings, coupled with poor academic and occupational performance, frequent job loss, and chronic work-related depression. Many clients minimize or avoid addressing their confrontational interpersonal styles, preferring instead to focus on new crises that surface each week, especially if these crises confirm existing dysfunctional core beliefs such as blaming others or blaming "the system." If this pattern has enabled the client to avoid taking personal responsibility for problems of interpersonal conflict at work, initiatives will need to be taken by the therapist to raise the issue of the client's failure to acknowledge or address long-standing confrontational patterns. The client's concerns with immediate acute problems are balanced by therapist concerns about long-standing cognitive and behavioral patterns linked to poorly resolved adult tasks. Subsequently, therapists seek to expand therapy goals in order to address life span developmental blocks. Ideally, as clients experience relief from presenting symptoms and complaints during the initial sessions, they will be motivated to address underlying developmental issues.

Clients are familiarized with the Developmental CBT approach and guided in conceptualizing their own problems within a Developmental CBT perspective. They may then collaborate with the therapist in designating targets for change. Like other CBT approaches, the therapist assumes the role of diagnostician, educator, and technical consultant. Therapists guide clients in conceptualizing their difficulties within a normative task-block framework. After developmental task blocks are identified, labeled, and analyzed, client and therapist carry out a joint brainstorming exercise to come up with ways to alter self-defeating pathways. Relapse prevention is enhanced by giving clients increasing responsibility for designing their own treatment plans, with the therapist as consultant. For example, clients may be asked what advice they would give to a person experiencing a similar blocked task. Clients become "trainees" who will eventually become their own therapists.

As a general rule, the therapist builds on client strengths in resolving past and concurrent psychosocial tasks, and many of the new developmental strategies have been designed with this in mind. More specifically, therapists seek to identify those times when their clients managed to temporarily deviate from their dysfunctional pathways and embrace more normative functional pathways. Working from the premise that clients may be led back to more serviceable pathways and that positive change is possible at many points despite early deviation from normative pathways, clients are encouraged to reflect back and identify those times in their lives when they managed to temporarily get back on track. They are then encouraged to resurrect some of their former coping strengths. Every effort is made to avoid using terms and official DSM-IV diagnoses that clients would find upsetting or discouraging, and that would increase the likelihood of the client's self-perception as mentally ill or sick. Instead, clients are encouraged to conceptualize their predicament as *stuck* versus *sick*.

SPECIAL FEATURES OF THE DEVELOPMENTAL PHASE

The new developmental assessment instruments to be described in Chapter 2 are used to identify developmental problem areas and to select targets for developmental therapy intervention. Major targets for therapy will be maladaptive developmental variations that have significantly disrupted or decelerated the client's ability to cope with normative milestones. A good yardstick for determining whether a task block is severe enough to merit therapy intervention is the extent to which the developmental disruption seriously jeopardizes the client's mental health and potential for resolution of other concurrent or future normative psychosocial developmental tasks. For example, a negative prognosis for future mental health would be predicted by developmental disruptions that interfere with performance of major life tasks such as completing one's education, establishing or advancing in a career, forming a stable long-term partner relationship, or practicing effective parenting. Since successful resolution of developmental tasks at earlier stages will affect a client's potential for mastering similar developmental tasks at later stages, therapists will seek to determine whether similar maladaptive cognitive and behavioral styles associated with past developmental blocks are still features of the client's current functioning. In the process, therapist and client will identify and address early maladaptive family of origin, peer, and school patterns that persist and maintain current difficulties.

By identifying and analyzing the origins and early manifestations of their difficulties in resolving particular normative developmental tasks, clients are better able to gain new insights into the factors that have played a role in maintaining the task difficulty over the years. Healthy cognitive reframing and behavior change is particularly likely when clients gain insight into their own role in maintaining the task difficulty and their reasons for adopting self-defeating pathways as a means of survival during early years. Similarly, as clients begin to understand that present problems are basically current manifestations of long-standing task difficulties and self-defeating pathways, they will be more motivated to try new approaches. As in other cognitive therapy models, there is an endeavor to identify and alter schemas driving self-defeating patterns, but in this approach the self-defeating pattern is a maladaptive developmental pathway. The client is helped to build new adaptive cognitive and behavioral patterns that will facilitate successful resolution of the impeded life task. Standard CBT techniques are useful for reframing maladaptive cognitive components maintaining the task block, such as distorted beliefs, causal attributions, traumatic early recollections, negative life themes or damaging self-evaluations.

In the process of reconceptualizing presenting problems and other symptoms in terms of their role in blocking resolution of identified normative psychosocial tasks, clients realize that difficulties with role demands are a challenge faced by most people to some degree. They become more optimistic with the realization that with regular teaching and practice sessions, they have the potential to alter underdeveloped life skills that are undermining their performance of age-appropriate tasks. Clients develop a better sense of control over their current situation when they begin to view themselves as stuck rather than sick and when they begin to reconceptualize their current predicaments as precipitated by gaps in acquisition of normative task skills — a predicament that can be rectified with the help of the therapist. They begin to grasp the notion of resurrecting their former strengths and more successful coping styles that helped them resolve normative developmental challenges in the past in order to get back on track.

SCOPE AND OBJECTIVES OF BOOK

Until recently, developmental psychopathology had been largely concerned with basic theoretical and empirical issues, but in recent years there has been an extended focus on applied developmental psychopathology. This book is meant to be a contribution to this endeavor. Chapters 4 through 6 will demonstrate the application of the developmental psychopathology perspective and specific assessment and change strategies to maladaptive patterns impeding performance of adult roles in occupation, social, and family functioning.

The developmental task difficulties identified in this book are based on clinical observation rather than empirical studies or a priori theories and represent a variety of common client task and role difficulties. Developmental CBT is not an attempt to provide a competing cognitive therapy model. Instead, it builds on previous cognitive therapy models and techniques while providing further assessment and therapy strategies to neutralize patterns interfering with resolution of normative adult tasks and roles. It seeks to provide a comprehensive assessment and therapy approach that addresses reciprocal influences of (1) client presenting problems, (2) Axis I and II symptoms, (3) external situational factors, and (4) psychosocial developmental task difficulties. The spectrum of developmental task blocks addressed in this book does not presume to be exhaustive but is meant to be a representative sample of types of clients encountered in an outpatient clinic practice who would be most likely to benefit from this approach.

Distinguishing features of the Developmental CBT approach are summarized in Table 1.2.

Table 1.2 Features of Developmental CBT

Feature 1. Incorporation of life span developmental psychology perspective and concepts of normal adulthood development and developmental psychopathology

Normal adult development:

The notion of early, middle, and mature adult developmental periods with component normative tasks, challenges, and transitions, in addition to child and adolescent tasks

Developmental psychopathology concepts:

The notion of inadequate resolution of normative life tasks as a major contributor to mental health problems

The notion of cumulative effects of inadequate developmental task resolution over the life span

The notion of reciprocal interaction between developmental task difficulties, heightened vulnerability to Axis I and II disorders, and vulnerability to nondevelopmental life stressors and situational crises

The concept of developmental pathways to competence versus maladaptive pathways to psychosocial task difficulties maintaining unresolved adult roles

Feature 2. Special emphasis on identifying and addressing residual effects of early family, peer, and school predispositions to adult developmental task difficulties.

Feature 3. Introduction of new developmental assessment and therapy strategies to be used in addition to standard cognitive therapy interventions. These have been designed to provide a comprehensive approach that methodically assesses and addresses the client's developmental task resolution history in addition to Axis I and II disorders and negative effects of nondevelopmental situational factors.

Feature 4. A focus on typical themes and descriptions of clinically observed characteristic behavioral coping styles and underlying influences and developmental pathways associated with various categories of adult developmental task difficulties in occupational, peer, partner, and family functioning.

Feature 5. Evaluation of therapy effectiveness will be measured in terms of the client's progress toward altering long-standing maladaptive pathways and successful negotiation of age-appropriate developmental tasks.

2

DEVELOPMENTAL COGNITIVE BEHAVIORAL THERAPY ASSESSMENT STRATEGIES

This chapter will outline a comprehensive Developmental CBT assessment approach, with special emphasis on new developmental assessment strategies. These strategies have been designed to highlight client difficulties in coping with age-appropriate psychosocial developmental tasks in current and previous life stages and are to be used in addition to traditional CBT strategies tapping Axis I and II symptoms. More specifically, new developmental strategies have been designed to meet the need for a *methodical* approach to identification and analysis of (1) normative task difficulties, (2) longstanding deviant pathways shaping and maintaining these difficulties, (3) their early influences and precursors, and (4) specific cognitive and behavioral features of the task difficulties and deviant pathways.

The developmental assessment approach investigates long-standing coping styles in areas of family, peer, school, and occupational functioning. Early influences impeding the developmental process may be factors such as family violence or dysfunctional child-rearing styles; maladaptive client interaction patterns with parents, peers, or teachers, role models to whom the client was exposed, or external factors such as low economic status, poor social support, or life accidents. Developmental variations that seem to have significantly disrupted the client's ability to cope with normative milestones will be noted by the therapist from the start of the therapy endeavor as the client describes reasons for seeking therapy.

The client's difficulties with current normative tasks are considered in light of previous difficulties in acquiring basic skills for resolution of peer, school, and family tasks during childhood and adolescence. Effective adult psychosocial task resolution at any given time is viewed as a cumulative process, progressing from mastery of basic skills during childhood and adolescence to mastery of similar but more complex skills during early, middle, and mature adulthood. An attempt is made to determine whether similar maladaptive cognitive and behavioral styles associated with past developmental blocks are still features of the client's current developmental task difficulties.

THE COMPREHENSIVE DEVELOPMENTAL CBT ASSESSMENT

Developmental CBT combines new developmental assessment techniques with older established CBT assessment strategies to investigate the following areas:

- Current functioning
  - Presenting problems
  - Current DSM IV Axis I and II symptoms
  - Current external stressors
  - Current Developmental Task Difficulties in areas of partner and social relationships, occupation, and family functioning
- Past Developmental history
  - Past Developmental Task Difficulties
  - Nonnormative crises contributing to task difficulties
  - Previous comorbid Axis I and II disorders contributing to normative task difficulties
  - Long-standing cognitive and behavioral–emotional patterns related to normative task difficulties
- Client strengths

The comprehensive nature of the assessment battery increases the likelihood of uncovering important aspects of the client's past and current functioning that may have otherwise gone undetected. Basically, for each presenting problem and comorbid Axis I disorder, standard CBT assessment techniques are used to identify relevant themes and behavior patterns. Following this, identification of blocked normative adult tasks is undertaken through a careful history of client functioning in occupational, partner, social, family of origin, and parenting roles. Cognitive and behavioral components of dysfunctional developmental patterns and pathways are targeted for change. Precursors linked to the blocked task are then investigated from childhood, adolescence, and earlier adult stages. This information is used to form a Developmental

CBT conceptualization that will be the basis of a therapy plan. This plan aims to first relieve acute symptoms and then neutralize dysfunctional patterns interfering with performance of current normative adult tasks and roles. An overview of the Developmental CBT assessment approach is shown in the Table 2.1.

ASSESSMENT

The comprehensive assessment is ongoing throughout the entire therapy process and yields a client history that enables the therapist to test hypotheses and to formulate a clear developmental conceptualization. The assessment consists of two overlapping phases. The first phase utilizes standard CBT assessment techniques to identify acute Axis I symptoms that require immediate intervention to restore adequate daily functioning. Standard CBT assessment techniques for identifying Axis II symptoms are also initiated at this time, such as those suggested by

TABLE 2.1 Summary of the Comprehensive Developmental CBT Assessment Steps

Step 1. Use new Developmental Assessment instruments, combined with standard CBT strategies to obtain a comprehensive picture of client's current and past psychological functioning. Obtain a developmental history of the presenting problems and comorbid Axis I and II disorders, in addition to a history of psychosocial developmental task difficulties across the life span.

Step 2. Identify and analyze cognitive, behavioral, and emotional components of current and previous developmental task difficulties. Designate core beliefs and self-defeating behavior patterns related to normative task difficulties for therapy interventions.

Step 3. Identify earlier family of origin, social, and school and occupational influences that have shaped and maintained the developmental task difficulties. These may include:

Family of origin influences, such as parenting style and parent–client interaction style, parental models, client perception of parents and siblings, and quality of parents' marital relationship

Peer influences, such as quality of relationships with same-sex peers and opposite-sex peers, dating patterns, and intimate partner relationships in adolescence and earlier adult stages

School and preliminary job influences, such as client's academic performance, parent and teacher evaluation of client's academic performance, teacher and classmate relationships, occupational performance, and boss and coworker relationships

Step 4. Formulate a developmental case conceptualization. This conceptualization includes identification of chronic dysfunctional coping styles linked to presenting problems, to developmental task difficulties, and to Axis I and II disorders from current and previous stages of the client's life. This developmental case conceptualization is then shared with the client, with requests for feedback, verification, and revisions.

Beck and Freeman (1990) and Young, Klosko, & Weisharr (2003). The second phase seeks to identify components of unresolved normative life tasks in the client's past history and current life and to determine the effects of these unresolved tasks on current presenting problems.

THE DEVELOPMENTAL ASSESSMENT

Developmental CBT is similar to other cognitive therapy approaches in its emphasis on identification of early origins of current self-defeating patterns, but with a particular interest in the early origins of adult life task difficulties and maladaptive developmental pathways. A developmental history is carried out to identify links between dysfunctional patterns contributing to the client's current task difficulties and earlier manifestations of similar patterns during childhood and adolescence. Once these self-defeating patterns are identified, they become the basis for cognitive and behavioral pattern-breaking techniques employed during the therapy change phase.

Examples of deficits maintaining task difficulties to be targeted for therapy include: (1) inadequate interpersonal skills for building and maintaining friendships, (2) inadequate skills for dealing appropriately with authority figures, (3) ineffective skills for daily interactions with peers and colleagues, (4) inadequate intimacy and couple-interaction skills necessary for initiating and maintaining satisfying romantic partner relationships and terminating destructive partner relationships, (5) inadequate self-discipline necessary for occupational mastery and satisfaction, (6) inadequate capacity for independent functioning necessary to break free from significant others or oppressive situations in order to establish a separate adult life structure, and (7) inadequate organizational skills needed to establish and maintain a healthy home environment.

Early family, peer, and school influences may compromise adult developmental task resolution. Dysfunctional relationships with parents, siblings, or peers may make it difficult for the child to negotiate primary childhood tasks such as forming affectionate family and peer relationships or fitting into peer and community groups. Examples of common clinically observed precursors of adult developmental task difficulties include: (1) insufficient exposure to same-sex or heterosexual peer-group activities during childhood and adolescence; (2) insufficient exposure to competent peer or adult role models; (3) academic under-achievement and negative school experiences; (4) stressful relationships with teachers or classmates; (5) abusive or unaffectionate parents, (6) incompetent parental role models lacking sufficient independence, resiliency, or interpersonal skills for daily coping; (7) exposure to destructive marital interaction styles or family violence affecting development of partner relationships skills; and (8) a chaotic early family environment lacking sufficient routine and parental expectations to shape responsible children.

PARENTING RESEARCH UNDERLYING DEVELOPMENTAL CBT STRATEGIES

For some clients, early origins of normative task difficulties date back to premature parent–child separations due to death or divorce, while for other clients they stem from daily exposure to inept child-rearing styles. Often maladaptive parent–child relationships persist into adulthood after the child leaves home. When children lack sufficient parental love, empathy, attention, and respect and are deprived of positive social experiences with peers, they may fail to develop the necessary skills for intimate partner relationships. They are more likely to develop Maladaptive Schemas of social isolation, alienation, deprivation, abandonment, or mistrust. Similarly, parents who provide too much assistance for the child make it difficult for the child to achieve sufficient autonomy and the ability to function independently in the world without continual support from others. Parents who provide too little structure, discipline, and expectations may make it difficult for the child to internalize reasonable expectations and reasonable limits, leading to occupational difficulties in adulthood.

Harmful family patterns affecting adult functioning identified by Bedrosian and Bozicas (1994) include ineffective parenting skills, *parentification* of children, boundary violations, chronic rejection, traumatic experiences, distorted cognitions, and distorted communication. These authors suggest that negative affective responses to major life events persist over time because the bereaved individual continues to process additional meanings and implications long after the precipitating event. Maladaptive belief systems and related behavior coping styles learned in the family of origin are viewed as mediators between early family dynamics and the child's ongoing developmental task difficulties.

Clinical research supports a strong link between family of origin dysfunction during childhood and adolescence and subsequent adult psychopathology (e.g., Bedrosian & Bozicas, 1994; Perris, Arrindell, & Eisemann, 1994; Young et al., 2003). Negative family factors such as parental abuse, boundary violations, or chaotic home environments have long-term effects on a child's basic beliefs about self, others, the world, and relationships. Adult psychiatry patients with a wide variety of psychological disorders report more adverse parental behavior than healthy offspring, including abuse, neglect, and inconsistent discipline (Bowlby, 1988; Burback & Borduin, 1986; Gerlsma, Emmelkamp, & Arrindell, 1990; Parker, 1988; Perris, 1988). Specific adult psychological disorders have been associated with particular parental child-rearing styles in the literature. For example, adult depression has been linked to the early loss of a parent with associated feelings of helplessness and to unstable relationships with parents during childhood. Parental rejection is particularly damaging in cases where children are told they are unlovable or incompetent (Bowlby, 1969; Beck, 1972). Similarly, a combination of insufficient parental affection and excessive parental control has been linked to interpersonal aggression in adulthood.

A summary of pertinent findings in the family of origin literature influencing the design of Developmental CBT assessment strategies is shown in Table 2.2.

OTHER CONCEPTS UNDERLYING DESIGN OF DEVELOPMENTAL CBT ASSESSMENT STRATEGIES

The developmental assessment instruments have been designed to tap the personal meaning that clients bring to negative events or conditions they have experienced. They also tap aspirations, goals, possible selves, and personal narratives with respect to the ways in which their lives have unfolded to date.

Stressful life events do not necessarily elicit adult crises per se, because the personal meaning that individuals attribute to significant life experiences is of primary importance (Cross & Markus, 1991; Franz, McClelland, & Weinberger, 1991; Gergen, 1977; Guidano, 1987). By tapping the client's personal developmental narrative, the therapist is able to discover a client's interpretation of adversity and positive and negative changes in one's own life.

The client's developmental self-concept with respect to "possible selves" is also worth investigating. Possible selves are motivators that function as incentives for future behavior, while providing an evaluative and interpretive context for the person's current view of self (Cross & Markus, 1991). In the process of successfully negotiating normative transitions and challenges across the life span, individuals construct possible selves that help motivate them toward desired ends and away from undesired outcomes and the threat of unfulfilled potential. In this way individuals may become active players in their own development. Possible selves are the blueprints for personal change and growth across the life span. For example, a stay-at-home mom who pictures herself as

TABLE 2.2 Family of Origin Factors Underlying Developmental CBT Assessment Strategies

- Dysfunctional schemas, emotions, and behavior patterns associated with the various characteristics of dysfunctional families may lead to recurrent life difficulties because of their interference with successful completion of normal developmental tasks.

- Each new developmental stage, with its new roles and responsibilities, demands cognitive and behavioral adaptation, thus challenging existing schemas and coping strategies. Individuals from dysfunctional families are more likely to have rigid cognitive styles and fear-driven, stereotyped coping strategies, thereby increasing the likelihood of difficulty with life transitions such as marriage and parenthood.

- Childhood acquisition of abnormal coping styles in dysfunctional families is an active process of devising cognitive and behavioral adaptations to the difficult environment, aimed at reducing pain and increasing a sense of well being. Children from dysfunctional families are likely to develop unwarranted faith in the ability of these abnormal coping strategies to relieve or remedy stressful conditions and to continue using these strategies even when they are no longer appropriate.

- Negative conditions in dysfunctional families, such as physical and sexual abuse, neglect, intense marital conflict, and parental alcoholism, tend to produce long-term effects for the offspring that may persist throughout the life span. These negative family conditions obstruct normal growth and development in children and adolescents, primarily by undermining self-worth and fostering the development of Maladaptive Schemas such as psychological threat or maladaptive information-processing styles such as denial and over-vigilance.

- Basic negative schemas linked to family of origin set the stage for the themes that are reflected in the person's thoughts, despite fluctuations in content that may occur across situations and developmental periods over the years. For example, a teenager who believes he is worthless may be preoccupied with poor physical appearance and peer rejection during adolescence, inadequate educational attainments in young adulthood, and inferior job status in middle age, different manifestations of the same underlying "I'm worthless" belief. Negative schemas and related behavior patterns foster ongoing psychopathology over the life span as they interfere with escalating demands of work, social life, marriage, and family.

a successful executive after her child leaves home may begin to prepare for this by taking university courses.

By comparing the possible selves of high satisfaction and low-satisfaction respondents across adult age groups, Cross and Marcus (1991) found that in every age group, low-satisfaction respondents' hoped-for selves tended to represent what was *missing* from their lives, such as being happy or content. Low-satisfaction respondents also mentioned fear of occupational failure, fear of being alone, of being lonely, of never being married, or of being widowed or divorced. Low-satisfaction respondents in younger age groups feared a meaningless life that was impossible to change. In general, life satisfaction has been found to relate to conventional social accomplishments: a long and happy marriage by midlife, children, and friends outside the marriage.

Self-concept is linked to the sum total of a person's evaluations of his or her abilities, competencies, successes, and failures across the life span (Suls & Mullen, 1982). These evaluations may be based on the reactions and opinions of other people (*reflected appraisals*), on self-generated attempts to assess the adequacy of one's own abilities, or both. Self-concept may be based on social or interpersonal comparisons with other people, as well as temporal comparisons, as, for example, when clients compare their present attainments with past performances.

NEW ASSESSMENT STRATEGIES

The instruments shown in Table 2.3 were designed to aid the therapist in gathering pertinent information about the client's performance of normative psychosocial tasks over the years, as well as earlier manifestations of the client's presenting problems, and comorbid Axis I and II symptoms. In addition to providing a methodical assessment of significant events in the client's life, these instruments have also been designed to tap the client's internal subjective interpretation of these events and to obtain information about the client's habitual coping styles.

Developmental assessment strategies were designed to be used throughout the therapy process as the need for more information arises. They need not be administered as part of an assessment during the first sessions of the therapy process, and it will not be necessary to use all

TABLE 2.3 Psychosocial Developmental Assessment Instruments

Instrument	Table
Child/Adolescent Normative Psychosocial Tasks	Table 2.4
Normative Psychosocial Tasks of Early, Middle, and Mature Adulthood	Table 2.5
Client's Current Life Evaluation	Table 2.6
Client's Developmental Task Review	Table 2.7
Stress Coping Style History	Table 2.8
Family of Origin Patterns	Table 2.9
Parent–Offspring Interaction Styles	Table 2.10
Peer Relationship History	Table 2.11
Intimate Partner Relationship History	Table 2.12
Client Perception of School Experiences	Table 2.13
Client Perception of Work Experiences	Table 2.14
Record of Dysfunctional Cognitive, Behavioral, and Emotional Patterns	Table 2.15
Developmental CBT Case Conceptualization	Table 2.16

of the instruments for each client. Some of the pertinent information will be obtained indirectly from client explanations and elaborations of their predicaments, their reasons for seeking therapy, and their past histories, without formal administration of the questionnaires. This information may be subsequently noted on the assessment forms between sessions. The instructions and individual items for the various instruments have been designed to serve as guidelines for obtaining important information.

Most of the instruments listed in Table 2.3 are designed to serve a twofold function: (1) as an assessment–interview instrument for collecting data and (2) as a therapy tool to teach the client to recognize and analyze his or her own cognitive, emotional, and behavioral styles. The therapist will use data obtained through the developmental assessment strategies to generate hypotheses about etiology and maintenance of long-term self-defeating patterns underlying the client's current distress and developmental task difficulties.

IDENTIFYING DEVELOPMENTAL TASK DIFFICULTIES

Since therapist familiarity with normative lifestyle tasks and roles is a necessary prerequisite for identification of client developmental difficulties, two of the new assessment instruments, shown in Tables 2.4 and 2.5, are useful charts listing major normative psychosocial developmental tasks across the life span from childhood to mature adulthood. These are based on the child and adult developmental literature cited in Chapter 1 and are meant to provide useful references for both the client and therapist in highlighting client developmental task difficulties.

The tables are designed to help the therapist determine how a client's long-standing maladaptive patterns are contributing to current problems. They also increase therapist insight into how certain behavioral styles have undermined the client's attempts to resolve normative developmental tasks and challenges during previous life stages.

Child and Adolescent Tasks

Psychosocial development is viewed as continuous across the life span. Clients manifesting psychological problems in adulthood have usually been hampered by early parenting and social influences in their attempts to negotiate major developmental tasks of childhood and adolescence. Table 2.4 shows normative psychosocial developmental tasks of childhood and adolescence.

During childhood, adolescence, and the early adult transition, the family provides nurturing and socialization, shaping adequate devel-

TABLE 2.4 Child/ Adolescent Normative Psychosocial Tasks

Psychological:
- Develop adequate autonomy
- Develop attachment, interpersonal connectedness
- Develop worthiness, positive sense of self (adequate sense of mastery)
- Develop self-discipline and self-control
- Develop reasonable expectations and limits (internalize society's values, norms, limits)

Social/peer relations:
- Learn basic social skills
- Develop friendships
- Participate in peer activities that create a sense of belonging and inclusion in pro-social peer groups with:
  - *Same-sex peers* (develop close friends)
  - *Opposite Sex Peers* (develop close nonromantic friendships; dating; initial romantic relationships

Occupational/school:
- Sufficient academic achievement and educational background in preparation for a viable occupational path
- Effective classmate relationships
- Effective relationships with authority figures (e.g., teacher, boss)

Family of origin:
- Adaptive mutually satisfying relationships with parents
- Increasing autonomy from parents
- Effective sibling relationships

opment of qualities necessary for the child to become a self-sufficient member of adult society. The youngster expands his or her social sphere from the family of origin to the community, which involves a wider peer group in school and neighborhood. Normally the child gradually becomes more industrious, disciplined, and skilled, while simultaneously resolving emotional struggles with the family. Puberty marks the shift from childhood to adolescence, initiated by bodily changes leading to sexual maturity. Adolescents must form stable relationships, acquire information and skills, and mature to a point where they internalize cultural mores and begin living independent adult lives.

Adult Tasks

Table 2.5, summarizing normative adult psychosocial developmental tasks, is based on the adult life span developmental literature. Therapists may expect to observe a great deal of variation in the way in which different clients attempt to negotiate the same adult developmental task.

Table 2.5 Normative Psychosocial Tasks of Early, Middle, and Mature Adulthood

Early Adulthood (ages 20 to 30/35)

Social/Peer relations:
- Form effective adult interpersonal skills
- Form mutually satisfying friendships

Occupation/Routine:
- Complete education
- Establish initial viable occupational path
- Establish health-enhancing daily routine
- Reassess initial occupational path and restructure if appropriate

Intimate partner relationships:
- Master effective intimate partner relationship skills; dating
- Select appropriate functional partner
- Partner commitment, engagement, cohabitation or marriage
- Terminate dysfunctional partner relationships
- Adjust to unwanted termination of romantic relationships

Family/Home:
- Establish healthful, functional home environment (single or couple)
- Responsible decisions about pregnancy
- Effective parenting: infants, children
- Maintain adaptive family of origin relationships and independence

Middle Adulthood (ages 30/35 to 50)

Social/Peer relations:
- Maintain effective interpersonal relationships in community, work setting
- Continue to maintain and build satisfying friendships

Occupation/Routine:
- Maintain health-enhancing daily routine
- Maintain occupational effectiveness; growth and development of midlife career path, homemaker/parent path, etc.)
- Reappraise occupation and restructure occupational path if appropriate

Intimate partner relationships:
- Maintain or establish satisfying functional partner or spousal relationship
- Reappraise, restructure, or terminate dysfunctional partner relationships
- Maintain satisfying single-life structure (divorced or never married)

Family/Home:
- Maintain functional home environment (single or couple)
- Effective parenting of children and adolescents
- Adjustment to end of reproduction cycle or unfulfilled parenting aspirations (e.g., childless, number of children)
- Maintain functional family of origin relationships and adequate independence

Mature Adulthood (ages 50 to 65)

Social /Peer relations:
- Continue to maintain effective interpersonal relationships outside family
- Continue to maintain and build satisfying friendships

—continued

Table 2.5 Normative Psychosocial Tasks of Early, Middle, and Mature Adulthood (continued)

Occupation /Routine:
- Maintain health-enhancing daily routine
- Maintain occupational path effectiveness
- Reappraisal of initial unrealistic or unfulfilled occupational aspirations, acceptance or restructuring of occupational path
- Preparation for retirement (gradual occupational disengagement, reordering occupational priorities, developing interests and activities to fill career void)

Intimate partner relationships:
- Maintain or establish satisfying functional postparenting partner relationship
- Reappraise, restructure, or terminate dysfunctional partner relationships
- Maintain satisfying single life structure

Family/ Home:
- Effective launching of adult children
- Restructure effective relationships with adult children
- Reappraise, restructure unfulfilled aspirations for children's development, relationships, accomplishments
- Maintain functional family of origin relationships and adequate independence (e.g., care for elderly parents, adjust to death of parents)
- Maintain functional extended-family relationships (in laws, grandchildren)

Client Life-Task-Review Instruments Three client life-review instruments are shown in Table 2.6 (the Client's Current Life Evaluation), Table 2.7 (the Client's Developmental Task Review), and Table 2.8 (the Stress Coping-Style History). These instruments have been designed to tap self-perceptions associated with satisfaction and dissatisfaction over the life span, client goals and aspirations at different life periods, and the degree to which clients perceive themselves as having sufficiently achieved these goals. They examine the personal meaning that clients attribute to setbacks and major changes, client evaluations of their lives to date, and client concepts of possible selves, or the way in which they picture themselves developing in the future (Cross & Markus, 1991). Table 2.6 is useful in identifying discrepancies between the client's preferred or ideal life structure and what has actually transpired.

Table 2.7 was designed to elicit client reports of past attempts to resolve normative developmental tasks, client perceptions and evaluations of negative or traumatic events in their histories, and client goals for future change. It is useful in revealing discrepancies between the client's ideal life goals and what actually transpired.

Table 2.6 Client's Current Life Evaluation

1. What is your life like now?
2. What are the most important parts of your life?
3. Who are the most important people in your life?
4. Where do you invest most of your time and energy?
5. What are your main goals (the main things you would like to accomplish or have happen in your life)?
6. How do you feel about your physical condition?
7. What do you enjoy doing most in life?
8. What are some things you would like to change to make your life more satisfying?
9. What situations or relationships in your life would you like to change if you could?
10. What activities or relationships would you like to add to your life? (These would include any types of activities or relationships that are missing from your life at the present time.)
11. What would your life be like today if it were the way you wanted it to be?
12. How would you like your life to be five years from now?

Table 2.7 Client's Developmental Task Review

Each stage of adult life is accompanied by common challenges or tasks that people have to deal with. The following questions will ask you to describe how you handled each of the following challenges.

Early and Middle Adulthood

1. What did you want to do with your life when you were in your late teens and early twenties? What was your first adult life plan? What were your hopes and goals for your adult life?
2. What where your views and hopes regarding marriage and family?
3. What were your views and hopes and goals regarding occupation or career?
4. What were your hopes regarding friends and social life?
5. What was your experience with leaving home and establishing an independent adult lifestyle?
6. What about your relationship with your parents, sisters, brothers, and others in your family?
7. How was your college or university experience?
8. How was your first occupation or job? What about changes in your occupation or career?
9. What about friendships and social life as a young adult?
10. What were your views about romantic relationships? What has been your experience with serious partner relationships and decisions about living together or marriage?

—continued

Table 2.7 Client's Developmental Task Review (continued)

11. How have you found living together or married life? (or, How do you find your single lifestyle?)
12. What are your thoughts about yourself as a parent? What about decisions to have children and experiences starting a family? Your experiences raising small children? Your experiences raising teenagers?
13. How has your progress been in terms of your own timetable for achieving personal goals for your life?
14. What were your views about conventional adult roles in our society with respect to romantic relationships, marriage, career, friendships, raising children, and relationships with elderly parents?

Middle and Mature Adulthood

15. What has been your experience as a parent?
16. At different times in their lives, some people reevaluate their lives and sometimes make changes. What has been your experience with making significant changes?
17. How have your children turned out?
18. What was experience of your children leaving home?
19. Looking back over the years, how has your chosen occupation or career path turned out for you?
20. Looking back, what has been your experience with romantic partners or spouse?
21. What has been your experience with your own parents over the years?
22. What about friendships over the years?
23. Looking back, what about your life in terms of your original goals, hopes, and aspirations? What about the future?

Rather than formally administer the items of this lengthy questionnaire, the therapist may choose to take a more informal approach by simply inquiring about the areas covered using the following abbreviated topic guidelines:

- First adult life plan
- Marriage and family
- Career
- Friends
- Leaving home
- Relationship with parents
- University or college experience
- First occupation
- Early adult friendships
- Romantic partner relationships
- Single lifestyle
- Marriage
- Timetable for achieving your goals
- Parenting experience
- Looking back: partner, peers, occupation, family

Table 2.8 Stress Coping Style History

1.What were the most stressful periods, events, or situations in your life?

2. What events or ongoing situations or relationships at home, at school or work, or with peers were most upsetting and stressful for you during your childhood years, teenage years, adult years? *(Record client's responses in columns 2, 3, and 4)*

Upsetting events and situations (column 2)

What did you perceive as the cause of the upsetting situations? (column 3)

What was your typical way of coping with the upsetting situation? (column 4)

Life Stage	Source of Stress	Interpretation of Causes of Stress	Coping Style
Childhood			
Adolescence			
Age 20–29			
Age 30–39			
Age 40–49			
Age 50–65			

EARLY PRECURSORS OF DEVELOPMENTAL TASK DIFFICULTIES

From a cognitive therapy perspective, affective responses to major life events have a significant impact on later development, whether a single traumatic event such as the loss of a loved one or chronic stress such as an abusive home situation. The purpose of the Stress Coping-Style History questionnaire is to gather information about negative life experiences or events in previous stages of the client's life. It taps client attributions of cause and client coping styles associated with the events. This information is useful since it is not necessarily the event per se that is of primary importance for long-term development, but the client's perception of the event. This instrument, shown in Table 2.8, taps the way in which the client has made sense of adversity, such as personal losses or family discord. It enables the therapist to form hypotheses about the origins of the client's dysfunctional schemas and behavior patterns. These hypotheses will subsequently be shared with the client in order to test their veracity and to obtain client clarification.

Early influences on adult mental health and on potential for resolving normative developmental tasks are found in family of origin, peer, and romantic partner relationships, as well as in school experiences. The six instruments shown in Tables 2.9 through 2.14 were designed to obtain detailed histories of client functioning in these areas.

Table 2.9 Family of Origin Patterns

1.	Who was living at home during your childhood and adolescence? Describe each person.
2.	How was anger expressed in your family?
3.	How was affection expressed in your family?
4.	What was the authority structure in your family? Who made and/or enforced the rules?
5.	Describe your relationship with your father. When you did something your father disapproved of, what typically happened?
6.	Describe your relationship with your mother. When you did something your mother disapproved of, what typically happened?
7.	Describe your parents' marital relationship.
8.	What are the things you did that earned your parents' approval? What are the things you did that resulted in your parents' disapproval?
9.	What were the most negative or painful experiences growing up in your family?
10.	What were the positive experiences?
11.	Describe your relationships with each of your siblings.

Identifying Family of Origin Dysfunction

Two assessment instruments have been developed to assist the therapist in identifying salient family influences linked to the client's current presenting problems and developmental task difficulties: the Family of Origin Patterns (Table 2.9) and the Parent–Offspring Interaction Styles (Table 2.10). The design of these instruments was based on clinical child and adolescent literature concerned with long-term effects of early parenting and family dysfunction on the child. The Family of Origin Patterns instrument relies on open-ended questions designed to elicit client perceptions of early family dynamics.

The Parent–Offspring Interaction Styles instrument is useful for eliciting data and for organizing information collected during therapy sessions. It may also be a useful therapy tool for guiding clients in identifying past or present interaction patterns with parents that have had negative long-term effects. It is a powerful tool for helping clients gain insight into the link between some of their own problematic behaviors and early exposure to dysfunctional or ineffective childrearing styles or parental models. It may also be used with clients who are parents themselves, whose major problems and current developmental task difficulties involve relationships with their children.

Table 2.10 Parent–Offspring Interaction Styles

Parenting Style	Offspring's Coping Style
Punitive, abusive parent	Feel inadequate, unworthy
	Retaliation
	Self-punishment
	Extreme guilt
	Approval seeking
	Adopt victim role
	Fearful obedience
	Temper outbursts
	Abusive
	Unaffectionate
	Social skills deficit
	Conduct disorder
Cold, unaffectionate parent	Approval seeking
	Excessive demands on others
	Easily offended
	Mistrust of others
	Unaffectionate
	Social skills deficit
	Cold, rejecting
	Lack of empathy
	Feel inadequate
	Empty, depressed
Coercive, controlling parent	Dependent on others
	Active /passive noncompliance
	Inadequate discipline
	Give in, defer to others
	Controlling
	Self-sacrificing
Over-protective, over-involved parent	Dependent on others
	Bored passivity
	Abdicate responsibility
	Self-sacrifice
	Manipulator
	Anxiety disorder
	Inadequate self-discipline
	Feel inadequate
Over-submissive parent	Self-centered, entitlement
	Impulsive pleasure seeking
	Conduct disorder
	Self-destructive
	Irresponsible
	Manipulate
	Demanding
	Poor self-discipline
	Drifting

—continued

Table 2.10 Parent–Offspring Interaction Styles (continued)

Parenting Style	Offspring's Coping Style
Neglecting parent due to physical or mental illness, parental absence (work demands, divorce, death)	Avoid forming close relationships Lack empathy Social skills deficit Excessive demands "Empty" depressed Excessive striving Manipulate Self-blame Drifting Anxiety disorder
Perfectionist parent (excessive expectations, demands on child)	Excessive striving Self-belittlement Guilt Give-up, escape pattern
Parent favors sibling	Anger problems Approval seeking Self-condemnation, Inadequate, unworthy
Dependent, helpless	Feel responsible for parent Self-sacrifice Guilt Helplessness Poor self-discipline
Parent somatoform disorder	Use illness as excuse for avoidance Irresponsible Anxiety disorder

FURTHER IDENTIFICATION OF PSYCHOSOCIAL DEVELOPMENTAL DIFFICULTIES

The instruments shown in Tables 2.11 through 2.14 have been designed to obtain client histories of social, intimate partner, school, and work experiences.

Table 2.11 Peer Relationships History

1. During **childhood**, what sort of relationship did you have with:
   - Classmates
   - Same-sex peers
   - Opposite-sex peers
2. What were your major activities outside of school as a child?
3. During your **teenage** years, what sort of relationship did you have with:
   - Classmates
   - Same-sex peers
   - Opposite-sex peers
4. What were your major activities outside of school as a teenager?
5. Were any of the following true for you during childhood or adolescent years?
   - Little or no engagement in activities with peers
   - Extreme shyness
   - Peer rejection
   - Embarrassment about physical appearance or another aspect of your self or life
   - Parents discouraged or prohibited involvement in activities with peers
   - No desire to spend time with peers
   - Failure to develop friendships
   - Little or no experience in activities in which peers of the opposite sex were present
6. Describe your best friend(s).

Table 2.12 Intimate Partner Relationship History

Describe the significant intimate partner relationships in your life to date.

Describe Partner and the Relationship	Positive and Negative Aspects of the Relationship	How and Why Relationship Ended

Table 2.13 Client Perception of School Experiences

1. Describe your school experience during childhood and adolescence.

2. Were you mainly successful or unsuccessful at school? Why?

3. How did your parents typically react to your school performance?

4. Describe your overall experience with fellow classmates. Describe problems you encountered with classmates.

5. Describe your overall experience with teachers. Describe problems you encountered with teachers?

6. Describe your postsecondary school experience at college or university.

Table 2.14 Client Perception of Work Experiences

PART I.

Describe each of your jobs or occupations over the years (including non-paying occupations such as housewife)

Briefly Describe the Job or Occupation and Duration (from when to when)	Good and Bad Aspects of the Job or Occupation	Reason for Termination of Job or Occupation

Table 2.14 Client Perception of Work Experiences

PART II.

1. Describe your **current** occupation.
2. How would you describe your current occupation with respect to the following:
   - Occupational satisfaction
   - Long-term career goals
   - Relationships with coworkers
   - Salary, benefits, job security
   - Occupational status
   - Potential for advancement
   - Demands on time and energy
3. What was your original occupational plan for your adult life?
4. What actually happened?
5. What changes have you made to your original occupational plan?
6. Do you have any regrets about previous occupational decisions?

Identifying and Recording Dysfunctional Cognitive and Behavioral Patterns

It is recommended that the therapist take notes during the sessions in order to keep an accurate record of three types of data:

- *Maladaptive cognitions* contained in client verbatim statements, reflecting their perceptions, attributions, predictions, assumptions, beliefs, or self-evaluations linked to identified problems or situations
- *Problematic behavior patterns* mentioned by the client or observed or hypothesized by the therapist during the session
- *Upsetting emotional response patterns* mentioned by the client or observed by the therapist during the session

The Record of Dysfunctional Cognitive, Behavioral, and Emotional Patterns (Table 2.15) is a simple data recording instrument designed to aid the therapist in keeping track of maladaptive cognitive and behavioral and emotional patterns observed or elicited using developmental instruments during therapy sessions.

BRIEF REVIEW OF COMMON COGNITIVE AND BEHAVIORAL TARGETS

This section presents a helpful guide for therapists in targeting relevant cognitive and behavioral data for analysis and change. The therapist will pay particular attention to characteristic themes and behaviors associated with Axis I and II disorders summarized in the following

Table 2.15 Record of Dysfunctional Cognitive, Behavioral, and Emotional Patterns

Client's Verbatim Statements (automatic thoughts, beliefs, attitudes, rules, assumptions)	Related Problematic Behavioral / Emotional Patterns
1.	1.
2.	2.
3.	3.
4.	4.

paragraphs. Therapists may expect to find considerable overlap between these components of Emotional and Personality Disorders and typical cognitive and behavioral presentations of various task difficulties across the adult lifespan.

Important categories of schemas and common issues and themes of therapy clients across Axis I and II disorders have been identified in the literature (e.g., Beck & Freeman, 1990; Stein & Young, 1993; Stein, 1992; Horowitz, 1988). These include:

- Cognitive schemas reflecting abstraction, interpretation, memories, self-evaluation, evaluation of others, expectancies, predictions
- Affective schemas (responsible for generation of feelings)
- Motivational schemas (wishes and desires)
- Instrumental schemas (prepare for action)
- Control schemas (self-monitoring, self-regulation, controlling relationships, controlling the external environment)
- Role schemas (position in relation to the world and one's culture)
- Relationship schemas (love, care, power, control, sexuality, status)

Beck and his colleagues have identified themes characteristic of clients with depression and anxiety disorders familiar to most CBT practitioners (e.g., Beck, 1963, 1964; Beck et al., 1979; Beck & Emery, 1985; Beck & Freeman, 1990; Beck, 1995; Freeman & Simon, 1989):

- Depression themes
  - Low self-esteem
  - Self-criticism and self-blame
  - Negative interpretation of events
  - Negative expectations for the future
  - Overwhelming responsibility
  - Desire to escape
  - Hopelessness
  - Lack of gratification
  - Anger or blame against person or agency
  - Helplessness, feeling of inadequacy
  - Feeling unlovable, undesirable, bad, unworthy, defective
- Anxiety themes
  - Personal danger (fear or threat of physical or psychological danger)
  - Loss of control
  - Exaggerated description of external demands and pressures
  - Misinterpretation of external or proprioceptive cues (e.g., panic attacks)
  - Fear of physical or psychological danger in a specific situation or circumstance (e.g., phobia)
  - Over-response to perceived sensory abnormalities
  - Ongoing thoughts that become cause for constant attention (e.g., obsessive thinking)
  - Belief that repetitive acts are necessary to ward off a threat (e.g., compulsive rituals)
  - Unreasonable fear that there is something seriously medically wrong

Identifying characteristic themes and coping styles of various personality disorders is particularly relevant because of the frequent overlap between components of personality disorders and developmental task difficulties such as dependence, social isolation, or entitlement. Cognitive and behavioral–emotional patterns linked to personality disorders have been identified in the literature by various practitioners (e.g., Beck & Freeman, 1990; Greenberg & Paivio, 1997; Linehan, 1993; Young & First, 1996; Young & Flanagan, 1998; Young & Gluhoski,

1996). For example, Beck and Freeman (1990) identify the following characteristic themes of clients with personality disorders:

- Statements reflecting self-concept
- Statements about rules the client lives by
- Client judgments of other people
- Statements suggesting deficiencies in interpersonal style
- Statements about the impossibility of changing ("I've always been that way")

Young and Flanagan (1998) have identified several early Maladaptive Schemas (EMSs) at the core of personality disorders. These broad, pervasive, lifelong themes regarding oneself and one's relationships with others may also be components of psychosocial task difficulties. Examples include the following:

- Abandonment/instability
- Mistrust/abuse
- Emotional deprivation
- Defectiveness/shame
- Social alienation
- Incompetence
- Vulnerability to danger
- Failure
- Entitlement/grandiosity
- Subjugation
- Self-sacrifice
- Approval-seeking
- Negativity
- Over-control
- Unrelenting standards

Young and First (1996) have also identified several dysfunctional schema modes characteristic of clients with various personality disorders. These dysfunctional schema modes run contrary to a healthy adult mode that typically nurtures, limits anger and impulsivity, and performs appropriate adult tasks.

- Vulnerable child (lonely, incompetent, defective)
- Angry child (enraged that needs are not met)
- Impulsive undisciplined child (difficulty delaying short-term gratification)
- Compliant surrender (subservient, approval-seeking)
- Detached protector (cuts off needs and feelings)

- Overcompensate (aggressive, grandiose, manipulative)
- Punitive parent (blaming self and others)
- Demanding parent (internalized strict rules)

DYSFUNCTIONAL COPING STYLES

Several authors have identified characteristic behavioral–emotional patterns of clients with personality disorders (e.g., Beck & Freeman, 1990; Greenberg & Paivio, 1997; Linehan, 1993; Young & First, 1996). The following list provides a useful tool for therapists in their analyses of blocked psychosocial developmental tasks:

- Aggression
- Anger, hate
- Attention seeking
- Avoidance (of evaluative situations)
- Autonomy (excessive)
- Competitiveness (excessive)
- Controlling
- Clinginess
- Compulsive
- Critical, intolerant, blaming
- Dominating
- Exhibitionism
- Exploitation
- Emotional regulation problems
- Emotional numbing
- Fearful, vulnerable
- Help seeking (excessive)
- Impulsive
- Inhibited, chronic over-control
- Irritable
- Labile
- Manipulative
- Overcompensating
- Overreact to perceived slight
- Passivity
- Resistance
- Recognition seeking
- Social isolation
- Self-focused
- Sabotaging
- Self aggrandizement
- Vigilance (excessive)

The Developmental CBT Case Conceptualization

Table 2.16 is a tool for organizing and analyzing pertinent data for the Developmental CBT case conceptualization. It may then be used for planning therapy strategies.

Table 2.16 Developmental CBT Case Conceptualization

I. Current Functioning

1. Presenting Problems

   Problem 1.

   Problem 2.

   Problem 3.

2. Current DSM IV Axis I and II Diagnoses

   Diagnosis #1 _____

      Related thoughts, beliefs and behavior coping patterns

   Diagnosis #2 _____

      Related thoughts, beliefs and behavior coping patterns

3. Current Developmental Task Difficulties

   Developmental Task Difficulty #1 _____

      Related thoughts, beliefs and behavior coping patterns

      Related self-defeating pathways

      Previous manifestations and early influences

   Developmental Task Difficulty #2 _____

      Related thoughts, beliefs and behavior coping patterns

      Related self-defeating pathways

      Previous manifestations and early influences

4. Current External Stressors

II. Past Developmental History

1. Past DSM IV Axis I and II Disorders

   Diagnosis #1 _____

      Related thoughts, beliefs and behavior coping patterns

   Diagnosis #2 _____

      Related thoughts, beliefs and behavior coping patterns

2. Past Developmental Task Difficulties: Childhood, Adolescence, Early Adulthood

   Past task difficulty #1_____

      Related thoughts, beliefs and behavior coping patterns

—continued

Table 2.16 Developmental CBT Case Conceptualization (continued)

   Related self-defeating pathways

Past Task Difficulty #2_____

   Related thoughts, beliefs and behavior coping patterns

   Related self-defeating pathways

III. Client Strengths

Successful coping strategies in past crises

Coping strategies during more successful life periods

Current coping skills

3

DEVELOPMENTAL COGNITIVE BEHAVIORAL THERAPY INTERVENTION STRATEGIES

This chapter will outline the Developmental Cognitive Behavioral Therapy (CBT) approach, with special emphasis on new developmental techniques designed to alter developmental psychosocial task difficulties. During initial therapy sessions, Developmental CBT resembles other cognitive therapy approaches in its reliance on standard CBT strategies of Beck and other practitioners for treatment of Axis I and II disorders and acute aspects of the presenting problems. Once the client is stabilized, the new developmental phase of therapy then addresses unresolved normative tasks interfering with the client's performance of adult roles.

A brief overview of the acute phase of the Developmental CBT model will be presented first, followed by a detailed discussion of the developmental phase of treatment, including an introduction to several new Developmental CBT treatment strategies. Table 3.1 summarizes the steps of the comprehensive Developmental CBT approach.

EDUCATING THE CLIENT ABOUT DEVELOPMENTAL CBT

The following is a standard introduction to Developmental CBT that may be presented to the client.

The Developmental CBT approach is meant to be a very practical, problem-focused therapy that addresses both recent problems as well as long-standing self-defeating patterns with origins dating back to childhood or adolescence. The initial goal of Developmental CBT is to bring about relief from the problems that led you to seek

Table 3.1 Steps of the Comprehensive Developmental CBT Approach

Initial Acute Phase

Address client presenting problems and comorbid Axis I Disorders. Use standard CBT strategies to alter cognitive and behavioral components of presenting problems and acute Axis I symptoms to stabilize the client's daily life. Then begin to address Axis II patterns linked to presenting problems using standard CBT strategies.

Developmental Phase

Step 1. Client Education and Developmental Task Difficulty Identification: Once the acute problems have been addressed, the therapist initiates the Developmental Phase. The therapist utilizes several of the new Developmental Assessment instruments as needed. Selection of developmental psychosocial task difficulties as therapy targets is based on the Developmental CBT assessment findings and case conceptualization (Table 2.16). The client is educated about the Developmental CBT approach, and the Developmental Task Difficulty conceptualization is then shared with the client. This conceptualization includes identification of chronic dysfunctional coping styles linked to Developmental Task Difficulties from current and previous stages of the client's life that are maintaining presenting problems and Axis I and II Disorders.

Step 2. Developmental Task Difficulty Analysis: This involves an in-depth analysis of developmental task resolution pathways:

- Explore in greater depth the identified psychosocial Developmental Task Difficulties and contributing cognitive and behavioral patterns.

- Explore previous Developmental Task Difficulties and maladaptive developmental pathways that have had an impact on current problems.

- Explore early triggers and origins of Developmental Task Difficulties identified in family, social, and occupational histories. Analyze ways in which these early influences have helped shape and maintain current developmental task difficulties and maladaptive pathways.

Step 3. Developmental Change Strategies: Therapist and client seek to alter patterns maintaining Developmental Task Difficulties using a combination of standard CBT strategies and new Developmental Strategies specifically designed to address psychosocial developmental task blocks. Emphasis will be on skill deficits and on teaching clients coping skills they failed to learn in earlier developmental periods. Emphasis will also be on helping clients shift to more adaptive pathways consistent with current psychosocial demands.

therapy and then to help you to gain insight into the way in which some of your long-standing patterns of coping have been self-defeating in that they have prevented you from living the life you want. The goal is to help you learn new, more effective ways of coping.

It is important to understand that a person's self-defeating patterns are influenced by the way the person perceives events and situ-

ations and that these perceptions are often inaccurate observations of the actual situations. Often these inaccurate perceptions take the form of negative or upsetting thoughts and emotions. Therefore, during therapy sessions, we will focus on your upsetting thoughts, which usually take the form of inflexible rules, distorted beliefs, or negative self-evaluations. We will also focus on your unwanted negative emotions such as sadness or anxiety. Negative upsetting thoughts and emotions are often linked to self-defeating behavior patterns that are actually maintaining the situations or conditions in your life that you want to change. We will focus on upsetting relationships with important people in your life, and we will look at the possibility of altering external aspects of your problematic situations.

During the therapy sessions we will work together to decide what to focus on, what changes need to be made, and what steps are necessary for bringing about these changes. Basically, I will be guiding you in analyzing aspects of your problems, introducing you to alternative ways of coping with these problems, and teaching you new coping skills. You will be asked to experiment with some new, healthier coping styles and skills in your daily life. Many of the techniques I will be teaching you can be used with various problems both now and in the future, and hopefully you will learn techniques that will enable you to become your own "therapist."

The initial therapy sessions will focus on current problems to help stabilize your daily life. Later sessions will focus on long-standing patterns that are no longer working for you that may date back to your early years and that continue to get in the way of your ability to function the way you would like in major adult roles.

Difficulties in coping with major child, adolescent, and adult roles may also be called developmental task blocks. *They refer to a person's difficulty in living up to cultural expectations or self-expectations for performing normal life tasks. Examples of major adult tasks and roles are (1) establishing a viable career or occupation, (2) finding a suitable romantic partner, (3) maintaining a mutually satisfying partner or marital relationship, (4) forming effective relationships with colleagues and friends, (5) functioning as an effective parent, and (6) maintaining satisfactory relationships with one's own parents and extended family.*

Even though some individuals do not adopt conventional life styles, most people still tend to evaluate themselves in terms of family, peer, or society's expectations for performing major adult roles in the proper time sequence. Often a person's self-defeating thought and behavior patterns are established early in life and evolved into maladaptive pathways that contributed to earlier difficulties with expected roles during childhood and adolescence. Although these pathways may have helped the person to cope temporarily with difficult situations, they subsequently become inappropriate when they no longer work for the person. Developmental task blocks in childhood, adolescence, or earlier stages of adulthood tend to have a residual negative effect on a person's ability to function effectively during the current adult stage. This is because some of the self-defeating thinking or behavior patterns may still be present.

Therefore, after there has been sufficient improvement in the acute problems that brought you to therapy and your daily life has become more stable, the focus of therapy will shift to difficulties with developmental tasks of your current stage of life and residual effects of past unresolved life tasks that may still be hampering you today. We will identify self-defeating thought and behavior patterns linked to your current task blocks, keeping in mind that these same patterns may have the potential to cause more problems in the future.

The important thing to remember is that these self-defeating pathways can be altered, even if they have been in existence for a long time. This second, developmental, phase of therapy will help you learn new effective patterns of thinking and interacting that will help you succeed in performing normal adult tasks and roles and will help ensure that you don't fall back into your former self-defeating patterns.

THE INITIAL (ACUTE) PHASE

The comprehensive Developmental CBT treatment approach begins with standard CBT strategies applied to client presenting problems and symptoms of Axis I and II Disorders. The proposed approach incorporates major features of Beck's cognitive therapy model, so a brief overview is appropriate. Features include the underlying cognitive theory (Beck, Rush, Shaw, & Emery, 1979; Beck & Freeman, 1990), cognitive models for case conceptualization (Beck & Freeman, 1990), and numerous treatment protocols for different client presenting problems developed by various adherents (e.g., Beck, Freeman, & Davis, 2004; Beck, 1995; Freeman, Simon, Beutler, & Arkowitz, 1989; McMullin, 2000; Padesky, 1995). Developmental CBT also adopts Beck's cognitive model of personality development, and a two-tiered treatment approach for Axis I and Axis II disorders — namely, an initial focus on symptom relief of acute symptoms of presenting problems and Axis I disorders, followed by a focus on Axis II disorders, especially core Maladaptive Schemas related to self and relationships (Young, Beck, & Weinberger, 1993). It is taken for granted that basic underlying features of standard CBT approaches are also adopted by the Developmental CBT approach. These include: (1) development of the therapeutic alliance and collaborative relationship, (2) client education, (3) assessment of client strengths and reinforcement of client contributions to positive changes, (4) problem-related coping skills training, (5) assignment of self-help personal experiments and other "homework" tasks to be carried out between sessions, and (6) relapse prevention strategies (Meichenbaum, 1994).

During initial sessions, the Developmental CBT approach relies on standard cognitive–behavioral interventions for treatment of Axis I disorders developed by various CBT practitioners over the years (e.g., Basco & Rush, 1996; Beck & Emery, 1985; Beck et al., 1979; Beck, 1995; Dattilio & Freeman, 2000; Dryden, 1990; Ellis, McInerny, DiGiuseppe, & Yeager, 1988; Epstein, Schlesinger, & Dryden, 1988; Freeman et al., 1989; Greenburger & Padesky, 1995; Padesky, 1995; Young et al., 1993). Similarly, the therapist may also utilize strategies from excellent publications on cognitive therapy for personality disorders (e.g., Beck & Freeman, 1990; Young, 1990). The Schema-Focused Therapy model of cognitive therapy was specifically developed by Jeffrey Young to address long-standing cognitive patterns called "Early Maladaptive Schemas" (EMSs) associated with various personality disorders (Young et al., 1993; Young & Klosko, 1994; Young & Gluhoski, 1996; Young, Klosko, & Weishaar, 2003). Young's Early Maladaptive Schemas, said to develop during childhood and to persist throughout a person's lifetime, characterize clients whose dysfunctional personality styles make them not only prone to anxiety and depression, but also less able to deal effectively with normal developmental psychosocial tasks, transitions, and common developmental crises. Finally, Developmental CBT has also been influenced by previous cognitive therapy models emphasizing the importance of a developmental approach to psychopathology that explores the historical roots of dysfunctional beliefs (e.g., Guidano, 1987, 1988; Guidano & Liotti, 1983) and by studies on the influence of early parenting styles on psychopathology (e.g., Perris, Arrindell, & Eisemann, 1994).

During initial sessions, the therapist uses open-ended questions to elicit more information about presenting problems and Axis I symptoms, including client perceptions of causes, underlying meanings (regarding self and others), duration, and severity of the problem. The therapist asks the client to give several examples of current problems and to describe related interpersonal interaction sequences in detail to identify cognitive, behavioral, and emotional components. The therapist then takes a history of the presenting problems to identify early origins. At this time, the therapist may also note components of presenting problems that seem to involve additional psychosocial Developmental Task Difficulties, to be targeted for the subsequent Developmental Phase of therapy. The therapist will then apply standard CBT techniques for crisis intervention and for relief from comorbid Axis I symptoms of presenting problems, such as debilitating depression or anxiety. A combination of medication and CBT techniques is frequently appropriate. Therapists are encouraged to generate their own lists of standard cognitive and behavioral techniques to use as a resource for treatment planning.

Once the client is stabilized, the therapist will begin to focus on characteristic long-standing maladaptive patterns or features of Axis II Disorders linked to presenting problems, namely, dysfunctional coping styles, themes, and early maladaptive schemes and modes. This provides a transition to the Developmental Phase because many of the same Axis II patterns will also be components of the client's developmental task difficulties. This is the time to put the presenting problems in the larger context of developmental task blocks that appear to be preventing the client from achieving the desired lifestyle and quality of life.

THE DEVELOPMENTAL PHASE

In addition to the need for the new developmental assessment instruments outlined in the previous chapter, there has also been a need for new developmental therapy strategies specifically designed to neutralize the negative consequences of previous unresolved tasks and increase potential for successful resolution of current and future developmental tasks. Some cognitive-restructuring strategies in the literature have sought to address the early roots of dysfunctional cognitive processes, without the underlying life span developmental perspective or focus on task blocks and maladaptive pathways of Developmental CBT. Examples include techniques designed to explore historical roots of dysfunctional beliefs (Guidano, 1987; Guidano & Liotti, 1983); techniques for reviewing, reliving, and reality-testing cognitions linked to childhood experiences (Beck and Freeman, 1990); Schema-Focused Therapy strategies combining life review, experiential, interpersonal, and behavioral techniques (McGinn & Young, 1996); and "historical re-synthesis" strategies (McMullin, 2000). In addition to this, Developmental CBT is interested the historical roots of the client's blocked psychosocial tasks and deviant pathways.

Changing a distorted anachronistic life theme or interpretation of a critical life event maintaining a dysfunctional developmental pathway presents a very difficult challenge since clients tend to adhere to familiar and habitual behavioral coping styles in spite of their damaging effect in the long run. Consequently, the new developmental analysis and change strategies to be introduced in this chapter have been designed to address not only current psychosocial developmental difficulties, but also delays from earlier stages in the client's life and potential blocks to resolution of future developmental tasks. These strategies, listed in Table 3.2, will be used (1) to educate clients about the contribution of psychosocial task difficulties to current problems, (2) to aid clients in identifying and analyzing cognitive and behavioral components of their psychosocial task difficulties, (3) to restructure dysfunctional developmental schemas, (4) to motivate clients to alter current chronic self-defeating pathways, (5) to teach clients new cognitive–behavioral life skills for developmental gaps and skill deficits impeding resolution of normative tasks, and (6) to neutralize residual negative effects of early family, peer, and school experiences that may be blocking successful task resolution in the current stage.

The application of these new Developmental CBT strategies to developmental difficulties in occupational, social, and family spheres will be further demonstrated in subsequent chapters. It is hoped that clients will start to feel more hopeful as they begin to apply former skills and newly learned coping strategies to current life transitions and challenges.

Table 3.2 New Developmental CBT Strategies

Developmental Analysis Strategies:
- Developmental Task Block Identification
- Developmental Task Block Analysis

Developmental Change Strategies:
- Developmental Task Resolution Planning
- Alternative Pathways
- Adaptive Versus Obsolete Coping Styles
- Developmental Deficit Skill Building
- Then and Now
- Current Life Structure Reorganization
- Fast Forward
- Future Developmental Stage Planning
- Negative Life Review Reframing
- Resiliency Training

DEVELOPMENTAL TASK-BLOCK IDENTIFICATION
Strategy Objectives

Clients are helped to identify their own past and present psychosocial task blocks or difficulties and self-defeating pathways in areas of intimate partner relationships and social, family, and occupational functioning.

Method

1. First the therapist identifies the client's task blocks and deviant developmental pathways on the basis of the ongoing developmental assessment. The following tables are useful references: Child and Adolescent Normative Psychosocial Tasks (Table 2.4), Adult Normative Psychosocial Tasks (Table 2.5), as well as special tables in Chapters 4 to 6 documenting typical themes and characteristic pathways associated with various psychosocial task difficulties in areas of occupation and in social and family relationships.
2. The therapist reintroduces the concept of developmental task blocks evolving into deviant pathways.
3. The therapist shares hypotheses about current and former task blocks with the client, followed by requests for verification and clarification.
4. Therapist and client target aspects of Developmental Task Difficulties for therapy intervention, and the client specifies goals for change with respect to each identified task block.

Client Example

The following example illustrates the Developmental Task Block Identification strategy.

At age 40, Richard was recently fired from his job as a waiter and found himself with no income and forced to reside with resentful "friends." He presented with anger, depression, and suicidal talk. The developmental assessment revealed a 20-year history of impulsively leaving jobs or being fired because of interpersonal conflict, followed by periods of unemployment and depression, long hours and desperate attempts to fight depression with all-night parties and "turning day into night" — a lifestyle that in turn precluded serious job-search activities. His school history revealed a pattern of disruptive classroom behavior, aggressive interactions with peers, and conflict with teachers. His father allowed him to leave school and take a factory job at age 16. This lasted only a few weeks because he soon became bored and impulsively quit before securing another job, setting a pattern of brief periods of employment followed by periods of unemployment that was to last for years. He "freelanced" as a rock musician and song writer for a while, and at different times he would move in with girlfriends who supported him temporarily until the relationships ended. At one point in his late twenties he briefly returned to school as a mature student with plans to complete qualifications for his high-school diploma and start university. Although he earned one credit, he soon became bored and failed to put forth sufficient effort, found himself failing his courses and in conflict with teachers, and dropped out.

Richard's presenting problems included his unemployed and homeless status and depression. Unresolved developmental tasks of adolescence included: (1) failure to acquire sufficient educational background for a viable adult occupational path, (2) failure to develop effective relationship skills with classmates and teachers, and (3) failure to develop adequate self-discipline necessary for successful academic performance. Blocked developmental tasks of early adulthood and current middle adult years included: (1) failure to form effective adult interpersonal skills, (2) failure to establish and maintain an initial viable occupational path, (3) failure to establish a health-enhancing daily routine, and (4) failure to establish a functional independent home environment. These were currently manifested in insufficient occupational commitment, coworker relationship problems, an impulsive job termination pattern precluding financial stability, and a chaotic daily routine currently affecting job-search activities.

DEVELOPMENTAL TASK-BLOCK ANALYSIS
Strategy Objectives
After developmental task blocks have been identified, client and therapist work together to analyze each unresolved task in order to identify cognitive, behavioral, and emotional components. Some of the components may be Axis I or Axis II symptoms such as debilitating anxiety or avoidance behaviors. Following this, client and therapist use Developmental CBT assessment instruments to identify earlier manifestations of the developmental task block and early family, social, and occupational origins and triggers. The roots of blocked developmental tasks can usually be found in childhood, adolescence, or earlier adult peri-

ods, so that the current block is essentially the recent manifestation of a chronic dysfunctional pathway. In most cases variations of dysfunctional child and adolescent coping patterns may still be maintaining the Developmental Task Difficulty. The benefits of guiding clients through self-discovery of earlier triggers and precursors of their current task blocks is that this process of discovery will highlight persistent thinking and behavior styles that still function as deterrents to achieving the kind of life they want today. Clients have a chance to reexperience and reframe their personal developmental task resolution history and thereby gain necessary insight into their past maladaptive styles affecting current presenting problems and concurrent Axis I disorders.

The client's analysis of his or her own psychosocial developmental task resolution history is used as a therapy technique to help the client reconceptualize current patterns within the larger framework of blocked normative adult tasks and roles. Insight into the origin of task blocks and specification of concrete cognitive and behavioral components of the difficulty lay the foundation for the subsequent process of client generation of goals and plans for resolving the developmental task and increase motivation for change. Clients also have the opportunity to identify periods in the past when they coped more successfully and to identify the skills that enabled them to do so. These strengths can be enhanced and called into play for resolving current developmental tasks, and clients will then be in a better position to develop new adaptive strategies for current and future functioning.

Method

Therapists may adapt the following explanation for the Developmental Task-Block Analysis:

> Your difficulty coping with your role as (e.g., student, employed worker, independent adult, spouse, parent, etc.) seems to be a major factor contributing to your upsetting emotional state. Certain things are expected of us by the society we live in, and if we fail to achieve them we often end up feeling sad, anxious, angry or unworthy. Your difficulty with this role is complicated by some of your long-term patterns that are self-defeating because they prevent you from attaining the type of life or relationships you want. Some of these self-defeating patterns are thought patterns, while others are behavior patterns, and most have been there for a long time. Changing these patterns sufficiently to enable you to have the life you want will take a great deal of motivation and discipline, but it can be done. It will involve first specifying precisely how you

want things to be and what you want to achieve in this role and then identifying the self-defeating patterns that prevent you from attaining your goals.

To address and resolve these developmental task blocks, you must first identify them, and then systematically pinpoint self-defeating past and present behavior and thinking styles contributing to the blocked task. We will also need to find out how these self-defeating patterns got started by looking back at earlier years in your life in your family and at your experiences and relationships outside the home with peers and classmates. Because of circumstances in your life, there may have been some essential skills you were unable to learn or master sufficiently when you were growing up, which you can still learn and master at this time.

This strategy is comprised of the following steps designed to guide clients through the process of identifying their inadequately resolved tasks of childhood, adolescence, or previous adult periods and examining cognitive, behavioral, and emotional components of their unsuccessful attempts at task resolution.

1. Use developmental assessment instruments described in Chapter 2 to obtain information about difficult periods in the client's life when the origins of task blocks were most likely to have occurred. Instruments include the Stress Coping Style History (Table 2.8), Family of Origin Patterns (Table 2.9), Parent–Offspring Interaction Styles (Table 2.10), and history of past peer, partner, school, and work functioning (Tables 2.11 to 2.14).
2. Identify early family, peer, and school influences and origins of the Developmental Task Difficulty.
3. Identify *current* cognitive, behavioral, and emotional components disrupting resolution of normative tasks today.
4. Identify earlier manifestations of these same components during previous life stages of childhood, adolescence, and recent adult periods.
5. Specify areas for change:
   • Dysfunctional cognitions that now need to be reframed from an adult perspective
   • Chronic behavior patterns contributing to the difficulty that need to be altered or replaced
   • Developmental skill deficits

Using Developmental CBT Assessment Instruments and Summary Tables as Therapy Tools for Historical Analysis

Many of the Developmental CBT assessment instruments were designed to function in two major ways: for collecting, recording, and summarizing data elicited through structured interviews, and for use with clients as tools for ongoing analysis. For example, new information obtained by the therapist during the sessions about the client's maladaptive thought and behavior patterns potentially linked to developmental task difficulties is first recorded and organized on the "Record of Dysfunctional Cognitive, Behavioral, and Emotional Patterns" (Table 2.15), and then targeted for therapy interventions. The instruments may be adapted by the therapist for use in teaching clients to analyze their current dysfunctional patterns and related early experiences.

Typical Early Influences

Therapists need to be familiar with typical early influences associated with various task and role difficulties. Some frequently observed influences affecting performance of a variety of normative tasks include: (1) inadequate opportunity for exposure to same-sex or heterosexual peer-group activities during childhood and adolescence, (2) inadequate exposure to competent effective adult or peer role models, (3) inadequate exposure to positive school experiences that prepare the individual for effective performance of adult occupational tasks, (4) a chaotic family environment without sufficient routine and parental expectations to ensure the child's development of self-discipline necessary for sufficient academic and occupational achievement, (5) exposure to destructive marital interaction styles of parents affecting the child's future partner relationships, (6) exposure to parental role models suffering from mental illness or lacking sufficient independence, resiliency, or interpersonal interaction skills, (7) chronic exposure to ineffectual or abusive parent–child interaction styles, and (8) ongoing exposure to negative or stressful teacher or classmate interactions affecting current performance in the work place.

Typical Skill Deficits and Pathways

Examples of underdeveloped coping skills linked to adult role difficulties that may be targeted for therapy include: (1) ineffective interpersonal skills for building and maintaining friendships or for dealing with authority figures, colleagues, or social interactions; (2) inadequate intimacy and couple-interaction skills necessary for initiating and maintaining satisfying partner relationships or for terminating destructive partner relationships; (3) inadequate self-discipline necessary for occupational success and satisfaction; and (4) inadequate capacity for independence and initiative necessary to break free from significant others or from oppressive situations in order to establish and maintain an effective independent adult life structure. If skill deficits are a feature, these are noted as targets for future life-skills training strategies designed by the therapist to facilitate client acquisition of skills inadequately developed during earlier stages.

Client Example

A historical analysis was carried out with Richard, and yielded the following additional details:

> Richard was from a small town and grew up in a chaotic family of five siblings. He had an aggressive alcoholic father and a disorganized mother who was unable to give the children adequate attention because of her difficulties in dealing with her husband. There were few consistent routines, rules, or regulations, and the home environment was not conducive to fostering self-discipline or effective study habits. The parents showed little interest in the children's school performance or attendance and left them to themselves. The family was shunned in the community because of the father's drinking problem, and the client reacted to taunts from peers by fighting back to prove that his family was as good as others, if not superior. With insufficient educational qualifications and few job prospects, the client adopted a pathway of impulsively quitting jobs when he became bored and becoming financially dependent on other people. This pathway continued into adulthood. He shunned entry-level jobs that he felt were below him, choosing to fantasize about a more glamorous career as a rock musician and successful song writer.

The client identified the following early manifestations of his impulsive job termination and aggressive interpersonal pathways:

- Childhood and adolescence
  - Aggressive attempts to prove self superior to critical peers
  - Quit school at age 16, drifting from job to job
- Early adulthood
  - Inappropriate occupational choice of rock musician
  - Failure to establish a viable career path
  - Chaotic lifestyle precluding prolonged steady employment
  - Abortive attempt to acquire further educational qualifications

Self-defeating themes and behavior styles identified by the client included:

- "I'm too good for menial jobs."
- "I should be able to 'strike it rich' without a college degree."
- "It's not my fault that I get fired. My bosses start the arguments."
- "Other people have an obligation to put me up at their homes since I would do the same for them."
- Acting impulsively when bored or angry.
- Chaotic daily life routine.
- Procrastinating job search hoping for a "lucky break."

Early influences shaping the dysfunctional pathways identified by client and therapist included:

- Parental neglect and chaotic home life: children's inadequate development of occupational self discipline
- Aggressive interpersonal style similar to father's in response to peer taunts
- Inadequate development of appropriate conflict-resolution skills
- Truancy ignored by parents, fostering adolescent pattern of manipulating the system

DEVELOPMENTAL TASK RESOLUTION PLANNING
Strategy Objectives

Once developmental task difficulties are identified and labeled, and cognitive, behavioral, and emotional components are pinpointed along with their earlier manifestations, clients are then assisted in devising their own plan for altering blocked tasks and maladaptive developmental pathways. The goal is for the client to propose a plan that he or she will be prepared to put into effect. The therapist may then propose appropriate interventions to implement the client's plan, drawn from new developmental strategies, as well as standard CBT interventions.

Method

The therapist introduces this strategy with the following:

Now that you have a better understanding of this, we will work together to devise a plan for learning and practicing new alternative healthier patterns that will work for you and help you attain the kind of life you want. In order to define what these healthy patterns will be, we will first need to decide the type of thinking and behavior patterns that would be more successful for you, and then you will need to learn and practice new skills associated with the healthier patterns. After you have learned and practiced these new skills, you will have the challenge of trying out these skills in your everyday life. You will need to persist with efforts to replace old self-defeating patterns with these new healthier thought and behavior patterns until you begin to have some success in resolving your task blocks and until you begin to see progress in achieving the life you want. It will take discipline because it is necessary to methodically observe your thinking and behavior patterns every day and systematically change self-defeating patterns and replace them with the new skills you will learn in the therapy sessions.

The therapist leads the client through the following steps:

1. Specify areas for change by asking yourself, "What do I want to be different in my life today?"
2. Identify and label each of the life tasks with which you are experiencing difficulties and specify how you would like to see each changed.
3. Identify chronic long-standing cognitive and behavioral patterns or "blocks" maintaining the Developmental Task Difficulty and identify self-defeating pathways that need to be altered.
4. Hypothesize about missing developmental steps and unlearned skills.
5. Identify and evaluate your current unsuccessful approach to achieving your goals. Ask yourself, "What am I doing wrong? Why isn't it working for me?" Identify the self-defeating thinking and behavior patterns that are contributing to your difficulty with each life task.
6. Identify former times when your life was better in terms of this type of life task. Ask yourself, "What was different during those periods when I managed to temporarily abandon my self-defeating pathway and function more effectively?"
7. Come up with a plan to intelligently do something about resolving the task, by designing practical steps that will help you learn missing skills that left gaps in your early development.
8. Apply yourself to learning new skills and patterns to alter self-defeating coping styles that are preventing you from moving forward with the task and remedying your situation. Make a daily effort to replace old patterns with new effective ones.

9. Keep a weekly record of daily activities to provide an ongoing evaluation of how well you are progressing toward realizing your goals.

Client Example

Richard identified the following targets and came up with the following task-block resolution plan for addressing his ongoing difficulty in maintaining a steady job and independent residence:

Current unsuccessful approach: Quitting a job before getting a new one; getting into arguments with coworkers; fantasizing about a career in a rock band

Self-defeating thinking and behavior patterns: "I can always get a better job." "This job is so boring I can't stand it." Impulsively terminating a job; allowing myself to get involved in arguments with bosses

Early dysfunctional pathways: Quitting high school before acquiring sufficient job or educational skills; drifting from job to job; living off of other people; quitting mature-student college program

Developmental skill gaps: Conflict resolution skills; persistence skills

Plan: Learn new ways to deal with bosses that don't lead to a conflict situation and being fired; learn self-discipline and persistence skills to maintain effective job performance

Larger life style changes: A more balanced life with my own place; possibly look into food-services training courses to increase my options in the restaurant business; continue to pursue rock music as strictly a hobby

After the client comes up with a plan, the therapist incorporates this into a larger, more detailed therapy plan using the Developmental CBT Case Formulation (Table 2.16) as a basis. Specific developmental strategies and standard CBT interventions are designated as interventions for each identified target. In Richard's case, the therapist targeted several components of his aggressive interpersonal style for therapy: (1) heightened sensitivity to hostile cues, (2) poorly developed empathy and sensitivity, (3) hostile attribution bias, (4) poor self-evaluation skills, (5) poor frustration control skills, (6) underdeveloped conflict negotiation skills, and (7) poor communication skills.

The therapist reviews the conceptualization and collaborative therapy plan with the client and asks for feedback. Periodic revisions in the detailed therapy plan are made to ensure that the client is willing and motivated to participate in the interventions.

Richard was helped to understand how maladaptive features of his relationships with coworkers were the culmination of long-standing aggressive interpersonal patterns dating back to his method of dealing with taunts from childhood peers. He realized that his aggressive response style was modeled on that of his alcoholic father, and his failure to develop mutually satisfying, trusting adolescent friendships was partially the result of inadequate exposure to more socially appropriate family role models.

THE EVOLVING DEVELOPMENTAL CBT TREATMENT PLAN

Incorporation of data into a comprehensive treatment plan is ongoing. After each session the therapist reviews and organizes session notes, adding new components of presenting problems and possible interventions for future sessions.

Information obtained through standard CBT assessment strategies and new developmental assessment instruments is first summarized on the Developmental CBT Case Conceptualization form (Table 2.16). Following this, the therapist selects or devises interventions for each target. For the Developmental Phase, the therapist begins to apply new Developmental CBT techniques to weaken dysfunctional patterns disrupting normal adult roles and to teach clients skills they failed to learn in earlier developmental periods until progress is made in resolving the current task. This provides the therapist with a provisionary treatment plan, which will be expanded and revised with each session.

Richard's developmental task resolution plan included goals of establishing a career plan that would ensure steady employment and enough money to maintain a decent home. He decided to accept an offer to temporarily live with his sister's family in exchange for regular baby-sitting and to attend a government job search and training program. He then listed beliefs and behavior patterns that could potentially sabotage his goals.

Richard's Developmental CBT treatment plan is shown in Table 3.3. It incorporates initiatives generated by the client, in addition to standard CBT strategies and new Developmental CBT interventions planned by the therapist. The Developmental CBT strategies included Alternative Pathways and Future Developmental Stage Planning to help Richard to draw on insight from past failures and missed opportunities to finally establish a viable career plan. The Adaptive Versus Obsolete Coping Styles strategy was used to teach him more effective ways of interact-

Table 3.3 Client Example of Developmental CBT Treatment Plan

PHASE ONE	
Targets	**Interventions**
Presenting problems:	• Job search skill training program;
• Fired from job, unemployed status;	• temporarily live with sister
• homeless, temporarily residing with resentful friends	
Axis I symptoms:	• Standard CBT interventions for depression
Axis II symptoms:	• Developmental Task-Block Analysis to
• Entitlement;	increase client insight into links between
• mistrust, inappropriate blaming;	Axis I and II symptoms and developmental
• impulsive response style;	task difficulties;
• recognition seeking	• Schema-Focused Therapy cognitive change techniques for Axis II symptoms

PHASE TWO	
Targets	**Interventions**
Task Difficulty #1	• Developmental Task-Block Identification,
Failure to establish an initial viable career path and to maintain steady employment; pattern of abruptly quitting jobs	Analysis, and Resolution Strategies; • Fast Forward to increase motivation for change; • Future Developmental Stage Planning
Themes and Beliefs:	• Standard cognitive techniques to alter
I can't tolerate this boring job. I'm too good for this job. I can get another job.	distorted thoughts and beliefs maintaining patterns of quitting adequate jobs prematurely
Self-Defeating Coping Styles:	• Standard behavior therapy techniques; fast
impulsively quitting jobs	forward five years
Previous Manifestations and Early	• Developmental Task-Block Analysis;
Influences: quit high school; quit jobs; quit mature-student college program	• Alternative Pathways
Task Difficulty #2	• Developmental Deficit Skill-Building
Aggressive interpersonal style with coworkers	Strategy to identify and target skill deficits in areas of conflict negotiation, empathic understanding, role taking; frustration control; accurate assessment of interpersonal situations.
Themes and Beliefs:	• Standard cognitive therapy change
I have to prove he's wrong and I'm right. If I ignore this it will show them they're right and I'm wrong.	techniques
Self-Defeating Coping Styles:	• Adaptive Versus Obsolete Coping Styles
provoke an argument; aggressive retaliation	
Previous Manifestations and Early	• Developmental Task-Block Analysis;
Influences:	• Developmental Deficit Skill Building
aggressive retaliation to peer taunts; aggressively challenge teachers; family stigma; aggressive parent role model; failure to develop friendships or effective interpersonal conflict resolution skills	

ing with work colleagues, and the Developmental Deficit Skill-Building strategy was used to improve job persistence and organizational skills. Current Life Structure Reorganization was used to alter his chaotic daily life pattern.

Once the plan is completed, developmental and cognitive and behavioral pattern–breaking techniques will be employed during the developmental therapy change phase. Therapist and client devise ways of evaluating outcome by means of homework assignments, such as having the client keep records of daily activities and upsetting thoughts.

ALTERNATIVE PATHWAYS

Strategy Objectives

Clients are encouraged to speculate about alternative pathways they might have taken during previous life stages that would have resulted in a more successful resolution of a developmental task challenge. Having clients hypothesize about the probable consequences of taking a different route in terms of their lives today is a first step toward finding an alternative pathway for the current manifestation of the task difficulty.

Method

The client is presented with the following:

1. Now that you have identified blocks to the resolution of your current life task challenges and have traced earlier manifestations and origins of the pathway you have chosen, imagine what your life would be like today if you had taken an alternative pathway.
2. Identify critical experiences underlying your choice of pathway. Speculate about your reason for choosing a particular pathway when you were faced with a difficult task or transition. How did the chosen pathway and your underlying beliefs help you cope?
3. What would have been a better pathway during your childhood and adolescence, during early adulthood, and today?
4. Suppose you were several years younger and in a position to take an alternative pathway. What would you do? How can you adapt this alternative pathway to your current situation?

Client Example

Richard considered what his life would have been like if he had followed a different occupational pathway that involved finishing high school and possibly going on to college or a job training course. He speculated that if his parents had insisted, he would have remained at home and persisted at schoolwork in spite of feeling bored and feeling the need for a more exciting life style. He decided that as a young adult it would have been better if he had taken a basic entry-level job, in spite of the modest salary, like most of his contemporaries and acquired new job skills and qualifications as he went along. He also felt that he would be better off today if he had persisted as a mature student in his late twenties and at least completed his high-school diploma at that time so that he would be eligible for a practical college co-op program, possibly in the food services area. He decided to finish his high school qualifications as a mature student, followed by a community college work–study program.

ADAPTIVE VERSUS OBSOLETE COPING STYLES

Intervention Objectives

This is used to help clients to alter their identified dysfunctional cognitive and behavioral coping styles that helped them survive stressful conditions during childhood and adolescence but that are now outmoded and working against them by maintaining developmental task difficulties. It is useful for altering a variety of maladaptive developmental patterns, such as self-defeating interpersonal interaction styles in social, work, and marital situations, dependency problems, and avoidance and escape patterns.

Method

1. Reiterate goals for resolution of the developmental task block.
2. The client is asked to provide detailed descriptions of problematic situations. Client and therapist then identify obsolete patterns from earlier developmental periods that are maintaining the current task difficulties.
3. Label current manifestations of the identified self-defeating pattern "Obsolete Coping Style."
4. Teach the client prerequisite skills for a more *Adaptive Coping Style*, appropriate for the current task challenge and developmental period. The client then practices this new coping style through role-playing during the session and in vivo between sessions.

Client Example

Richard's goal was to find a new job and maintain it for three months without getting fired. He was aware that conflict with bosses and coworkers was his major stumbling block in terms of job continuity but did not know what to do about it. Components of his self-defeating interpersonal style that escalated conflicts were labeled "Obsolete Coping Style." Richard gradually came to realize that his future success in maintaining employment would depend on a shift away from his current manifestation of an Obsolete Coping Style he had resorted to as a child in response to peer harassment. Components of this self-defeating style that were currently escalating conflicts were his repeated efforts to prove himself to be right or superior and his tendency to misinterpret the thoughts and actions of others as malevolent. Another Obsolete Coping Style was his tendency to abruptly terminate a potentially good occupational situation when feeling stressed, bored, or angry. These were all labeled as his Obsolete Coping Style. The therapist helped him develop alternative functional patterns that were labeled "Adaptive Coping Style." He was taught to reconsider and alter angry reactions by inhibiting angry responses and replacing them with neutral responses and to pay attention to and acknowledge the other person's viewpoint both verbally and nonverbally. He was also taught to inhibit the urge to abruptly resign from a job by putting off a decision for at least one week in order to increase his chances for maintaining steady employment. Table 3.4 summarizes this process.

DEVELOPMENTAL DEFICIT SKILL BUILDING

Intervention Objectives

The goal here is to identify missing normative developmental steps and assist clients in learning new skills to compensate for gaps in their early psychosocial developmental histories. This strategy is designed for clients who have embarked on maladaptive pathways because of failure to master basic prerequisite life skills during childhood, adolescence, or early adulthood. Treatment of the client's current task difficulty will necessitate acquisition of basic skills as a preliminary step for mastery of the more complex skills required in the current life stage. It is particularly well suited for aggressive clients such as Richard, whose poorly developed conflict-resolution skills precluded job continuity. It is also useful for clients with other forms of underdeveloped interpersonal or friendship skills precipitating a social-isolation pathway, including clients with difficulties forming intimate relationships. The Developmental Deficit Skill-Building strategy may also help clients lacking basic

Table 3.4 Client Example of Adaptive versus Obsolete Coping Styles

Trigger	Obsolete Coping Style	Adaptive Coping Style
Person using a judgmental, dictatorial, or condescending tone to tell me I'm wrong	• "I must prove I'm better than him." • Try to convince person I'm right; protest; say too much	• Neutral response (e.g.. "That's one way of looking at it.") • Nod silently without comment • Inhibit urge to debate the issue
	• Overly sensitive to slight; take things too personally (e.g., "That was a put-down, I can't let that go by.") • React defensively (demand proof; demand to know what I did wrong; counter everything the other person says)	• Adaptive self-talk (e.g., "Remember your long-term goals and let it go, count to 10." "This isn't forever." "Don't bite on every hook." "Assume that no criticism was meant." "Listen carefully to what the other person is saying.") • Verbalize respect for some aspect of the other person's opinion • Summarize the other person's view • Observe how other coworkers handle this person or how they diffuse potential conflicts, and try out their strategies • Neutral voice • Excuse self and politely leave the room if necessary to avoid angry outburst
	• "I can't work with this idiot." • Resign from the job abruptly and dramatically	• Remain in the work setting for the remainder of the day • Adaptive self talk ("I will put up with this discomfort and keep focused on my work." • "Remember your resolution to never leave a job before finding a new one.")

skills for adequate job performance, such as self discipline, persistence, or efficient time management. Basically, the therapist uses information gleaned from the life history assessment to identify and educate the client about under-developed or missing coping skills underlying unresolved psychosocial tasks. The therapist then designs step-by-step skill-building strategies to facilitate client acquisition of necessary skills. The client is helped to understand how skill gaps have precluded more effective coping styles and pathways for resolving the identified psycho-social tasks.

Method

The steps of this strategy are as follows:

1. The therapist uses Developmental CBT history question-naires to obtain information about early experiences and pos-sible early origins of the client's current Developmental Task Difficulty.
2. The therapist postulates missing developmental steps or skill deficits in the client's earlier life stages on the basis of clinical observation and familiarity with psychosocial developmental literature on normal acquisition of basic life skills (e.g., Carter & McGoldrick, 1989; Deeter-Deckard, 2001; Linehan, 1993; Young, 1982.)
3. Clients are helped to understand how inadequate opportu-nities to learn basic skills in the past are linked to their present difficulties with current, more complex tasks.
4. Therapist and client identify developmental gaps, early influ-ences, and maladaptive coping pathways adopted by the client in previous developmental stages.
5. Therapists then educate clients about the contrast between their developmental histories and more normative early histo-ries that facilitate acquisition of particular life skills.
6. Clients may be asked to observe people they know who have been successful in handling a particular developmental task and to identify adaptive skills possessed by others that they have failed to learn. This enables the client to participate more fully in compiling a list of missed skills and steps that he or she will need to master.
7. Therapists propose skill-acquisition goals for identified tasks and devise methods of teaching these skills, incorporating standard CBT skill-building techniques.
8. Clients practice the new skills during the sessions and between sessions in their daily lives.

Although this strategy may incorporate established CBT skill-build-ing techniques, it differs from standard CBT approaches by providing a developmental perspective. Clients are helped to gain insight into maladaptive processes or pathways responsible for their skill defi-cits, to contrast these with normal developmental pathways fostering adaptive skill development, and to seek to rectify earlier developmental gaps during their current life stage.

Client Example

Tom was a middle-aged post office employee who had been unsuccessful in his ongoing attempts to initiate a romantic partner relationship. He had been raised by an anxious, demanding single mother who prohibited her son from participating in social activities. He had been excluded from activities with the opposite sex during adolescence, resulting in underdeveloped heterosexual relationship skills. This precipitated years of embarrassment and self-imposed social isolation. His current repertoire consisted of inappropriate techniques for approaching women that were considered "politically incorrect." He was extremely shy and never learned to converse with girls during his adolescent years. He rarely participated in mixed group activities and never had a date. This pattern of social isolation continued into his twenties and thirties. He had no female acquaintances and no relationships with female work colleagues. In his free time, he spent long hours in solitary pursuits. He resorted to answering personal ads for companionship in the newspaper. He was also introduced to a few potential partners through a dating agency but either rejected them all as not beautiful enough or alienated them by raising the inappropriate topics on the first date.

Through the use of Developmental CBT assessment techniques, the client was helped to view his current heterosexual skill deficit in the context of underdeveloped communication skills and a long-standing social-isolation pathway dating back to childhood. The client's unsuccessful approach with women was broken down into component skill deficits. Underdeveloped conversation skills was one skill-deficit area, involving problems initiating conversations, communicating interest, experiencing true empathy, and conveying empathic understanding. The therapist then collaborated with the client to produce the following list of skill-building activities:

1. Learn and practice basic conversation skills during the session (e.g., skills for initiating, maintaining, and ending a conversation).
2. Learn and practice social perception skills during the session, using specific situations from the client's daily life:

- Increase client's ability to make accurate perceptions and attributions about the meaning of the other person's words and actions.
- Increase client's ability to make accurate social judgments about what is *appropriate* to say and do in social situations.
- Increase client's ability to use feedback from the other person's behavior to decide the appropriate way to proceed.

3. Initiate conversation with a work colleague.
4. Phone an old acquaintance (any age) and talk for five minutes.
5. Initiate an activity with a work colleague.
6. Attend a mixed social group activity to increase the likelihood of meeting appropriate partners and learning appropriate social interaction skills by observing others (e.g., clubs, coffee breaks).
7. Develop a platonic friendship with a woman.
8. Observe potential partners interacting with other people to get some idea of what the person is like before deciding if it is appropriate to ask for a date.
9. Learn and role-play heterosexual interaction sequences during the session (e.g., talk about one's own experiences; encourage the other person to talk; ask leading questions; show interest in what the other person says).
10. Initiate a brief conversation with a potential date.
11. Ask for a date.

THEN AND NOW
Intervention Objectives

The purpose of this strategy is to help clients distinguish between their own successful and unsuccessful handling of current and past developmental task challenges. They are asked to recall periods in their lives when they were coping more successfully with a similar developmental task or transition and to isolate components of past coping styles that worked for them. They can then build on these earlier strengths by resurrecting their former coping skills for use today with a current task challenge.

Method

Clients are asked to recall previous situations during earlier life stages when they experienced similar negative emotions and other difficulties when attempting to negotiate a developmental challenge. The therapist leads the client through the following steps:

1. Close your eyes and bring to mind earlier difficult periods in your life during childhood, adolescence, or earlier adult periods when you experienced similar task challenges and negative emotions. Describe each of these situations.
2. Describe your coping style in each of these difficult situations.
3. Next, recall a stage in your life when you think you were coping better with similar task challenges. What were the major reasons for your more effective coping style at that time? Identify components of your effective coping style.
4. What are the main differences between then and now in terms of your coping style? What worked better for you? What coping styles were least effective?
5. Which of your effective past coping techniques would help you today?

Client Example

The client was a 43-year-old unemployed woman who presented with depression and a history of panic attacks. She had been living at her mother's home since she quit her job shortly after her relationship with her boyfriend ended two years ago. The developmental analysis revealed that as a teenager she had felt responsible for looking after her divorced mother. She often feigned illness in order to be at home with her mother — a practice condoned by the mother, who felt safer with her daughter nearby. She had attempted to attend university out of town but dropped out and returned home. She was offered a job by a relative, which she accepted in spite of reservations about her ability to sustain adequate attendance because of her panic attacks. She joined an exercise group, managed to make a few friends, and had a boyfriend for the first time in her life. When the opportunity arose, she decided to move into an apartment with a girlfriend. In spite of occasional panic attacks and her mother's pleas that she return home, she managed to cope independently and to hold down a job for three years. Later she was obliged to give up her apartment when her girlfriend got married. She decided to move in with her boyfriend rather than return to her mother's home. However, shortly afterward the relationship began to deteriorate, her panic attacks worsened, and she returned to live with her mother.

The client stated that her most successful period was during her twenties when she was single, living independently from her mother, and working steadily for three years. Effective components of her life at that time were: (1) assertive resistance to pressure from her mother to return home, (2) financial independence, (3) persistence at a job in spite of periodic panic attacks, (4) social activities, and (5) less preoccupation with somatoform symptoms. Closer analysis revealed the following components of her current unsuccessful coping pattern: (1) social isolation, (2) financial dependence on mother, (3) giving in to mother's demands on her time, (4) catastrophic thoughts fostering resistance to finding another job (e.g., "I can't move out of Mom's home and live alone because I'll have panic attacks." "The thought of working again is impossible right now due to my anxiety." "I have to look after my mother she's getting old and this comes first.").

The client identified the following former successful coping behaviors that she hoped to resurrect: (1) initiate job search activities in spite of worries about panic attacks interfering with job attendance, (2) rejoin the hiking group, (3) reduce frequency of doctors' appointments, and (4) search for a new apartment mate and set a target date for moving out of mother's home.

CURRENT LIFE STRUCTURE REORGANIZATION

Intervention Objectives

This strategy is used to help clients whose life structures are inappropriate for their current life stage or detrimental to resolution of current life tasks. Clients are encouraged to take a comprehensive look at their current life and to generate specific goals for a more satisfying, healthful, and appropriate life structure. Clients are helped to understand that they may have to make significant alterations in their own behavior and in their external environment in order to achieve these goals. This strategy is particularly suited for clients whose daily activities and routines are immature or prematurely old for their current life stage or are at odds with the life they wish to be living. Examples include clients with hectic or chaotic lifestyles interfering with work or with interpersonal relationships or clients with too few meaningful or effective activities in their daily lives, fostering a sense of emptiness or despair.

Method

The therapist leads the client through the following steps:

1. Describe the way you would like your life to be today.
2. How do you think your life structure *should* be at your particular time of your life or life stage?

3. Describe the person you'd like to be today in terms of how you would like to be functioning in the following areas:
   - Social relationships
   - Partner (spouse) relationship
   - Occupation (career)
   - Family life
   - Recreation
   - Psychological and spiritual status
4. What activities are appropriate at your age, and what activities would you like to be pursuing in the above areas? These will be labeled your "preferred activities."
5. Record your current morning, afternoon, and evening activities for the past few days. Label these your "actual activities." Roughly estimate the amount of time per day devoted to each of these activities.
6. Roughly estimate how much time per day was spent in your preferred activities over the past few days.
7. Compare the proportion of time you spend in your actual activities in the various areas with the proportion of time spent in your preferred activities. Note discrepancies between what you would *like* to be doing, and what you are *actually* doing.
8. Use this information to plan daily activities and a daily life structure with an increased amount of time spent in preferred activities that will be more in keeping with the daily life you would like to be leading.

Client Example

Joseph was a 61-year-old bachelor who was living with his elderly mother. She was suffering from advanced dementia and required 24-hour care. Over the past few years he had gradually given up his former social and recreational activities to spend most of his free time with his mother. His siblings participated very little in their mother's care and were critical of Joseph when he began to make arrangements for admitting his mother to a nursing home when he felt he could no longer provide adequate care for her. Joseph was also disappointed in the fact that he was the only one of the children who failed to marry and raise a family. Although his job had been satisfactory, and he had been an avid golfer and gourmet cook in the past, retirement was now "looming," and he despaired at the thought of carrying on as his mother's full-time caregiver. He had discontinued most of the activities that had made his life meaningful and was unable to recover his former optimism and zest for living.

Joseph realized that he spent most of his free time alone at home, watching television and coping poorly with his mother's demands and the inevitable chaos. Almost no time was spent in his preferred activities, such as playing golf, spending time with friends, or having small dinner parties. Table 3.5 summarizes his goals for change on the basis of the discrepancy between the proportion of time spent pursuing his current daily activities and time spent pursuing preferred daily activities:

Table 3.5 Client Example of Current Life Structure Reorganization

Areas	Current Daily Activities or Situations	Preferred Daily Activities or Situations
Social relationships	Alone; no social activity	Renew regular contact with former golf friends and pursue a new activity with potential for making new friends
Partner relationship	Ongoing ruminations about lack of a companion or soul mate	Invite female friend to a concert
Occupation	Work satisfaction; dreading retirement	Prepare for retirement by adopting a four-day week and resuming golf on Fridays
Family/Home	Evenings and weekends spent looking after mother; chaotic home environment; ongoing futile attempts to gain sibling cooperation in finding a facility for mother	Independently select a facility for mother and settle her into a nursing home; reestablish serene home environment.
Recreation	Inadequate physical activity; weight gain	Resume golf and cooking for friends; join an exercise class at the golf club
Psychological /Spiritual status	Depressed, angry	Begin attending church groups again

FAST FORWARD

Intervention Objectives

The purpose of this technique is to increase client motivation to resolve current developmental task blocks or to avoid potentially disastrous lifestyle changes. It is particularly well suited for helping clients make major lifestyle changes that are necessary for mental health, such as terminating a destructive partner relationship or a stressful job situation or altering ineffective parenting styles that are no longer working. It may also be used to help clients who are considering life changes that would disrupt a healthy pathway, such as clients who are considering leaving a stable family situation for a new unsuitable partner. Clients are instructed to anticipate the developmental challenges of their current and future life stages and to weigh the costs and benefits of maintaining or changing the status quo in light of these challenges.

Method

Clients are helped by the following questions to anticipate the consequences of either maintaining or changing the status quo:

1. If your current life structure persists unchanged, what will your life be like in 5 years time? In 10 years time?
2. List the pros and cons of retaining (or changing) the status quo in terms of quality of life for all persons involved, such as children, partner, and extended family.
3. What are the tasks of your next developmental stage? How will your current decision affect your ability to deal with the developmental tasks of future stages?
4. How would you like your life to be in 5 years time? In 10 years time?
5. Which of your beliefs, behavior patterns, or earlier life influences are affecting this decision?
6. What plans would you make to change the status quo (or to retain the status quo with some improvements to your current situation)?

Client Example

Dan had been living at home with his divorced mother while involved in a relationship with an unfaithful woman for over 10 years. His girlfriend denied her infidelity and insisted she wanted to marry him eventually. However, Dan was close to 50 years old and wanted to marry and start a family. He repeatedly vowed to leave her but was unable to follow through. Dan hypothesized that in five years he might still be stuck in the same jealous turmoil, waiting for his girlfriend to make up her mind, and still living at home with his mother. He was earning a good living and was ready to move on to the next stage of life as a family man and realized that for this to happen he would need to find a partner with similar commitment to marital fidelity, family, and children. He felt that the consequences of retaining the status quo may be the loss of an opportunity for marriage and family. He realized that his fear of dating, fear of not being able to find someone else, and fear of another failed relationship were keeping him in the same rut and that his unassertive approach with strong demanding women such as his girlfriend and his mother was a long-standing self-defeating pattern. In the end, Dan decided that anything would be better than remaining in this relationship for another five years.

Dan was helped to generate the following steps in a plan to implement his decision to break off the relationship and attempt to find another partner.

- Break off current relationship.
- Recovery period for six months with no self-imposed pressure to date. During this time, reconnect with old friends and with single friends on a regular basis.
- Start taking the initiative to meet someone else by asking friends for assistance and by getting involved in new activities.
- Begin to date more seriously. Establish basic criteria for a suitable partner (e.g., faithful, family oriented, kind to my mother, accepting me as I am without pressure to change).
- Establish a time line of two to three years to meet a suitable partner and marry.

FUTURE DEVELOPMENTAL STAGE PLANNING
Intervention Objectives

This strategy is designed to help clients think ahead to their next developmental stage and to help them begin to plan for that stage. Clients are helped to anticipate future tasks and challenges that they will have to face in major areas of daily life, with particular emphasis on areas in which they are experiencing difficulties. In the process of anticipating future stages of current developmental tasks and roles, clients will be in a better position to identify areas in which they may lack necessary skills, and will be motivated to change self-defeating patterns as a preventative measure.

Method

1. What are the tasks and challenges you will be faced with in your next stage of life (i.e., middle age, mature adulthood, postretirement, old age)?
2. What are the tasks you will have to cope with (1) in your role as a parent, (2) in your relationship with a partner or spouse or as a single unattached person), (3) in your work or daily occupation, (4) in your social relationships, and (5) in extended family relationships?
3. Which of your thought and behavior patterns associated with current or past task difficulties might lead to potential future task difficulties?
4. What skills will you need to develop to master these future-stage tasks or roles?

Client Example

Marilyn was a 38-year-old divorced mother who was having difficulty controlling her 11-year-old daughter. Marilyn had taken on extra waitress work in the early evenings, leaving her daughter in the care of a neighbor. However, the daughter had become increasingly defiant about coming home when Marilyn returned from work, manipulating her mother into allowing her to remain outside with neighborhood peers later and later each night. Marilyn suspected that these peers were already experimenting with drugs. The developmental analysis revealed that Marilyn had never known her father and was raised by a mother who was too preoccupied with the men in her life to pay sufficient attention to her daughter. As a result, Marilyn grew up without appropriate restrictions or curfews. She vowed to be a better parent for her own daughter but lacked a role model for effective parenting. In her attempts to give her daughter the attention she herself lacked in her own childhood, Marilyn had established a long-standing pattern of capitulating to the daughter's whims and escalating demands.

Marilyn was helped to anticipate the tasks and challenges she would be faced with as she entered middle age, especially with respect to parenting. She realized she would need to develop effective parenting skills necessary for controlling her daughter's teenage rebelliousness and for ensuring that her daughter developed values that would increase the likelihood that she would complete high school and would form friendships with peers with similar academic goals. Marilyn realized that these challenges would not be met if she continued her over-submissive parenting style that currently allowed her daughter to associate with peers who had too much freedom. She acknowledged the need for help in learning a more assertive parenting approach that had less to do with proving her devotion by giving in to her daughter and more to do with implementation of a sufficient daily routine, structure, rules and expectations. In other areas, Marilyn decided that her work hours would have to be restricted to daytime shifts, in spite of a decrease in pay, and that her week-night socializing would need to be curtailed so she could be available to provide her daughter with sufficient after-school and evening supervision, as well as assistance with homework.

NEGATIVE LIFE-REVIEW REFRAMING
Intervention Objectives

This intervention is used to alter a client's negative self-evaluations with respect to previous developmental task failures. It is used with clients whose ongoing regrets and ruminations about past failures prevent them from moving on to resolve the developmental tasks of their current stage. Typical preoccupations are with past job loss or demotion, with absent or unsuccessful partner relationships, or with disappointment at the way in which the children have turned out.

Method

The therapist introduces this strategy with the following explanation of the negative life-review predicament:

> *Each society has cultural expectations about appropriate behaviors, tasks, and roles that should be performed at certain ages and stages of life. There are also cultural standards for what constitutes success or failure in these roles. From childhood on, people are exposed to society's expectations of age-appropriate behavior and social timetables dictating milestones such as the time to become independent from one's parents, the time to establish a career, the time to marry, and the time to start a family. People develop self-expectations based on societal values, timetables, and criteria for success, and if they feel they haven't lived up to these expectations, they may conclude that the way in which they have lived their life is somehow inferior or unworthy. Even though some people do not choose to conform to conventional social expectations, they may still continue to evaluate their life choices and pathways in terms of conventional societal expectations.*

The therapist then proceeds with the following steps:

1. The client is helped to reconceptualize events, situations, and beliefs linked to the negative life review within a developmental life span perspective. Clients are asked to view their disappointments about unresolved tasks, unfulfilled adult roles, and past mistakes within a larger context of common (and often inevitable) ups and downs of normal life span development. Perceived failures may be reconceptualized as learning experiences that may prove helpful in coping with current tasks. Clients are asked what they have learned from their mistakes and how they may now benefit from this insight.

2. Long-standing thought and behavioral coping styles underlying the negative life review are then identified and treated with standard CBT techniques, especially techniques designed to address symptoms of personality disorders. Common components of a client's negative life review are revenge-seeking, extreme guilt, self-punishment, victim role, dependency, blame, and beliefs about irreversible damage. The therapist uses cognitive therapy techniques to guide the client in generating more-positive interpretations of events or conditions of past years, so that the client begins to view past failures as constructive setbacks that do not necessarily diminish self-worth.

3. As the client is guided toward a gradual acceptance of past decisions and consequences, there is a new focus on client achievements and adaptive reordering of priorities in the current life stage. Clients are encouraged to come up with strategies that may be used at the present time to right past wrongs, such as reestablishing contact with estranged adult children or with an estranged parent.

The Negative Life-Review Reframing strategy may also be applied to patterns of chronic debilitating ruminations stemming from early traumatic emotional memories. Many clients present with long histories of angry ruminations about childhood traumas or chronic stress, accompanied by underlying beliefs that the negative experiences have somehow rendered them mentally "sick" or abnormal and prevented them from resolving psychosocial tasks and living a normal life. In many cases they have abdicated responsibility for attempting normal tasks and roles.

A common cause of negative life review is lingering memories of traumatic family situations experienced during childhood, such as abuse or parental alcoholism. Residual negative emotional memories may also stem from peer or school experiences or from isolated traumatic events.

The common thread of the negative life review is the client's preoccupation with the unfairness of the situation, "what others did to me," and the impossibility of ever being normal. This hopelessness keeps the client in a perpetual victim role and interferes with the client's ability to master normative life tasks in various areas.

Typical categories of themes and schemas are vulnerability, defectiveness, shame, mistrust, and abuse (e.g., I'm abnormal; I can't ever have a good life; I must always suffer because of what was done to me; nobody would ever want me). These underlie behavioral patterns of giving up and blaming past injustices when the going gets rough and failing to pursue social relationships, romantic relationships, or career opportunities. The pathway involves angry ruminations about intractable defectiveness. During childhood and adolescence, this preoccupation with self-pity and hopelessness may have blocked opportunities for achieving interpersonal connectedness, self-confidence, worthiness, participation in peer activities, formation of deep friendships, or adequate school achievement. When the negative life review involves long-standing blame, hopelessness, and helpless passivity, the first step is to identify and explore reasons for the client's inability to let go of the traumatic experiences sufficiently to attempt age-appropriate tasks. Following this, clients are helped to examine long-standing beliefs about the permanence of their resultant mental instability and helplessness to create a more desirable life. The validity and consequences of continuing to blame current misfortunes on cruel or neglectful parents or other traumatic situations that occurred in the distant past is then raised. This outmoded negative life review is then contrasted with a more adaptive coping style that involves countering helplessness and blame schemas and assuming some responsibility for perpetuating the debilitating passive victim role over the years. It also involves a decision to take responsibility for creating a more desirable life and acquiring the necessary skills for resolving neglected tasks in social, occupational, and family spheres.

Client Example

The client was twice divorced and in her late fifties when she presented with depression secondary to her inability to leave her current alcoholic husband because that would mean another failed marriage. She hated herself for being so dependent on her husband, and she continually berated herself for past involvement in extramarital affairs that led to the breakdown of her first two marriages. She admitted that her current marriage was intolerable but was reluctant to leave her husband, primarily because she feared being judged harshly for a third failed marriage. She also ruminated about her estrangement from her only daughter, who continued to blame her mother for leaving her father, breaking up the family, and ruining her childhood. The daughter hated her mother's current husband and refused to allow the grandchildren in her mother's home.

The client was helped to see how her guilt about past decisions and her preoccupation with the stigma of a third failed marriage jeopardized her chances for a peaceful health-enhancing future life structure. Ruminations underlying irreversible aspects of her past were preventing her from addressing her current abusive marital situation. The Developmental Task-Block Analysis helped her see that her dependent personality style, dating back to her inappropriate reliance on her mother well into her early adulthood years, had led to marriages to aggressive, controlling men who provided the shelter she sought. She was then helped by the Fast Forward strategy to assess the consequences of remaining with her abusive husband for the remainder of her life, and she eventually was able to make a decision to end the relationship. She was then helped by the Current Life Structure Reorganization strategy to establish an adequate independent life structure. Cognitive therapy techniques were used to help her decrease time spent ruminating about her failure as a parent and to increase her tolerance of her daughter's aloofness and blame. She sought to atone for her past neglect of her daughter by offering to set aside time each week for babysitting the grandchildren. Assisting her daughter in this way helped her shift her focus away from her daughter's painful accusations and her failure as a parent to her positive role as grandmother, helping to raise her grandchildren.

RESILIENCY TRAINING

Intervention Objectives

This intervention is useful for helping clients adjust to common developmental or transitional challenges, such as unwanted termination of a job or partner relationship, departure of grown children from home, or separation from children following divorce. For many therapy clients, these normative transitions or events prove to be ongoing unresolved crises, disrupting any semblance of normal daily functioning for months or even years. The Resiliency Training Strategy also has a *role redefinition* component that may be used to prepare clients to cope more effectively with difficult role transitions or future changes.

It is well suited for clients who are stuck at transitions from marital to single status, from married custodial parent to divorced noncustodial parent, from parent of compliant loving small children to parent of rebellious teenagers, from employed to retired status, or from stay-at-home mom to working mother. Moos and Schaefer (1986) identify five major sets of adaptive tasks necessary for managing a life transition or crisis:

- Establish the meaning and understand the personal significance of the situation.
- Confront reality and respond to the requirements of the external situation.
- Sustain relationships with family members and friends as well as with other individuals who may be helpful in resolving the crisis and its aftermath.
- Maintain a reasonable emotional balance by managing upsetting feelings aroused by the situation.
- Preserve a satisfactory self-image and maintain a sense of competence and mastery.

These tasks were helpful in designing the Resiliency Training Strategy.

Method

1. Help the client reconceptualize the crisis within a larger life span developmental perspective of normative developmental challenges and crises accompanied by increased vulnerability to stress. Help the client to understand that temporary developmental crises are considered within normal limits and that these crises provide an opportunity for growth as the person resolves the crisis and moves on. For example, the painful end of a relationship may be reconceptualized as a common occurrence in the "*intimate relationship pathway*," or in the search for a life partner, and a person may be expected to experience several relationship failures before meeting and marrying a compatible mate. Similarly, termination of a job can be reframed within a life span perspective of normal career development that involves job loss from time to time.

2. Generate a plan to maintain coping and mastery in other areas of daily life, while using problem-solving skills to address this transition. The Current Life Structure reorganization strategy may be helpful here.

3. The concept of role redefinition is introduced next. Provide the client with an explanation of the process of giving up the former role and moving on to define and develop the new role in the best way possible. The new role will be designed to incorporate and adapt the same client values, goals, and healthy routines that were associated with the former role. Emphasize the futility of clinging to a past role that is no longer feasible and the importance of creating a new manifestation of the former role that will have potential for satisfaction and a sense of accomplishment in the future as the role is mastered.

4. Identify cognitive and behavioral components of the situation that are blocking the client's potential for accepting the situation and moving on to a new stage, such as anger, fear of being alone, disorganization, or social withdrawal. For example, a divorced spouse may be unable to achieve adequate *emotional divorce* after several years because of unreasonable hopes for reconciliation and ongoing attempts to spend time with the former spouse. Similarly, a client may be unable to move beyond a job loss after a reasonable length of time because of a futile preoccupation with suing the former employer that is curtailing search for a new job.

5. Help the client identify features of the former role that were associated with a sense of mastery and positive self-esteem, including client values, aspirations, routines, and social networks. These essential sources of positive feedback for the client may be identified by asking, "What qualities or aspects of your past role were associated with positive feelings about yourself? What parts of the former role were particularly satisfying?" Help the client incorporate these features into the new role so that elements associated with former role satisfaction are retained to some degree.

6. Help the client identify positive role models who seem to be coping well with similar predicaments and roles. Ask, "Do you know a person in a situation similar to yours who seems to be coping well? What qualities does this person have? What practical coping strategies does this person use? How does this person view the situation? How can you incorporate some of these coping strategies into your own situation?"

7. Help the client design a step-by-step plan for implementing the new role. Ask, "What are the necessary components of the new role that will help you to move on with your life? What skills do you need to develop for your new role?"

Client Example

Jim had been suffering from severe depression since his wife unexpectedly left him three years before and began living with her new boyfriend. His wife retained the family home and had custody of their daughters on weekdays, so that her boyfriend had become a stepfather to the girls. After the separation, Jim made no effort to contact friends or to pursue his former initiatives for advancement at work. In fact, he avoided supportive friends, work colleagues, and family because of embarrassment and humiliation and failed to initiate activities to fill the void created by the absence of daily childrearing activities. Although his former wife had made it clear that there was no chance of reconciliation, Jim was unable to accept this and continually devised excuses to drop in on her at home and to reiterate his plea that she return to him "for the sake of the family." Because of his hopes for a reconciliation, Jim had put very little effort into making his apartment comfortable, and he felt sad when his daughters resisted spending time there. As time went on he was gradually seeing less and less of the girls. He resented the stepfather's "negative" influence on his daughters and despaired that there was no hope of raising mentally stable, successful children in a broken home.

Jim was helped through Resiliency Training and role redefinition to make a more adaptive transition from full-time father and major provider in a comfortable family home to divorced father living in a second "family home" with significant participation and influence in his children's lives. He identified three crucial features of his former role that were now absent from his life and responsible for his despair: time spent in daily childrearing tasks, time spent planning and building a career and work relationships to ensure the best opportunities for his children, and the satisfaction of being part of a traditional family with two loving parents.

The client was helped to regain remnants of the supportive network that he had neglected for the past three years. This involved reconnecting with family, old friends, and work colleagues. Cognitive therapy techniques were used to address his unrealistic preoccupation with winning his wife back and his belief that successful childrearing was an impossible feat for divorced parents. He was helped to move through the process of divorce, and implement the necessary steps he had avoided for three years, such as informing friends, family, and children about the finality of the marital separation.

Following this, Problem-Solving techniques were used to help him create a more satisfying single-father life structure by generating solutions to his predicament of too much time on his hands and too little participation in his daughters' daily activities. He was helped to specify missing aspects of his former role that continued to foster his sense of loss and depression. He identified: (1) absence of a daily family routine (i.e., the dinner hour, assisting daughters with homework, watching T.V. together, bedtime stories), (2) absence of a comfortable home environment with the children's friends coming and going, and (3) absence of sufficient influence over his children's lives to ensure healthy routines and exposure to important values. He then persuaded his wife to change the custody arrangement so that he would have the children on weekdays on alternate weeks. He also decided to move back into his old neighborhood to be near to his children's school and friends and to transform his new apartment into a comfortable, attractive second home.

APPLICATION OF DEVELOPMENTAL CBT STRATEGIES

In keeping with the goal of assisting clients in resolving normative life tasks, this chapter has presented several new Developmental Change Strategies specifically designed for this purpose. The following chapters will demonstrate application of these new Developmental CBT strategies to a variety of occupational, social, and family problems. Chapter 4 will address various developmental difficulties in occupational functioning. Chapter 5 will demonstrate the new Developmental CBT approach with developmental blocks in various areas of social and interpersonal functioning, while Chapter 6 will address developmental difficulties in partner and family relationships.

4

MALADAPTIVE DEVELOPMENTAL PATTERNS AFFECTING OCCUPATIONAL FUNCTIONING

This chapter will focus on treatment of clients who present with difficulties establishing adaptive adult daily routines and carrying out occupational roles. Adult occupational roles in this book will refer not only to career paths, but also to "filler" jobs; college, university, or job-training programs; housewife and parenting roles; volunteer work; serious artistic or sports endeavors; and other vocational and leisure paths through which people derive meaning. Normative and maladaptive developmental patterns and pathways affecting adult occupational functioning will be contrasted, as will processes that underlie adaptive occupational functioning at different stages of life span development.

NORMATIVE OCCUPATIONAL CHALLENGES ACROSS THE LIFE SPAN

Studies of normal adult development highlight several distinct occupational tasks and patterns of early, middle, and mature adulthood (Levinson, 1978, 1996; Okun, 1984; Cross & Markus, 1991; Tamir, 1986; Cohler & Boxer, 1991; Turner, 1980). The occupational tasks, transitions and challenges described in the following paragraphs are considered normative and affect most people to some degree. Dysfunctional occupational patterns often start out as prolonged or severe difficulties with resolution of these normative occupational tasks and challenges.

The young adult must make a first formulation of a life plan, in the form of general intentions and goals that can be implemented, and from which he or she can derive a sense of security and competence. Young adults may fail to do this either because they formulate elaborate and rigid, but impractical, plans that defy implementation or because they opt for scarcely articulated life plans that will likely be questioned in later stages of adulthood. The young adult must also achieve sufficient autonomy from family of origin to move away and develop an independent functional adult life style. This involves taking responsibility for oneself, establishing a healthful routine, making a commitment to a viable occupational or career path, and striving with some enthusiasm and self-discipline toward attaining occupational goals.

By middle adulthood, most people have committed to a career or occupation and are now faced with the daily challenge of maintaining occupational satisfaction and mastery. People with satisfying work situations at midlife mention excitement, challenge, satisfaction with work outcomes, creativity, recognition for achievements, and sufficient financial outcome. A common challenge at this stage of life is the decision to either remain in one's initial occupational path if it has become unsatisfactory for one reason or another or undertake the challenge of changing jobs or career path. After age 40, a person is no longer a junior member of the adult work scene and must begin to form a niche as a more senior member. In addition, added financial burdens develop as one's children reach late adolescence and prepare for higher education, precipitating decisions about those components of their early adult occupational aspirations that need to be modified and those that are best maintained.

Men and women in their middle years may become preoccupied with decreased potential for occupational advancement. Midlife occupational crises during the forties decade, or later, may involve perceived gaps between initial career aspirations and actual achievements. Psychological adjustment of middle adulthood may center around unattainable components of the person's initial career goals. Unattainable goals may be the result of physiological changes or external factors such as an economic recession, so that a major midlife occupational reappraisal and lifestyle revisions may be necessary. Adjusting to the limitations of one's youthful goals may involve acknowledging one's limitations and recognizing one's illusions. An important task of middle adulthood is adjustment to realistic limitations of some aspects of one's initial long-term life plan.

Research suggests that most men will experience some difficulties in their developmental progression in one or more of the three central spheres of life: work, family, and social relationships (Tamir, 1986). In the occupational sphere, job or professional options may become more limited during middle adulthood. If men or women have not achieved the success they have been seeking, they will likely be disappointed. They will have to reassess their careers and decide where they should go from here. Some will increase the amount of time devoted to work because retirement is looming with its demands for long-term financial security. For others, work satisfaction will no longer be the most important criterion for a sense of well-being, and they may seek some degree of disengagement from work. There may be a trade-off between occupation and people, between objective accomplishment and interpersonal relationships. Attempts to deal with these disappointments may lead to a turning point and a decision whether to continue in one's job, to change professions, or to invest less in occupation and more in family, leisure, community, or other aspects of life. Some will be unable to change jobs and will persevere but become psychologically detached from their jobs.

In general, occupational challenges for women in middle age are somewhat different from those of men. Although conflicting career and parenting demands affect men to a certain degree, Western women have traditionally had to deal with the stress of coping with multiple, conflicting demands of career, homemaker, wife, and mother. Women who have chosen the homemaker role will find themselves with more and more free time as the children approach late adolescence. They may be faced with decisions about seeking paid work outside the home. There may be disagreement between husband and wife about the wife's decision to work. Mothers with careers may have to come to terms with the myth of the successful career woman, namely that having it all is possible: career, marriage, family, and leisure. If she fails in one of these areas, she may perceive herself as incompetent. In spite of the feminist media, some women are so stressed by career demands that they have little sense of competence or satisfaction with career, marriage, or family. Divided loyalties or occupational overload are typical as women attempt to cope with simultaneous parent, homemaker, and job demands. A woman may feel the need for a drastic restructuring of her life but lack the necessary skills, energy, resources, or circumstances to bring about change.

Further occupational challenges surface during mature adulthood. A new awareness of time running out is common at this time. Concerns revolve around failure to attain socially desired roles and status in occupation. Preoccupation with physiological changes of aging or fear of being overtaken by illness may also surface and affect occupational performance.

CATEGORIES OF OCCUPATIONAL
DEVELOPMENTAL DIFFICULTIES

The remainder of this chapter will describe difficulties in occupational functioning characteristic of therapy clients who have been unable to resolve normative occupational challenges sufficiently to maintain mental stability and carry on effectively. Occupational stress affects a substantial proportion of people. Some studies suggest that up to 50% of middle-aged men find work damaging to self and unrewarding, and this may be linked to alcoholism, depression, burn-out, marginal work performance, early retirement, or a search for inappropriate youthful excitement (Levinson, 1978).

While many occupational presenting problems are linked to the dimension of competence or mastery of the occupational endeavor, coexisting personality or clinical disorders such as depression, anxiety, and substance abuse may also interfere with occupational performance. Occupational functioning may be compromised by interpersonal problems with coworkers or authority figures or by autonomy issues such as insufficient independence from family of origin to facilitate establishment of adult occupational initiatives.

Categories of common occupational presenting problems and occupational developmental difficulties to be addressed in this chapter include the following:

- Occupational depression and anxiety
- Problems *establishing* an initial viable adult occupational path
- Problems *sustaining* occupational effectiveness
- Job termination and demotion adjustment difficulties

These categories are not mutually exclusive, and there will be considerable overlap between them for some clients.

CHARACTERISTIC OCCUPATIONAL PROBLEMS OF
EARLY, MIDDLE, AND MATURE ADULTHOOD

The incidence of particular types of occupational problems varies with the age and life stage of individual clients. With young-adult clients, one would expect a higher incidence of inappropriate educational or job-choice decisions, vague, poorly defined occupational goals, difficulties initiating a job search or application to an academic program, and difficulties achieving financial independence. Any of these problems may persist into middle adulthood or arise at later adult stages, but with somewhat different manifestations.

For clients in middle adulthood, one would expect a higher incidence of dissatisfaction with an initial occupational choice, difficulties restructuring an unsatisfying career path, or difficulties coping with off-time transitions. Off-time transitions may involve returning to college or taking an entry-level job in one's thirties when fellow students or colleagues will be much younger. Homemakers attempting to pursue a career after a long absence from the work force may also seek therapy during the middle adult years.

A characteristic occupational _____ y of late adulthood is acceptance of _____ realizing initial career goals. _____ th anxiety about impending _____ meaningful activities to fill _____

_____ gories of occupational problems _____ stage, some types of occu-_____ to clients in all life stages, _____ These include inadequate _____ discipline or persistence, _____ les of occupational problem _____ ent academic or job-skill _____ al path, difficulty coping _____ ders or depression, and _____ e due to incongruence _____ n, perceptions of one's _____ or unattainable career _____ relationship problems _____ blematic during early,

_____) ANXIETY

_____ mastery of occupa-_____ es are often exacer-_____ with occupational _____ ctivity, hopelessness, _____ s, or avoidance patterns. Clients typically _____ pts to help them build new adaptive career paths if it means giving up protective avoidance behaviors, rituals, or safe daily routines.

Occupational Depression

Occupational depression is characterized by themes of failure, incompetence, perfectionist standards, and overwhelming responsibility. In terms of Beck's *cognitive triangle* of depression (Beck, 1963), depressive occupational themes may reflect a view of oneself as worthless with respect to career accomplishments, a view of one's current occupational situation as cruel or punishing, or a view of one's occupational future as hopeless. Clients whose occupational problems are linked to depression may complain that their jobs are too menial or meaningless, that the work environment is intolerable, or that they feel unworthy at work. They may complain of insomnia, somatic symptoms, or poor concentration interfering with work performance. There may be patterns of social withdrawal, avoidance of coworkers, substance abuse, or dependency curtailing effective occupational performance. Feelings of failure may precipitate avoidance of occupational challenges, and there may be a tendency to give up prematurely when the going gets rough.

Examples of typical depressive occupational themes from case histories are shown in Table 4.1.

Early Influences Linked to Occupational Depression and Anxiety

Typical early developmental influences linked to occupational depression and anxiety in adulthood may be found in home, school, and peer experiences. With respect to family of origin, clients who develop occupational anxiety as adults may have been exposed to overprotective or over-involved parents who foster the child's anxious school avoidance and demands for parental rescue. Clients raised by parents with mental health problems may have developed anxious preoccupations with the parent's well-being, or they may have developed emotional disorders similar to the parent's, interfering with school achievement. Unrealistic parental expectations may have led to anxious academic striving on the part of the child, interfering with academic task application. Perceived peer or teacher criticism may precipitate social withdrawal at school, rebellion, or school avoidance.

Table 4.1 Typical Themes Associated with Occupational Depression

Negative view of current occupational situation: My job has no meaning, job is too menial; intolerable coworkers, job demands overwhelming

Negative view of self in occupational role (failure, incompetence, defectiveness, social undesirability themes): I'm failing at my job, I'm worthless; it's all my fault the job failed; my boss thinks I'm incompetent; I've let everyone down; I don't know what I want to do, so I can't plan a career; there's no job I can do; I can't ever work; I'm ashamed of my job, don't want to tell others what I do; if I commit to a challenge I'll fail

Negative view of occupational future: I'm stuck in this intolerable job forever; I've failed in my past jobs and I know I'll fail if I try again

Interventions for Occupational Depression

Client and therapist first identify schemas and behavior patterns currently maintaining the occupational depression, such as subjugation, failure, or defectiveness schemas; depressive inactivity; opting out in response to occupational challenges; or social withdrawal in occupational settings. Standard CBT techniques for depression may then be applied to alter these patterns at any point in the therapy process, such as those outlined in texts by Beck and his colleagues (e.g., Beck, 1963, 1976; Beck, Rush, & Shaw, 1979). Following this, client and therapist use new Developmental Analysis Strategies to identify early predisposing factors and child and adolescent manifestations of the client's deviant developmental pathways leading to current occupational depression. Various early maladaptive pathways may lead to similar outcomes in terms of chronic depression curtailing acquisition of occupational skills.

Occupational Anxiety

Clients whose occupational problems are linked to an anxiety disorder may complain of uncomfortable physical symptoms affecting work performance, such as palpitations, shortness of breath, or fear of a panic attack that necessitates abruptly leaving the workplace or classroom. Clients may express fears about breaking down at work or school and not being able to fulfill job or academic obligations. Anxious clients may avoid an occupational setting altogether or engage in time-consuming compulsive rituals that disrupt job performance. Features of panic disorder, phobias, obsessive–compulsive patterns, or general anxiety disorders will become evident as clients provide specific examples of their occupational problems. Three frequent manifestations of occupational anxiety include: (1) task overload anxiety, (2) procrastination anxiety, and (3) workplace avoidance.

Task Overload Anxiety   Dysfunctional patterns in this category are linked to schemas of unrelenting standards, self-sacrifice, and unassertiveness. Self-sacrificing clients set unrealistically high performance standards, fail to live up to them, and then condemn themselves for failing to do so. They have a tendency to take on more than their share of responsibility and then become overwhelmed and unable to work efficiently. They may routinely work overtime or make excessive revisions to work in progress. Unassertive clients are unable to say no to unfair demands on their time. They reluctantly commit themselves to too much work out of fear of negative boss or colleague evaluations.

Even if they manage to complete the work, they end up feeling angry about having been manipulated.

Procrastination Anxiety   These clients usually set unrealistically high or perfectionist standards for themselves and then are blocked when attempting to start work on a project or assignment. They end up waiting until the last minute to get started, jeopardizing job performance. They fail to arrive at work on time or to meet deadlines. They may lack basic skills for breaking work tasks down into small, manageable steps and for creating a workable plan that can be successfully implemented. They are unable to decide where to start, so put off doing so until the last minute. In the process they become increasingly anxious about the possibility of not completing the task adequately. At the same time, they condemn themselves for failure to act, for poor last-minute performance, or for giving up altogether.

Workplace Avoidance   Anxiety or somatoform symptoms may interfere with the person's ability to get to or from the work or classroom setting or to remain in the setting long enough to complete occupational tasks. Clients in this category may put pressure on a spouse, parent, or friend to accompany them to work or to "rescue" them from the work setting when their anxiety gets too high. Typical anxiety themes linked to occupational attendance problems are vulnerability, need for accompaniment or rescue, and social phobia themes about colleagues' negative evaluations. Typical anxiety behaviors include phobic reactions, panic attacks, and obsessive–compulsive rituals that consume large chunks of work time. Somatoform symptoms may also be linked to occupational attendance problems. The person routinely decides to stay home because he or she feels too weak to go to work. These clients typically fear getting sick or otherwise embarrassing themselves in the work setting or classroom. At times they fear that their symptoms will be exacerbated to a point where they could lose control. Typical themes of clients suffering from occupational anxiety are shown in Table 4.2.

Interventions for Occupational Anxiety

Treatment of anxiety symptoms may be an important prerequisite to altering the long-standing occupational developmental difficulties addressed in the remainder of this chapter. Standard CBT techniques to reduce the severity of specific anxiety symptoms such as panic attacks, phobias, and Obsessive–Compulsive Disorder (OCD) rituals have been outlined in the literature (e.g., Beck & Emery, 1985; Guidano & Liotti, 1983; Padesky, 1994; Freeman, Simon, Beutler, & Arkowitz, 1989). CBT

Table 4.2 Typical Themes Associated with Occupational Anxiety

Vulnerability, dependence and enmeshment themes: I won't be able to perform my job; I'll break down; colleagues will see my craziness; I can't stay at work when I think I'll go crazy, faint, have a heart attack; I won't be able to concentrate; I can't ever commit to a job because of my panic attacks; I can't get to work alone; I won't ever be able to work because of my panic attacks, my illness; I can't stay at meetings

Social anxiety themes: People know I always miss work; they're judging my work

Defectiveness, incompetence, failure themes: I'll never be able to finish this; I won't be able to cope with this; I'm spinning my wheels, getting nowhere; this assignment is too much for me; I'll never be able to do this; I'm out of my depth

Unrelenting self standards themes: I must spend more time on this than others; I must do a superior job; I can still do more, another revision

Subjugation themes: (This assignment is unfair, but I can't say no; I have no choice or I won't get promoted; I'll be fired

Initiation blocks: I do my best work at the last minute; I'll think about it tomorrow; I can't start until I feel motivated; I don't know where to start on such a big project, too much is expected; I must do these several things before I start the project

Perfectionist, obsessive indecision themes: I must do this perfectly; I can't make any decision or start this job before exploring every possible option and exploring all possible outcomes

skill-building interventions may also be applied to all three manifestations of occupational anxiety. For example, task overload anxiety may be treated with assertiveness training, time management, and cognitive change techniques for unrealistic self-imposed standards that lead to task overload. Procrastination anxiety may be treated with self-monitoring training to combat indecision and to break down tasks into manageable steps. Similarly, school or workplace avoidance may be alleviated by social-skills training.

Once Axis I disorders are addressed by standard CBT strategies, the Developmental Phase of therapy addresses chronic self-defeating anxiety patterns jeopardizing occupational performance over the years. Maladaptive Developmental Pathways and their early influences are identified using Developmental Analysis Strategies and are designated as targets for therapy. Developmental Change Strategies may then be applied in an attempt to deflect clients from long-standing dysfunctional pathways. For example, the Developmental Task Resolution Planning and Current Life-Structure Reorganization strategies outlined in Chapter 3 may help clients take steps to reorganize their lives to reduce stress, set priorities, regularize daily schedules, and explore less stressful jobs or academic programs. The Adaptive Versus Obsolete Coping-Styles strategy may be used to teach clients to observe, consult, and emulate coworkers who are more successful in managing occupational stress. The Then and Now strategy may be used to identify and resurrect anxiety-control techniques adopted by the client in the past that allowed adequate occupational functioning or facilitated resolution of other developmental tasks or transitions.

Table 4.3 shows typical case-history examples of deviant developmental pathways associated with occupational depression and anxiety.

PROBLEMS ESTABLISHING AN INITIAL VIABLE OCCUPATIONAL PATH

A primary task of early adulthood is establishment of an initial viable occupational path. This is usually dependent on a health-enhancing routine that is conducive to performance of occupational tasks. Although more common among young adults, clients at different adult stages may present with ongoing difficulties initiating and committing to a viable occupational path. This may be manifested in failure to pursue and secure a first job or failure to achieve financial independence. For young adults in the student role, difficulties may be manifested in

Table 4.3 Maladaptive Developmental Pathways Associated with Occupational Depression and Anxiety

Occupational failure pathway: Rejecting parent or excessive parental academic expectations: child internalizes unrealistic academic standards or develops academic defectiveness and failure schemas, anxious academic striving, underachievement, opts out when faced with academic challenge followed by temporary relief but self-condemnation, hopelessness, subsequently sets unrealistic occupational goals in adulthood, opts out when faced with adult occupational challenges, condemns self for inadequate occupational performance

Occupational social sensitivity pathway: Perceived teacher or classmate criticism or rejection: child becomes overly sensitive to slight, develops personal defectiveness schemas, social alienation or withdrawal, avoidance of school activities, may opt out with inadequate educational attainments or development of occupational skills for acceptable adult occupation, perceived criticism of adult superiors and work colleagues, avoidance patterns in occupational setting affecting occupational effectiveness

Occupational avoidance and/or dependence pathway: Early trauma or overprotective or anxious parent: child develops vulnerability schemas accompanied by anxiety and somatoform symptoms in school setting, dependent on parents, school avoidance history or demands for parent accompaniment or rescue, academic underachievement secondary to truancy or quitting school, excessive time spent in solitary activities, may develop chaotic routine or self-soothing patterns such as substance abuse, ongoing dependence on parents in early adulthood, failure to establish independent adult occupational path and financial independence failure to initiate university application or gain university acceptance, academic underachievement, inappropriate choice of a postsecondary educational path, or failure to complete educational prerequisites for an acceptable career. Those who have chosen the homemaker–parent path may present with problems establishing a healthful routine, unreasonable dependence on a spouse, or failure to provide adequate child care. Middle-aged homemakers may seek therapy for difficulties returning to work and establishing an initial occupational path outside the home at this later stage after the children have grown.

Depression or anxiety disorders may be important components of the problem. These may be manifested in avoidance patterns or insufficient initiative to implement the normal process of selecting a particular occupational path, obtaining the necessary qualifications, implementing job-search tasks, following through with job interviews, and subsequently securing a job and entering the work force. Clients may encounter blocks at any stage of this process, such as failure to complete sufficient academic prerequisites for their desired career paths. This may be due to difficulties initiating the necessary application process for college or university entrance or for job-skills training programs. Some young clients apply but give up after receiving rejection notices from universities or stubbornly refuse to pursue alternative second or third choices. Instead they simply drift. Other clients appear to be in a holding pattern, failing to enter the work force while waiting to meet a partner who will support them and relieve them of the need to work.

Some clients in this category present with entitlement or self-aggrandizement schemas that serve to exempt them from the difficult process of preparing for a career or securing a job. They may blame external factors for their failure to initiate a job search. Some clients will have failed to attain sufficient physical and psychological separation from parents for an independent adult life structure. Middle-aged clients may still be financially dependent on their family of origin. Ongoing failure to establish a viable occupational path negatively affects other major areas of an individual's functioning, jeopardizing potential for satisfying social relationships, intimate partner relationships, or family relationships.

Two frequent blocks to establishing an initial occupational path are discussed below: (1) prolonged dependence interfering with the process of leaving the family home and (2) a chaotic lifestyle precluding a functional occupational path.

Prolonged Dependence on Family of Origin

Although ongoing dependence on family of origin is more common in early adulthood, some middle-aged adults may still be unsuccessful in leaving the parental home and continue to be financially and psychologically dependent on parents well into their thirties or forties. Depression, anxiety disorders, and self-discipline problems are common underlying features.

Normative patterns of leaving home in the late teens or early twenties involve physical, financial, and psychological independence. The young adult takes the first steps toward separate living arrangements and financial independence, establishing a new adult home base. A desire to pursue college, university, or a first job are common reasons for leaving home, as well as decisions to marry, cohabit, or set up independent living arrangements with friends.

Successful separation from family of origin is predicated on previous acquisition of adequate social, occupational, and independence skills during childhood and adolescence. The young adult will need to have acquired the necessary educational background to embark on a job or career, as well as skills for independent living and for development of effective peer relationships and intimate partner relationships. Healthy interaction styles learned in the family of origin help shape these skills. Adequate separation is a two-way affair that begins in adolescence, with the parents gradually letting go and encouraging the son or daughter to take more and more responsibility, while the young person assumes increasing independence. When the parenting style has been over-controlling or over-protective, it will be up to the young adult to overcome parental barriers to independence.

Partial financial dependence on parents may continue for several years while the young adult attends university or works at a low-paying job. Successful transitions to adult roles are often facilitated by parental sponsorship of postsecondary education for young adults through financial support and by ongoing emotional support during a prolonged period in which parents and adult children reside together because of financial necessity (Hussong & Chassin, 2002; White, 1994). During difficult economic times, an increasing number of young adults continue to live at home for longer periods of time or return to live in the parental home temporarily after having initially moved out. As a result, the actual physical and financial separation from parents is often achieved at a later age than was typical in the past. Consequently, the young adult who continues to live in the parental home must somehow manage to achieve a sufficient degree of adult status and equality with parents, as well as adequate psychological separation. Similarly, the university student who maintains an independent residence while remaining financially dependent on parents will still need to achieve independence in life-management functions, decision-making, and social choices. An important prerequisite for an independent adult life structure is willingness to take responsibility for solving ones own problems and a shift away from a childhood pattern of blaming others for disappointments when things go wrong. The process of leaving home normally involves consultation with parents about the transition and parental assistance with implementing the move.

Difficulties with the Leaving-Home Transition   Those who continue to live at home and remain financially dependent and psychologically enmeshed with parents may cite duty to needy parents as the justification for their ongoing dependence. Common early developmental influences include exposure to over-submissive, over-protective, or guilt-engendering parents or to parents with mental health problems. Often there is a history of dependence during childhood and adolescence, academic underachievement, social isolation, or school avoidance with tacit parental compliance. Anxiety disorders may also contribute to a client's ongoing failure to leave the parental home, as, for example, in the case of a phobic client who required parental accompaniment to university classes.

Problems with this transition may also result from an adolescent's premature departure from home before independence and occupational skills for adult roles are adequately developed. The premature departure may be catalyzed by family conflict or disorganization and is usually accompanied by negative feelings of anger, sadness, anxiety, or guilt. Some young adults achieve physical independence without psychological independence from parents, such as those who run away from home or get involved in impulsive disastrous marriages, pregnancies, or substance abuse. They may appear to be independent until they encounter financial or emotional difficulties and consequently look to their parents to rescue them.

Disorders of Routine Affecting Establishment of a Viable Occupational Path

A health-enhancing daily routine is a necessary prerequisite for successful establishment and maintenance of viable occupational roles across the life span. A person must establish and maintain daily routines that minimize sources of stress, promote mental health, and allow sufficient time and energy for mastery of occupational demands. Clients who have difficulty establishing healthful daily routines may sleep too much or too little or may sleep during conventional daytime work hours. They are often impulsive or oppositional. Some adopt a reckless pleasure-seeking lifestyle characterized by problems of self-control, substance abuse, excessive pleasure seeking, drifting from place to place, sexual promiscuity, or involvement in antisocial pursuits. Other clients with chaotic daily routines are depressed, inactive, and easily bored. Some suffer from conditions of inadequate nutrition, rest, or shelter, or they may be homeless, freeloading off of friends and acquaintances until they are asked to leave. Extreme financial incompetence, brief spurts of employment followed by job dismissals, and impulsive job-change decisions are common features.

Some typical themes of clients with problems establishing an independent adult occupational path and routine are shown in Table 4.4.

Early Influences Associated with Problems of Occupational Initiation and Sustained Occupational Effectiveness

Hardships during childhood and adolescence have been found to predict poor work outcomes for both men and women in midlife (McClelland & Franz, 1992). Occupational functioning is centered primarily on school performance during childhood and adolescence, and difficulties at school have also been linked to subsequent occupational difficulties in adulthood (Roeser & Eccles, 2000).

Prolonged difficulty implementing college-application or job-search tasks or securing a first job may be an outgrowth of earlier unresolved tasks, such as adolescent failure to develop self-discipline and efficient work patterns or failure to achieve adequate independence from family of origin. Unresolved adolescent tasks may also contribute to difficulties sustaining occupational effectiveness over the years, a topic to be introduced in the next section. Negative childhood influences contributing to ongoing occupational task difficulties may be linked to early family, peer, or school experiences. By diminishing the youngster's success in resolving normative school-related tasks, these negative influences set the child on a deviant path that will eventually curtail occupational effectiveness in adulthood.

Family of Origin Factors Maladaptive childrearing styles linked to school difficulties include over-submissive, overprotective, punitive, and neglectful parenting. Adults with occupational task performance problems may have been raised in families where an anxious, overprotective parent tended to rescue the child by becoming too involved in the child's school work and placing too little emphasis on the child's

Table 4.4 Typical Themes Associated with Problems Establishing an Initial Occupational Path

Dependence themes: I can't work as long as mother needs me at home

External blame themes: New immigrants are taking all the jobs from us; employers are corrupt; female bosses have it in for me; every time I make a career plan, somebody shoots it down and ruins my chances

Excuses for chaotic routine: I'm not a morning person; I do my best work after midnight; I can't work before noon

Defectiveness themes: I'm too fat (stupid, unworthy) to apply for the job; coworkers will learn my shameful secrets; if I commit to it I'll fail; I've always failed and always will

Social alienation themes: I can't stand a job where you have to deal with people; I could never fit into the corporate image; I don't really like being around people and their disgusting habits

Vulnerability themes: What if I get a job and then get sick? Things might come up and I'd have to miss work

Rigid job criteria: I can't tolerate meetings; I'm not a morning person; I don't want to invest too much effort

Self-aggrandizement/and entitlement themes: It's against my principles to take a job like that; why should I take that job when I could make double the salary; only losers do those kinds of jobs

Magical thinking: If I wait long enough, a good job will come along

independent efforts. Some may have had parents who were neglectful or under-involved, creating a chaotic family environment with inadequate structure, routines, and supervision needed to foster good study habits and self-discipline in the child. There may have been a single parent, overwhelmed by family demands, or a mentally unstable parent unable to give sufficient time and attention to parenting. Some clients with job-task application difficulties in adulthood were exposed to permissive parents who had low academic expectations for the child or low expectations for the child's initiative in taking responsibility for homework. Parents may have placed excessive demands on the child for academic achievement or compared the child unfavorably with more successful siblings, so that the child eventually rebelled or gave up. There may have been a history of school attendance problems, based on somatoform complaints or other manipulative ploys to avoid school, often with parental compliance. Finally, clients with a history of parental abuse, neglect, or insecure parent–child attachment may have resorted to aggressive interpersonal styles or social withdrawal, thereby jeopardizing school success. In addition to maladaptive child-rearing skills, early school difficulties may be related to domestic violence, financial hardship, chronic unemployment, job loss, divorce, or parental psychopathology (Cicchetti, Toth, & Maughan, 2000).

School Factors School difficulties during childhood and adolescence may have been associated with perceived teacher criticism or peer ridicule, leading youngsters to label themselves as "stupid" or "undesirable" and to social withdrawal or school avoidance. There may have been a history of oppositional or disruptive classroom behavior combined with low academic-achievement motivation. Associations with classmates with similar patterns of work avoidance or truancy may have been a factor, increasing academic failure, conflicts with teachers, and under-involvement in positive extracurricular peer and school activities (Deater-Decker, 2001). There may also have been an absence of positive school patterns associated with academic success such as task persistence, choice of moderately challenging tasks, positive conduct in the school setting, attribution of academic success or failure to oneself, a belief in one's own academic competence, and high value on academic success (Roeser & Eccles, 2000).

Client Example: Occupation Initiation Difficulty

The following example illustrates the Developmental CBT approach to altering long-standing maladaptive developmental pathways interfering with the client's ability to establish an initial functional adult occupational path.

> Marie was a 25-year-old woman who sought therapy for depression linked to her ongoing failure to secure a first job and independence from her mother. During her early years, her anxious mother had worried excessively about her daughter's safety when she was outside the home. Marie's father was an abusive alcoholic husband, and as a child Marie felt responsible for the safety and well-being of her mother. As a teenager, Marie was anxious at school and started faking illness in order to stay home from school to be near to her mother. Her mother was comfortable with this and continued to be an over-involved and overprotective parent, seriously curtailing Marie's ability to develop independence. Marie's absences from school resulted in academic failure, and she subsequently dropped out of school, remained at home, and worked occasionally as a cleaning person. Later, in a desperate attempt to escape from her violent family environment, Marie moved in with her boyfriend in spite of his history of substance abuse. Financial necessity forced her to take a job at a daycare center, but when this relationship broke up after a few months, she quit her job and found herself back in her parents' home, suffering from panic attacks, increasingly housebound, and still unable to

initiate a job search. After two years, she was still unemployed, occasionally going out with friends, and waiting to be rescued.

Presenting problems included depression, panic attacks, and inadequate job skills and educational qualifications. Developmental Task Difficulties identified by client and therapist were ongoing dependence on family of origin, failure to initiate a job search and commit to an initial job path, and inappropriate criteria for partner selection. Underlying beliefs were reflected in the following themes: "Mom needs me at home to help her handle dad." "I need someone to look after me" (dependence). "I can't move out and live alone or work because of my panic attacks." "I've been through so much, I can't think of working until I get rid of these panic attacks" (vulnerability). Dysfunctional coping styles included depressed inactivity and extreme reluctance to leave the house.

Standard CBT techniques for anxiety and depression were first applied, including anxiety-control techniques to reduce symptoms of panic attacks and activity scheduling to alter depressive inactivity. Behavior skill training, role rehearsal, and vocational assessment interventions were used to teach job-search skills. Cognitive techniques were applied to alter core schemas of vulnerability, dependence, and incompetence. However, although these standard CBT interventions brought some relief from anxiety symptoms and depression, Marie remained trapped in the dependent adolescent life structure she hated.

The Developmental Phase   Through use of the Developmental Task-Block Identification and Analysis strategies, the client pinpointed two Maladaptive Developmental Pathways leading to her current difficulties with early-adulthood tasks of independence from family and initiation of a viable occupational path. She labeled the first her "dependence pathway": over-protective mother makes teenage daughter her confidant and ally against dad; mother sanctions client's truancy in attempts to keep the daughter close by; Marie's truancy leads to academic failure and her decision to drop out of high school; Marie suffers years of unemployment and depressed inactivity, living at home isolated from people her age. An extension of the dependency pathway was characterized by her inappropriate partner selection based on dependency needs, her short-lived attempts to live independently, marital stress leading to panic attacks, and eventual return to the safety of her parents' home. A second dysfunctional pathway was labeled her "chaotic lifestyle pathway": lax inconsistent parental discipline during adolescence; client develops a chaotic life structure and fails to develop adequate occupational self-discipline and persistence; poor academic results cause client to give up with inadequate educational foundation for financially viable career; client adopts a self-soothing daily structure of too much sleep and ongoing depression stemming from negative occupational self-concept and hopelessness regarding her occupational future.

Once Marie understood how these Maladaptive Developmental Pathways had interfered with resolution of normal occupational, partner relationship, and independence tasks, she could see how quitting her job when stressed by the break-up of her relationship and her retreat home to mother followed by an episode of depressed inactivity fit into her old self-defeating patterns. She realized that independence from her mother had been incomplete, having never progressed through the sequence of steps necessary for achieving normal autonomy during adolescence. She also realized that she had never developed the self-discipline and persistence skills necessary for a successful job search and securing a first job.

Motivation to change was first enhanced by the Fast Forward strategy. Marie realized that there was a good chance that she would still be financially dependent on her parents and still living with them five years from now. With the help of the therapist, Marie then used the Developmental Task-Resolution Planning strategy to formulate a plan for finally taking steps to alter the above pathways. Her goals were to learn job-search techniques, secure a permanent job, and subsequently move into an affordable apartment situation with two girlfriends who were looking for a third roommate.

By means of the Then and Now strategy, she identified a more successful period of her life when she had been able to prevail over her depressed inactivity and dependence on her mother. This involved her successful departure from the family home to live with her boyfriend, even though the relationship did not work out in the long run. She recalled how she had achieved independence by gradually spending more and more time away from home. She first began spending individual nights at her boyfriend's apartment in spite of her mother's protests that she was afraid to be left alone at night. This was followed by weekends and gradually whole weeks at her boyfriend's place, which gave her the confidence to move out completely. She decided that she could begin this same strategy at her girlfriends' apartment. She also identified her only successful job initiative. When she found herself in desperate financial need, she had been able to downplay her anxious fears of a panic attack long enough to walk into a day care center advertising a position and accept the job.

The Developmental Deficit Skill-Building strategy was used for independence training. Marie was helped to identify and then learn essential skills she had failed to acquire as a teenager, including assertiveness techniques to combat her mother's requests for company and her manipulative "sick" behaviors. With the help of a graded task-assignment intervention, she gradually increased time spent away from home with contemporaries by joining the YMCA for exercises classes. This later extended to joining her girlfriends for a night out at a restaurant.

The Developmental Deficit Skill-Building strategy was used next to address Marie's failure to proceed through the normal steps of selecting and committing to an initial occupational path. Marie was gradually taken through the process of (1) preliminary identification of interests, (2) translating interests into possible occupations, (3) choosing the most compatible career path, and (4) educating herself about skills necessary for the chosen occupation. At the end of this process she had a working career plan in fashion sales and decided to pursue this further by participating in a job-search program at the YMCA. This was a major step for Marie in light of her anxiety disorder, but she managed to attend the first session in spite of fears of panic attacks, using her new anxiety-control techniques. She persisted for three months until she learned the appropriate skills and attended a job interview.

With the help of the Developmental CBT strategies, Marie was able to see where she was coming from and predict where she would end up in the future unless she took steps to shift away from what had become a comfortable dependency pathway. She realized that a first serious job and a concrete career path would be her salvation. Within the next month she managed to secure a job in a dress shop and was therefore forced to adopt an organized daily routine. Her new job provided not only an independent income, but also a new social support group that gave her the courage to subsequently move out of her mother's house the next year.

PROBLEMS SUSTAINING OCCUPATIONAL EFFECTIVENESS

Clients in this category differ from those in the first category in that they have been successful in securing an initial job or admission to a postsecondary education program but have been unable to sustain effective occupational functioning over time. Problems sustaining occupational effectiveness may stem from a variety of factors such as insufficient self-discipline and task persistence, often with features of entitlement, difficulties with coworkers, chronic job dissatisfaction, or inappropriate occupational choice. Individual clients may manifest more than one of these difficulties, with roots dating back several years.

Many similarities exist between student problems and job task performance difficulties in adulthood. These include avoidance of occupational task challenges, inadequate persistence in the face of task difficulty, inadequate participation in work events, and poor attendance. Clients experiencing difficulties in applying themselves effectively to academic or job tasks often manifest long-standing deficits in self-discipline and persistence. They become restless, intolerant, and bored when tasks become too demanding. They may act impulsively to avoid discomfort when the going gets tough. They have difficulty inhibiting the urge to give up or escape to more pleasurable pursuits long enough to get the job done. Poor planning and organizational skills may also be features of the problem.

Entitlement beliefs may underlie occupational task-application problems. Clients with entitlement beliefs feel that they should have special privileges and be exempted from the rules that govern other workers. They should not have to start at the bottom with an entry-level job and work their way up. They should not have to perform mundane job tasks they consider to be beneath them, and consequently put forth insufficient effort to complete these unappealing tasks. They may seek to manipulate the situation, to cover up, or to make excuses for inadequate effort. They may shun entry-level jobs, rely on unrealistic expectations for lucky breaks, or develop other patterns of abdicating responsibility for putting in sufficient time and effort expected of others in the same position. Self-aggrandizement schemas may be manifested in inflated beliefs about their superiority in comparison with colleagues.

Interpersonal problems with coworkers may also undermine occupational effectiveness. They may make inappropriate challenges or demonstrate provocative behaviors with superiors that alienate employers, curtail promotions, or precipitate job termination. Some clients repeatedly get into self-defeating debates or altercations with employers that affect occupational functioning. Analysis of these encounters may reveal attempts to compensate for perceived occupational inadequacy or for insufficient educational attainments, self-discipline, or job experience. They may also make inappropriate attempts to become too familiar with coworkers or attempts to manipulate or impress colleagues and prove their superiority by pointing out coworkers' flaws. Workplace effectiveness may also be compromised by social anxiety, feelings of inferiority, or beliefs that coworkers are critical or unfriendly. This may lead to insufficient interaction with colleagues that is necessary for efficient job performance.

Chronic job dissatisfaction may curtail occupational effectiveness. Clients from entry-level positions to CEO may complain that they hate their jobs but are unable to make a change. They may be uncertain about the merits of initiating a job change because of financial reasons, fear of failure, or concerns that they lack sufficient energy or job skills to cope with a new job. This predicament may persist over a period of months or years, with the person feeling helpless to improve the situation. These clients complain of intolerable stagnation, failure, and burnout. Some report that they have reached a plateau and dread the thought of continuing in their job for the next decade or until retirement. Similarly, homemakers experiencing empty nest syndrome after children leave home, artists, or others with home-based occupations may wish to return to the work force outside the home but are unable to take the step. The common thread with this type of client is an ongoing failure to initiate the desired change, often accompanied by depression. This distinguishes them from those who *have* been able to address the task of reassessing and restructuring an unhappy occupational situation. This adaptive reassessment pattern usually begins with increasing occupational dissatisfaction followed by reevaluation and, finally, a decision to either continue with the status quo with alterations or to implement a decision to make a change.

Clients stuck in the unhappy predicament of chronic occupational dissatisfaction are frequently young adults who experience an urgent need to make a change from an unsatisfactory initial occupational path but are unable to do so. This age-thirty predicament is common enough to be considered a normal passage and does not fit the label of developmental task block unless the decision process is unduly prolonged. Sometimes it is a component of disenchantment with a more comprehensive life structure, involving dissatisfaction in areas of partner, family, or peer relationships in addition to occupation. Some older clients with chronic occupational dissatisfaction are suffering the consequences of a lifelong pattern of taking brief filler jobs but never committing to a serious occupational path that offers sufficient meaning, remuneration, and positive occupational esteem.

Some clients with chronic occupational dissatisfaction have made inappropriate career choices. They may be locked into jobs that are far below or above their capabilities, so that they are embarrassed about their situation or overly stressed. Some have insisted on occupational paths that are unavailable to them for one reason or another and stubbornly refuse to entertain alternatives. They may have failed to gain acceptance into a particular academic program or have failed to secure a coveted job but have refused to accept a second choice. Other clients have a clear idea of what they want to do but are impeded because their desired occupation is incongruent with expectations of family or friends. Some clients choose occupations that are incompatible with their natural abilities, personality styles, financial needs, or other factors, such as those who find themselves in demanding careers with high status and financial remuneration but who lack the required self-discipline, cognitive abilities, or initiative to succeed. Many clients lack a clear awareness of necessary career prerequisites, such as a need for more academic or job-skill training.

Client Example: Insufficient Occupational Task Application

The following client's work performance over the years was repeatedly hampered by inadequate task application combined with interpersonal problems with colleagues.

Martha was approaching her 50th birthday when she presented with anger, shame, and depression about her low-status marketing job with a large corporation. She complained that her income had been insufficient for the past 20 years and was bitter about being denied the VP position she felt she deserved on the basis of her superior intellect. As a young woman she half-heartedly applied to a local university but was denied acceptance because of poor secondary school results. Too lazy to pursue the university option further, she shunned the drudgery of completing a university degree in favor of a job in marketing and what she thought would be a lucrative business career. Marketing was a highly competitive field, but Martha was not prepared to put in the long hours of work necessary for the promotions that were achieved by more industrious colleagues. In an attempt to catch up, she enrolled in evening courses at a business college but dropped out when she became depressed following a failed romantic relationship. She resorted to her former high-school pattern of attempting to talk her way out of difficulties caused by her poor work effort and sought to convince others of her superior intellect and the wisdom of her decision to forgo unnecessary university training in favor of practical experience. She alienated people with her "superior" argumentative style and need to win every debate.

With insufficient business training, Martha was forced to continue in her entry-level marketing job. Although she saw this as a temporary measure, with her poor work effort, it soon became permanent. Martha had failed to complete any major projects over the past eight years, and she now compared herself unfavorably to more financially successful colleagues with MBA degrees who she considered her intellectual inferiors. Over the years she had made a few abortive attempts to take short courses in business but either failed the exams or dropped out of the course. She also shunned opportunities for special projects at work that would have led to promotions, unable to persist at challenges that required ongoing discipline and commitment.

Components of the client's task application deficit were her poor self-discipline, poor effort, and her "superior" aggressive interpersonal style in the work setting. Relevant themes included the following: "Only losers do mundane tasks" (entitlement). "My job has no status, it's embarrassing" (failure). "Other less intelligent colleagues are taking all the business" (anger/blame). Dysfunctional behavior patterns included procrastination, poor organizational skills, avoidance of challenging tasks, insufficient effort, and inappropriate manipulation.

The Developmental Phase The Developmental Deficit Skill-Building strategy was first used to help Martha analyze components of her task-application difficulties over the years. Martha realized that during the time when she should have been developing self-discipline, she was instead relying on her mother to finish her school projects for her. Her self-discipline deficit had precluded successful completion of postsecondary school credits and subsequently curtailed career advancement. This new understanding increased her motivation to participate fully in standard CBT techniques applied to the above target behaviors and beliefs. These included time management for poor self-discipline, poor organizational skills, and avoidance of occupational tasks; realistic goal setting for anxiety and indecision fostering procrastination; and cognitive change techniques for failure and entitlement schemas.

The Developmental Blocks Identification and Analysis strategies uncovered a long history of inferiority linked to childhood embarrassment about her working-class family and exclusion from peer groups she sought to join. This had precipitated entitlement and self-aggrandizement schemas to compensate for her low status and later for her lack of university education. This culminated in a lifelong pattern of alienating people in her attempts to convince them of her superiority.

A developmental history of her poor self-discipline revealed an over-involved and over-valuing mother who provided inadequate expectations for school achievement and who convinced her daughter that she was more intelligent than her peers. The mother took over major school projects, allowing Martha to "slack off," in her own words. Poor self-discipline and persistence at academic tasks were early patterns, as was a history of successfully talking her way out tough situations. Martha recalled that she argued with teachers routinely to get a higher mark and to get out of as much work as possible. She continually attempted to gain classmates' approval by acting superior but found that peers would drift away. Over the years, she had been good at selling herself at school and work but poor at following through with assignments and challenging job tasks. She usually opted out rather than risk failure. Unresolved tasks of childhood and adolescence were manifested in poor self-discipline and insufficient academic attainments for an acceptable career. Blocked tasks of early adulthood were manifested in her failure to attain postsecondary education and failure to establish a viable career path. Her failure to establish effective interpersonal relationships with colleagues represented another unresolved task, a problem to be addressed in Chapter 5.

Therapist and client identified two maladaptive developmental pathways underlying Martha's poor occupational performance over the years. The first was labeled "superior–entitled pathway," beginning as an attempt to neutralize feelings of family inferiority with childhood peers and fostered by her mother's insistence that Martha was smarter than other children and the mother's willingness to do her daughter's homework. This precipitated Martha's pattern of inadequate application to schoolwork and beliefs that her intellectual superiority excused her from having to complete tedious homework assignments. The client was still relying on her "superiority" as a strategy for neutralizing feelings of occupational, educational, and class inferiority and for justifying her poor work effort. In addition, her superior attitude towards colleagues continued to preclude formation of effective work relationships.

Martha labeled a second deviant pathway the "fear of failure pathway." When faced with challenging tasks at school and subsequently at work, she tended to give up rather than risk failure. Her chronic inability to complete projects or to embrace occupational challenges fuelled a sense of hopelessness and a belief that it was too late to change. She was also reluctant to accept her limitations in realizing her initial lofty goals and to address her fears about her life after retirement. She realized that the above pathways had interfered with the early adulthood task of establishing a viable occupational path and the subsequent task of reassessing her initial occupational path when she first realized that it was not working for her in her early thirties and making the necessary changes at that time by successfully completing the business courses she needed for advancement. Her current challenge was the task of reappraising her occupational path once again in late middle age and making the necessary changes to ensure a more positive self-evaluation in the occupational domain.

The Fast Forward strategy was used to increase the client's motivation for change. She was encouraged to hypothesize about the quality of her next life stage as she approached retirement age if her occupational situation was not addressed. She predicted that she would be unable to retire and would have to continue working after age 65 because of insufficient finances.

Future Developmental Stage Planning was initiated to help Martha explore alternatives to her current work situation. She listed four alternatives: (1) 10 more years of the status quo, waiting for the elusive promotion, (2) a new career in real estate that would involve more schooling and breaking into a new field, (3) early retirement and moving in with her mother, and (4) remaining with her company and attending evening classes for one year to earn a business diploma that would guarantee a promotion. She chose the latter alternative because it would allow her to build on her current experience instead of starting all over. It also increased the likelihood of an adequate pension if she managed to attain the business qualifications and earn a higher salary over the next few years.

The Then and Now strategy helped the client identify similarities in her current and earlier stages. She recalled her adolescent fear of failure underlying her tendency to shun academic challenges, combined with her poor self-discipline, and her attempts to convince others that her superior intelligence entitled her to passing grades without putting in the required effort and hard work. This pattern had led her to forgo university in favor of holding out for a lucky break. Following this, she was asked to identify times in her life when she had been more effective and positive about her occupational situation. She said the only time was in her early twenties when she was enrolled in business courses and still harbored plans to complete a university business degree. This was before she was faced with the realization that her temporary menial job was, in fact, permanent. She said that her most unsuccessful periods of occupational functioning were her present situation and the earlier period when she gave up on her courses following the break-up of her relationship.

With the client's new understanding of the above behavioral patterns and pathways from childhood through to the present adult stage, the Developmental Task Resolution Planning strategy helped her devise ways to remove current blocks to improving her career prospects at her current life stage. She knew that her current task was to reappraise and restructure her unsuccessful occupational patterns. Her immediate goals were to complete at least one major project in the next month to enhance her chances for promotions and to counter her daily tendency to procrastinate with her new time-management skills. Her long-term goal was to increase her likelihood of realizing her earlier hopes for occupational advancement by once again enrolling in evening classes. She was able to view her predicament in terms of the mature-adult developmental task of reappraising and restructuring initial unrealistic and unfulfilled occupational goals. Martha scaled down her aspirations for a VP position in favor of a more modest and realistic goal of becoming a section leader. Given her task-application difficulties, she felt that this was within her capabilities and would provide an adequate increase in salary. In the process of scaling down her aspirations, Martha made some headway in moving from her fear of failure pathway and superior–entitled pathway, to what she termed her new "modest–realistic" pathway. Over the next year, Martha was able to persist with her evening classes and earn a business credit, which for her was a substantial accomplishment.

Client Example: Inappropriate Occupational Choice

Another client presented with agitated depression related to his failure to achieve any degree of success in his chosen career as a freelance artist working from home.

> Ron complained of being extremely unproductive and depressed at age 35. He had difficulty getting out of bed and getting started in the morning. As the day wore on he became more and more anxious and usually abandoned his efforts to paint by late afternoon, followed by self-condemnation for being a failure. After dinner he would again attempt to work, without success, so that in essence he was putting in an eight-hour working day with nothing to show for it. His pattern of occupational underachievement dated back to childhood when he was diagnosed with Attention Deficit Hyperactivity Disorder (ADHD). Chronic school failure led to a pattern of procrastination in high school that continued when he entered a business course at community college. It became so severe that he left college after one year and announced to his family that he had decided to freelance from home.
>
> Ron currently found himself unable to fall asleep at night, ruminating about his low level of productivity and often slept in until noon the next morning. This pattern had persisted for years, but he refused to consider the possibility that he had made the wrong career choice. This was in keeping with his determination to prove to his father that he could be a success as an artist.

Although he sought therapy, Ron felt guilty attending sessions because they were interfering with his work time.

Standard CBT techniques were first used to treat acute depression and anxiety symptoms precluding even minimal productivity or effective daily routine. Techniques included activity scheduling, self-monitoring, time management, and cognitive therapy techniques for depression and anxiety. These techniques helped alleviate Ron's emotional symptoms to the extent that he regained sufficient stability in his daily life to proceed to the Developmental Phase of therapy.

The Developmental Phase By means of the Developmental Task Block Identification and Analysis strategies, the client and therapist identified three major early-adult task difficulties that Ron had failed to resolve: (1) establishing a viable career path and occupational effectiveness, (2) establishing a health-enhancing daily routine, and (3) reassessing and restructuring an initial unsuccessful occupational choice. Further analysis revealed more information about the long history of poor academic performance that preceded his career problems. This began with his poor study habits and underachievement secondary to his biologically based hyperactivity syndrome. He had been diagnosed with ADHD at age nine. During adolescence this was compounded by a chronic pattern of extreme procrastination that Ron resorted to in his attempts to cope with the painful consequences of daily failures. This was further complicated by his father's high academic standards for his son, which Ron began to impose upon himself as he approached adulthood. This led to certain failure, since Ron's poor self-discipline prevented him from even getting close to achieving these standards. Ron labeled this self-defeating pattern his "perfectionist–procrastination pathway." He was able to see the discrepancy between his long-standing self-discipline deficit and pattern of perfectionist procrastination and the demands of his freelance career that required a high degree of discipline, initiative, and ability to cope with long hours of social isolation each day. Ron also identified a lifelong pattern of unsuccessful attempts to earn his father's approval.

Ron had a long history of disappointing his father because of his poor academic record. When Ron was a child, his father repeatedly told Ron that he was stupid and that he would never amount to anything. He discounted Ron's ADHD diagnosis and learning disability and attributed his son's academic failure to laziness. The father's academic expectations continued to be unreasonably high. On top of this, the father always compared Ron unfavorably to a cousin his age. The cousin, who had always been an honor student, completed university and initiated a successful home-based business career. Ron's father talked about his nephew as "the son I never had."

Ron realized that his refusal to even consider another career was one example of his ongoing unsuccessful attempts to prove himself to his father by insisting that his decisions were right and that his career choice was comparable to his cousin's. Ron labeled this his "approval-seeking pathway." He realized that gaining his father's approval was an impossible task that had less to do with his own inadequacy than with his father's distorted belief that a parent should withhold approval to ensure a son's continual striving for excellence. This helped Ron to weaken his old pattern of stubborn resistance to changing initial decisions. In this case Ron's habitual resistance to change was working against him, maintaining a career path incompatible with his weak self-discipline and initiation skills. At the same time, it discouraged him from considering a career path of his own choice that would be more in keeping with his strong social skills.

The Current Life Structure Reorganization strategy was used to help Ron to carry out a comprehensive evaluation of his current lifestyle. He found that his actual time spent painting was less than one hour each day, compared to his preference that he paint for at least six hours on week days. He also found that he was spending virtually no time pursuing other preferred activities: spending time with friends, dating, and sports. Instead, his most time-consuming activities were sleeping and "spinning his wheels," trying unsuccessfully to paint. Ron was persuaded to shape a preferred life structure. He decided on a maximum of four hours of productive painting daily, a sleep schedule from 11 pm to 8 am, daily jogging, and time allocated for socializing on weekends. By following this schedule, Ron made some headway in restoring a healthier balance to his daily life.

The Developmental Deficit Skill-Building strategy was then used to educate Ron about gaps in his life in the normative developmental process of choosing a career path. His difficulty with the task of establishing an initial viable career was partly due to his failure to progress through the essential steps of exploring career options, making an informed choice, and attaining educational prerequisites. He realized that his inappropriate occupational choice had not been well thought out but had been a snap decision to deal with the humiliation he suffered after failing at college. It was also an attempt to match his cousin's success at freelancing and ultimately to meet his father's expectations.

Ron was taken through the normal steps necessary for career-change decisions and for choosing a second more appropriate occupational path. This included: (1) preliminary identification of interests, (2) translation of these interests into possible occupations, (3) analyzing the fit between his personality and various career alternatives, (4) choosing the best alternative for a new career path, (5) attaining the necessary academic and job skills for the chosen occupation, and (6) entering the work force or an educational training program.

The client was asked to speculate about educational qualifications, skills, and relevant personality styles necessary for various careers. He was also helped to look for inconsistencies between each career possibility and his own skill strengths and weaknesses (namely, his problems with self-discipline and initiative). Ron realized that freelancing was at odds with his personality and that he would do best in a job that offered more structure. He decided to explore this further and set aside five hours each week for career search activities at a career development center. With his new insight, Ron was able to deviate from his approval-seeking pathway enough to decide for himself without being controlled by fear of his father's reaction. He took a position teaching art to adults for five hours each day at a local community center, in spite of his knowledge that his father would consider this job to be "below his capabilities." This required him to get up in the morning in time to be at work by 10, and once he got into the routine he began to feel better. The job also left some time to paint each day, but Ron found that he did not really want to. Instead, he sought to expand his teaching career. He found himself enjoying his students and experienced a feeling of mastery as he noted their progress.

Chronic Unemployment

Perhaps the most extreme manifestation of problems sustaining occupational effectiveness is chronic unemployment. Therapy clients of various ages and stages present with depression secondary to chronic failure to maintain adequate steady employment. Underlying anger and anxiety disorders are common features of frequent or lengthy unemployment.

Some clients present with a pattern of impulsively quitting jobs before securing a new position. Often these clients have a problem with coworker relationships and are frequently fired or denied promotion because of aggressive or inflexible interpersonal patterns. Other clients suffering from social anxiety may leave an adequate job prematurely because they perceive others as judging them harshly. Many lack a well-thought-out, long-term occupational plan and will take new jobs with the intention of staying for only a short time. Some are periodically on unemployment insurance or other sources of social assistance and may be playing the system, but in the long run, they suffer periods of shame and depression.

Chronic unemployment patterns are frequent presenting problems of clients in middle and mature adulthood years. For some, persistent unemployment may be an outgrowth of an earlier adopted lifestyle that was considered more acceptable at a younger age. During adolescence, a cavalier attitude toward homework, attendance, and school achievement may have gained them status in some peer groups. Later, during early adulthood, an itinerant "hippy" lifestyle may have been enviable, but is no longer deemed acceptable at later stages of life.

Many of the characteristic behavior patterns and themes of the chronically unemployed are components of occupational developmental difficulties addressed in previous sections. Typical behavior patterns include problems of daily routine, social withdrawal, substance abuse or other self-soothing patterns, financial dependence, inadequate self-discipline, low initiative, aggressive interaction styles, procrastination, impulsivity, low tolerance for boring tasks, and resistance to exploring occupational alternatives.

Chronically unemployed clients tend to blame external factors for their predicament while minimizing or denying their own role in failing to search for work until employment is secured. Low achievement motivation and entitlement beliefs are common. Many chronically unemployed clients are supported financially by a spouse, family member, or other person but still feel embarrassed and dissatisfied with their ongoing unemployed status. Some present themselves publicly as free spirits or nonconformists while inwardly evaluating themselves as worthless failures. When the unemployed status persists, depression is usually a feature, with underlying defectiveness, failure, and social alienation schemas.

Typical themes from case histories associated with chronic unemployment are shown in Table 4.5.

Client Example: Chronic Unemployment

Dysfunctional daily routines and entitlement beliefs are often important components of chronic unemployment, as shown in the following example. In addition to periodic financial dependence on family of origin, this client's occupational functioning was impeded by several developmental difficulties over the years, in areas of occupational initiative, independence, daily routine, and task application.

Table 4.5 Typical Themes Associated with Chronic Unemployment

Depression themes: (hopeless occupational situation): It's too late for me to start a career; it's impossible to get a job

Defectiveness themes: My c.v. has gaps in it; I have never been disciplined enough to succeed at a job; I'm too embarrassed about being unemployed so long; I'm not qualified enough to apply for this job; I've always been destined to fail

Entitlement themes: These jobs are below me, too menial, boring; I'm not a nine-to-five person; I can't stand working with idiots

Rigid job criteria: It's against my principles to take a low-paying job when I should make double the salary; no other occupation is acceptable

Unrealistic occupational goals: What I really want is to be a rock singer; I've always wanted to be a doctor; I could start my own business and make a lot of money

Magical thinking: I'll buy a business after I win the lottery; I can do a deal and make a million

Abdication of responsibility: I can't do anything about it, the system has to change; I leave it to fate

Avoidance themes: I must be cured of my anxiety first before I can begin to think of looking for a job; mother needs me at home; I need to fix my computer first

Vulnerability themes: I'd go crazy cooped up at an office all day

External blame themes: New immigrants are taking all the jobs from us; employers are corrupt; employers don't listen to me during interviews; female bosses have it in for me; every time I made a career plan, somebody shoots it down

Elizabeth was a 44-year-old woman who was unemployed and considering the option of enrolling in a welfare job-training program. However, she was uncertain about whether she would be able to stick to a regular routine. Although she had succeeded at high school with minimal effort, her poor effort, disorganized life structure, and substance abuse contributed to academic difficulties at the university level, and she did not bother to finish. Afterwards she drifted from place to place, partially supporting herself with a series of waitress jobs, supplemented by financial donations from her parents. This continued for years, with ongoing failure to establish a stable routine conducive to a long-term career path. She lived with three different partners over the years and eventually had a daughter by a man she met in her travels. After a short time the relationship broke up, and after years of drifting and cheap accommodation, Elizabeth suddenly found herself faced with the necessity of permanent employment in order to support herself and her child. Although they were separated, the child's father was determined to participate in raising his daughter. Elizabeth had not bothered to initiate a formal separation agreement and was now ambivalent about the father as a caregiver. At the same time, she was afraid of the responsibility of taking sole custody of her daughter.

The client's presenting problems included her unemployed status, insufficient finances for raising a child, ongoing dependence on her parents for money, and insufficient job experience and educational background for a job she considered to have appropriate status and remuneration. Components of her chronic unemployed status designated as therapy targets included her pattern of rejecting entry-level jobs as below her, her chaotic daily routine interfering with job search initiatives, and job-search avoidance patterns that involved distracting activities consuming large chunks of her time each day.

Underlying themes and behavior patterns included some of the examples listed in Table 4.5. These included her talk about lucky breaks (magical thinking), numerous excuses for putting off a proper job search such as the need to borrow money to buy a computer first (procrastination), her insistence on an unrealistically high salary given her minimal educational qualifications and work experience (entitlement), and her talk about the hopelessness of ever getting work again after her pathetic occupational performance over the years (occupational depression).

Standard CBT interventions included cognitive techniques for altering depression schemas (Beck et al., 1979), and Schema-Focused Therapy techniques for altering failure and entitlement schemas (Young & Klosko, 1994). Activity scheduling and self-monitoring were then used to help the client to make improvements in her chaotic routine and slovenly living environment. This was subsequently followed by job-search skill training.

The Developmental Phase   After several weeks there were some improvements, but the client had still not undertaken a serious job search. Therefore, the Developmental Phase was initiated using developmental assessment instruments to obtain a history of different aspects of her presenting problems, including an occupational and family of origin history to discover the roots of her poor self-discipline, procrastination patterns, and job-search avoidance.

> Elizabeth had been raised in a family with a depressed mother and a remote father who had minimal involvement with his daughter. She was left on her own with few limits or expectations with respect to academic responsibilities or school attendance. Elizabeth's early exposure to lax and inconsistent rules precluded

a normal developmental pattern of increasing academic self-discipline. Instead, the client developed an expedient pattern of manipulating teachers, parents, and environmental factors to avoid schoolwork. During that time Elizabeth also befriended similar low-achieving peers. After leaving school, Elizabeth's tendency to drift persisted into her early and middle adulthood years so that she never managed to establish a practical, financially solvent occupational path or secure partner relationship.

The Developmental Block Identification and Analysis strategies were used to identify and analyze unresolved tasks dating back to childhood. Blocked tasks identified by the client and therapist included: (1) adolescent tasks of acquisition of self-discipline and sufficient educational background for a workable career path; (2) early adult tasks of financial independence from parents, establishment of a responsible adult routine and career, and commitment to a healthy intimate partner relationship; and (3) additional middle adult tasks of maintaining a functional home environment and effective parenting. Through this process, the client was able to identify what she termed her "adolescent drifting pathway." She realized that this had been facilitated by her parents' lax discipline and low expectations, her associations with similar rudderless peers over the years, and her failure to establish either responsible career initiatives or a stable intimate partner relationship.

The Fast Forward strategy was used to enhance motivation for change. The client was asked to speculate about her life in five years time if her undisciplined life structure and unemployed status persisted. The client's goals, elicited as part of the Developmental Task Resolution Planning, strategy were to secure and maintain steady employment for the next 10 years, to be living in her own apartment with her daughter in 6 month's time, and to begin putting money aside for her daughter's education.

The client was helped by means of Current Life-Structure Reorganization to move from what was essentially an irresponsible adolescent lifestyle to a life structure more appropriate for middle age. She was asked to consider what changes she might make in areas of occupation and routine, partner relationship, parent role, and home environment. She was helped to create a more effective, healthful lifestyle and routine conducive to regular daily work hours, to take advantage of the job-retraining program for the next three months, and to establish a formal separation and custody agreement with her former partner, while allowing him to take over as major caregiver during the week so she could attend classes. She decided to remain temporarily in her rooming house residence to earn money for expenses by working as a waitress two evenings per week.

These strategies helped Elizabeth make the shift from an adolescent drifting pathway to what she labeled her new "responsible adult pathway." Over the next few weeks she managed to stick to her job-training program, which subsequently led to a permanent job in food services. She now found herself able to tolerate a conventional lifestyle and actually began to enjoy it. In the following months she was able to take over more of the parenting responsibilities and was eventually able to afford an apartment for herself and her daughter.

JOB TERMINATION AND DEMOTION ADJUSTMENT DISABILITIES

The clients in this category do not have a pattern of chronic unemployment but are experiencing the prolonged negative repercussions of job loss or demotion and are unable to adjust after a reasonable amount of time. Some clients are still ruminating about a lost job several years later, accompanied by depression and anxiety. These clients lack sufficient resilience to pick up the pieces and move on. Anger and revenge themes are common. Clients may be more concerned with sustaining the victim role or with retaliation against the system or former coworkers than they are with securing another job. Typical behavior patterns include prolonged failure to explore future employment options or undertake a job search, prolonged sick role, exaggeration of job-loss trauma, plans to sue the former employer or colleagues, repeated demands for employers to justify their decisions, social isolation, and self-soothing behaviors such as alcohol abuse.

Characteristic themes from case histories are shown in Table 4.6. Categories include unfair treatment, self-pity, revenge, escape, and depression themes. These beliefs play a role in keeping the anger alive and justifying reasons for failure to move on to another job or occupation.

Client Example: Job Loss Adjustment Difficulties

The following client was still consumed with anger about having been fired from her job two years before.

Patricia was in her mid-fifties when she sought therapy for depression and anger. Two years earlier her boss had terminated her job as a receptionist, as well as the jobs of two of her colleagues, stating that it was part of a company downsizing initiative. Patricia claimed that she was suddenly let go with no reasonable explana-

Table 4.6 Typical Themes Associated with Job Loss or Demotion Adjustment Difficulties

Abdication of responsibility: They fired me unfairly, why should I look for another job; it's my boss' responsibility to find me another job

Blame external factors: Coworkers wanted me out, they always took advantage of me; my former boss has ruined my chances for ever getting another acceptable job

Hopelessness themes: It's impossible to find another job, why try; nobody can help me; I don't dare try another job, I'll get fired again; I just want to disappear; now I'm too old and tired to try again; I have no control over what happens to me)

Exaggeration of job loss consequences: My former life was perfect before this happened; what happened has ruined my chances for ever having a successful career or life again; I don't make plans, because when you are fired and try again something bad always happens

tion after working for the company for eight years without any problems. After the dismissal she refused the company's offer of a job-search support program. She suffered from depression and agoraphobia, rarely leaving home, and became dependent on her former husband for financial support. She stopped attending her bridge club and failed to return friends' phone calls. She continued to ruminate obsessively about her unfair dismissal, but subsequent information suggested that her poor attendance and interpersonal conflicts with management may have been contributing factors. Patricia refused to explore future job possibilities, claiming that her misfortune was not her fault.

The major components of Patricia's job-loss adjustment difficulties were negative ruminations about the impossibility of future employment, depressive inactivity, debilitating anxiety, job-search avoidance blocks, and social isolation. Underlying beliefs were reflected in the following themes: "I did nothing wrong and they took my job away … I'm a victim of the system" (external blame). "I'm waiting for insight as to what job I should go after … I need another vocational assessment first … I have to feel useful before I can become active in another job" (job search avoidance excuses). "It's my boss' fault and his responsibility to find me another job" (abdication of responsibility). "I'll never have a successful career again … I've wasted my life" (negative occupational future).

Standard CBT techniques were used for depression and anxiety symptoms and underlying vulnerability schemas that were interfering with job search initiatives. This was followed by activity scheduling for depressive inactivity, graded task assignment for social withdrawal secondary to embarrassment about unemployment status, and problem solving to combat decision paralysis. Attempts to initiate resume-writing and job-search skill training interventions were unsuccessful because the client refused to participate or to even discuss future options. The strength of her resistance was so strong that it suggested a need to explore the possibility of maladaptive developmental pathways leading to her current predicament.

The Developmental Phase Developmental CBT assessment instruments revealed the following history.

> Patricia's mother suffered from an anxiety disorder and had been totally dependent on Patricia's father. However, the father had died when Patricia was 14, and her mother then became severely depressed. She began to drink was unable to function as a parent or to perform rudimentary household chores. Patricia began missing school and took over all aspects of housekeeping, hoping that her mother would appreciate this and spend more time with her. Unfortunately, her efforts were largely unnoticed. Patricia developed the attitude of "nobody cares, why should I?" and withdrew from school and friends. Although she eventually resumed sporadic school attendance, the girl's misfortune became a topic of conversation, and peers avoided her out of embarrassment. Patricia suffered her first panic attack at school and began staying at home, where she became inactive and depressed. This coincided with the onset of perfectionist compulsive rituals that functioned to bring some order to her chaotic home environment and to ward off future family tragedies.

With the help of the Then and Now strategy, Patricia recalled a similar situation during her late twenties when a negative experience with critical coworkers led to frequent absences from work. This led to elevated anxiety manifested in a fear of using the subway, demands that her former husband accompany her to work, and eventually, resignation from her job. Patricia was able to identify the similarities between these two incidents during her adult years and her earlier adolescent pattern.

Through the Developmental Task Block Identification and Analysis strategies, the client realized that the traumatic loss of her father combined with her mother's inability to provide adequate nurturance had led to Patricia's unsuccessful striving for attention from what was essentially a neglecting, alcoholic mother. This was the root of an intense anger and stubborn resistance to getting better that surfaced periodically over the years when stressful situations arose. Unresolved adolescent tasks identified by the client involved her failure to achieve a sense of connectedness with her mother and/or psychological independence from her mother and her difficulties persisting with school responsibilities during times of stress. Unresolved adult tasks included her periodic failure to reappraise and restructure unsuccessful occupational situations and failure to cultivate and maintain supportive friendships over the years.

Patricia labeled this pattern her "angry–anxious–paralysis pathway." She then recalled that in the previous situation in her late twenties, after quitting her job she eventually got her life back on track when she entered a business training program to upgrade her skills. She labeled this healthier pattern a "resilient survivor pathway."

The client was then helped by the Resiliency Training Strategy to conceptualize her recent job loss as a fairly common occurrence in the ups and downs of a career, rather than a tragedy. She was asked to speculate about what she could have done differently to maintain continuity in other areas of her daily life and concluded that she should have continued her routine social activities and should have attended the job-search support program to provide some daily structure and to acquire additional occupational skills. Patricia was able to identify the self-defeating preoccupations listed above as fueling her old "nobody-cares-why-should I?" theme and anxious withdrawal pattern contributing to her paralysis. She was encouraged to identify her major strengths and to put them to work to overcome this pattern. Patricia was proud of her organizational skills and methodological approach to work and was persuaded to practice these skills as a member of a vocational support group in the community. She was also taught techniques to increase social anxiety tolerance and social-interaction skills as a buffer for future occupational disappointments. Her new friendships in the vocational support group and participation in the group's job-search initiatives were the first steps in Patricia's transition to the adaptive resilient survivor pathway.

SUMMARY OF MALADAPTIVE DEVELOPMENTAL PATHWAYS ASSOCIATED WITH ADULT OCCUPATIONAL PROBLEMS

Clients manifesting the various occupational developmental difficulties addressed in this chapter share many of the same early histories and behavior patterns. There are also many similarities between the early developmental pathways. Therapists may find it useful for future reference to compile a list of typical client developmental pathways associated with problems establishing and maintaining viable occupational paths, similar to the one shown in Table 4.7.

Table 4.7 Examples of Maladaptive Developmental Pathways Associated with Adult Occupational Difficulties

Task application deficit pathway: Parental psychopathology, neglect, poor parental models of self-discipline, or chaotic home environment (inadequate routine, parental supervision, or academic expectations for the child): child fails to develop adequate self-discipline, schoolwork avoidance during childhood and adolescence, low interest in or value on schoolwork, inadequate homework or classroom application, academic challenge avoidance, inadequate task persistence, academic underachievement or failure, inadequate educational attainments for acceptable occupational path. **Adult pattern:** insufficient application to adult occupational tasks, low interest in work tasks, low tolerance for boring routine tasks, diversions to avoid work demands, seeking to cover up

Occupational entitlement pathway: Over-involved, over-submissive, or over-valuing parent (parent exaggerates child's abilities; inadequate parental expectations for child's independent completion of school tasks and academic achievement): child learns to manipulate parent to avoid schoolwork, expects special treatment from teachers, fails to complete school tasks independently, may disregard school rules or have pattern of truancy, fails to obtain educational qualifications for desired occupation status or acceptable job. **Adult pattern:** inadequate application to adult job tasks, impostor pattern (talks way into a job; loses job when fails to deliver, anger and blame for perceived unfair treatment)

Oppositional and defiant occupational pathway: Rejecting, punitive, abusive, over-submissive, or neglecting parent, inadequate parental supervision, lax or inconsistent discipline, inadequate academic expectations: child oppositional, defiant at school, disruptive classroom behavior or conflict with teachers, disregards school rules and school assignments, truancy, may be impulsive and stimulus-seeking, close association with similar underachieving or disruptive peers, under-involvement in pro-social school activities, may leave school prematurely with inadequate educational attainments or underdeveloped occupational skills, drifting. **Adult pattern:** inadequate application to adult job tasks, interpersonal conflicts with colleagues, fired from jobs, externalizes blame for job failure, hostile attributions

Anxious avoidant occupational pathway: Overprotective anxious parent, child develops anxiety disorder and school avoidance, academic underachievement secondary to truancy. **Adult pattern:** financial dependence on parents in early adulthood, job search and occupational fears, ongoing failure to enter the work force or postsecondary educational program

5

MALADAPTIVE DEVELOPMENTAL PATTERNS
AFFECTING SOCIAL RELATIONSHIPS

This chapter will demonstrate the Developmental CBT approach with developmental patterns impeding the formation of satisfying and effective social relationships across the life span. Adult clients with social problems present with a wide range of maladaptive social interaction styles. For example, dysfunctional social interaction patterns of personality disorders described in DSM IV include unfounded distrust of others, exploitation of friends and associates, deliberate detachment from social relationships, excessive social anxiety and avoidance, deficits in social and emotional interaction skills, deceitfulness, indifference to the pain of others, intense anger and aggression, inappropriate attention or approval seeking, and inappropriate attempts to control others. As would be expected, dysfunctional social pathways may impede client performance of adult roles and tasks in several related areas of daily functioning, such as intimate partner relationships, educational and occupational performance, and parenting roles.

As children grow older, their social world expands and peer groups become increasingly important as standards for self-evaluation, with a gradual orientation toward social comparisons and conformity with one's peers (Suls & Mullen, 1982). Problems with peer acceptance and relationships in childhood have been found to predict behavioral maladjustment in adolescence and adulthood (Masten & Coatsworth, 1995; Hartup, 1983; Putallaz & Dunn, 1990). For example, children who have difficulty getting along with their peers are more likely to experience subsequent difficulties with the law, with drugs, and with academic adjustment and to be fired from jobs for behavioral reasons as adults (Putallaz & Dunn, 1990). However, social support derived from close confiding friendships moderates the impact of negative everyday stressors (Cohen & Wills, 1985). Youngsters with a difficult family history or difficult school experiences, who have nevertheless managed to form satisfying peer relationships, are also more likely to successfully negotiate normative psychosocial tasks and transitions.

The focus of this chapter will be limited to a discussion of the Developmental CBT approach with three maladaptive social interaction styles commonly observed in therapy clients. These will be referred to as (1) the angry–aggressive social style, (2) the superior–entitled social style, and (3) the anxious–awkward social style. These social interaction styles are not mutually exclusive, and there will be considerable overlap for some clients. For example, one client with a diagnosis of Borderline Personality Disorder manifested components of the angry–aggressive and the superior–entitled patterns combined with approval-seeking features of the anxious–awkward style. The initial focus of the Developmental CBT approach will be dysfunctional behavior patterns and core schemas underlying the client's current maladaptive social style. This is then followed by an analysis of the influences shaping and maintaining developmental pathways culminating in the client's current social difficulties.

NEGATIVE EARLY INFLUENCES AND EXPERIENCES

Negative family of origin influences such as family violence, parental mental illness or alcoholism, and ineffective child-rearing styles tend to jeopardize a child's social development. Typical family histories of adult clients with social interaction problems include parents who were punitive, rejecting, neglectful, unaffectionate, over-protective, or over-submissive or parents who were poor role models such as socially avoidant parents. There may also be a history of exposure to early trauma such as sexual abuse, marital discord or divorce, parent desertion, or death of a parent. A child with dysfunctional parental role models learns maladaptive interaction patterns and socialization styles in the home, which increases the likelihood of peer rejection and exclusion from healthy social networks. This limits the child's exposure to positive peer socialization experiences that normally facilitate acquisition of *social intelligence* and effective interpersonal styles (Hartup, 1983). Child and adolescent friendships provide an ongoing milieu for fine-tuning interpersonal skills over the years.

An early family environment with emotionally distant, rejecting, or abusive parents fails to provide sufficient security, sense of belonging, caring, or modeling necessary to prepare the youngster for satisfying, trusting adult social relationships (Rokach, 1989). Attachment theorists emphasize that the establishment of secure parent–child bonds during childhood is essential for children to develop the capacity for warmth and closeness in their own social relationships. Disruption of early family bonds increases the likelihood of subsequent emotional and interpersonal difficulties and loneliness. Parent psychopathology may also disrupt the child's social development. For example, children of alcoholics have an increased incidence of depression, anxiety disorders, and anger problems that decrease their capacity for friendship (Bedrosian & Bozicas, 1994; Johnson, Sher, & Rolf, 1991; Perlman, 1987; Russell, Henderson, & Blume, 1985). Typical early peer and school experiences predicting unsatisfactory adult social relationships include a history of peer rejection or harassment and patterns of social anxiety, social isolation, school avoidance or phobia, school failure or underachievement, conflict with teachers and classmates, antisocial behavior, and insufficient involvement in age-appropriate peer-group activities. The latter may be due to a variety of reasons such as extreme shyness, parental prohibitions, or embarrassment about physical appearance or family stigma.

NORMAL PATHWAYS TO ADAPTIVE SOCIAL DEVELOPMENT

Normal social development is predicated on the youngster's capacity to form cooperative relationships with pro-social peers during childhood and adolescence. Children are required to learn and apply appropriate rules of social behavior that will be rewarded by close friendships. Having stable friendships and a "best friend" in childhood can function as a buffer to ameliorate deleterious effects of a troubled home environment or periodic peer harassment. Children not only develop dyadic relationships with several close friends, but are also involved in small groups of friends and larger groups within their classrooms and neighborhoods. Consequently, they must learn rules for friendship in both small and larger peer groups. Since attitudinal and behavioral norms vary to some extent across social settings, children must learn subtle variations in appropriate social behavior and rules for successful relationships in pairs, small groups, classroom, and playground (Deater-Deckard, 2001).

Linehan (1993) identifies three major areas of interpersonal skill development: cognitive social skills, emotional skills, and overt behavioral skills. Cognitive social skills include social sensitivity, and social judgment. Social sensitivity is the ability to discriminate what is happening in a given situation and to make accurate attributions about the other person's behavior. Social judgment is the ability to generate behavioral responses that will be effective in a given situation and the ability to evaluate the probable effects that these behaviors will have on people.

Emotional skills involve both emotional range and affect regulation. Appropriate emotional range is neither too flat (as when a person avoids or disowns emotion) nor too intense, excessive, or labile. Similarly, affect regulation skills enable a person to match a particular emotional response to a particular situation.

Behavioral skills include effective strategies for asking for what you need, saying no, and coping effectively with interpersonal conflict. Self-management is another behavioral skill that controls, manages, or otherwise changes inappropriate social responses.

Clients who have deviated from normal socialization pathways have probably failed to acquire crucial interpersonal skills during their early years. Table 5.1, adapted from Linehan (1993) and Deater-Deckard (2001), provides a useful assessment tool for targeting areas of social skill deficits.

ADDRESSING MALADAPTIVE PATHWAYS OF SOCIAL DEVELOPMENT

The therapist begins by identifying components of a client's deviant interpersonal pathway, such as failure to engage in casual activities with peers and failure to develop same-sex friendships during childhood and adolescence. Next, the therapist targets deficits in crucial interpersonal skills underlying adult interpersonal problems, such as emotional regulation problems, social information processing problems, inadequate knowledge about prerequisites of effective peer relationships, or distorted self-perceptions. The therapist will then devise ways of helping the client learn various aspects of successful social functioning that he or she has failed to master, using standard CBT techniques. Examples of useful techniques include:

- Role-playing skill training to foster empathy
- Conflict-resolution skill training
- Active-listening skill training (e.g., reflect back, inhibit own interruptions, elicit and validate other person's views)
- Anger-control techniques
- Conflict de-escalation techniques (e.g., neutral statements, self-deprecating humor)
- Emotion-regulation skill training
- Social-problem-solving training
- Distress-tolerance skill training

Table 5.1 Adaptive Interpersonal Skills

Cognitive social skills:
- Knowledge about social relationships (through adequate experience in interpersonal situations)
- Social sensitivity skills (accurate attributions)
- Accurate perceptions about potential for suitable friendships
- Social judgment skills (ability to generate appropriate social behaviors and predict the outcome)
- Social perception skills (ability to make accurate attributions about other people's motives, judgments)
- Social self-regulation skills (ability to use feedback to monitor own behavior)
- Knowledge about appropriate behaviors for specific situations
- Self-perception skills

Emotional skills:
- Adequate emotional range
- Emotional regulation skills

Behavioral skills:
- Active listening skills
- Anger control techniques
- Conflict de-escalation skills
- Eliciting other person's views, opinions, giving equal time
- Use of self-deprecating humor
- Inhibition of tendency to jump to conclusions
- Self-talk to diffuse negative emotional reactions
- Problem-solving skills for stressful social situations
- Nonverbal social behavior skills (e.g., facial expressions and gestures)
- Assertiveness skills
- Appropriate self-disclosure
- Conflict negotiation and resolution skills
- Self-management skills for anger-provoking situations
- Conversation skills (greeting, raising appropriate topics, acknowledging another person's point of view or feelings)
- Empathy skills

Source: Adapted from Linehan, 1993; Deater-Deckard, 2001

DEVELOPMENTAL CBT STRATEGIES

In addition to standard CBT social-skills training techniques, therapist and client will seek to identify and analyze early experiences that set the client on a deviant socialization pathway that shaped the ineffective social-interaction patterns underlying current social problems. Early experiences may include a history of anxiety or depression in the school setting, rejection or victimization by peers, or daily exposure to dysfunctional family role models or family violence. More specifically, the focus will shift to (1) identifying predisposing maladaptive patterns or pathways, (2) educating clients about normal social skills that they seem to have failed to acquire at earlier developmental stages, and (3) increasing client understanding of the way in which maladaptive social interaction patterns have been instrumental in either curtailing his or her capacity for forming adult friendships, or limiting effective interpersonal functioning in school, work, or community settings.

THE ANGRY–AGGRESSIVE SOCIAL STYLE

The angry–aggressive social interaction style is characterized by inappropriate blaming, criticism, name calling, threats, provocations, confrontations, emotional outbursts, insistence on having the last word, and attempts to dominate or control social relationships. There may be repeated demands for justification of another person's point of view, followed by failure to attend sufficiently to the other person's explanation. Insistence on having the last word is typical. Characteristic themes reflect mistrust, abuse, blame, failure to empathize, helplessness, harsh judgment of others, entitlement, and angry ruminations about personal injustices.

Passive–aggressive patterns may also be present. These may be manifested in contradiction, compliant defiance, or covert assertiveness. Passive–aggressive clients often present as stubborn malcontents who resist unappealing routine tasks, complain of being misunderstood and unappreciated, scorn authority, and dwell on personal misfortune. These clients may routinely seek to downgrade others or to turn one person against another. Typical patterns include sulking, silent treatment, guilt-engendering statements, and resistance to others' attempts to be helpful. They may refuse to get better and remain indefinitely "sick" to prove a point. In fact, these clients may deliberately isolate themselves from friends or sabotage friendly initiatives. As therapy clients, they are often determined to fail.

Early Influences and Precursors

Typical early manifestations of the angry–aggressive style include child and adolescent histories of Oppositional Defiant Disorder (ODD), Conduct Disorder (CD), or Attention Deficit/Hyperactivity Disorder (ADHD). Early predisposing factors commonly include chronic family stress or violence, maladaptive parenting, extreme marital discord, and parental alcoholism or mental illness. Parents may be punitive, abusive, unaffectionate, or neglecting. Children exposed to family violence may grow up feeling inadequate, angry, or unloved and may seek retaliation. Aggressive family role models may be combined with parental disciplinary styles that are overly strict, fostering angry, fearful obedience. In some cases discipline is lax and inconsistent, enabling children to manipulate the parents.

Typical early social experiences include peer rejection, harassment, bullying, association with aggressive or antisocial peers, and inadequate exposure to gentle pro-social peers. There may also be a history of conflict at school, academic underachievement, or truancy.

Client Example

Judy complained of unfair treatment from her boss and friends at work. She had been locked in a power struggle with her boss for several weeks following a routine yearly performance evaluation that the client considered unflattering. Afterwards she burst into tears and accused him of deliberately trying to ruin her career. She refused to cosign the evaluation, refused to speak to her boss, and initiated a charge of harassment against him. When senior management refused to go along with this, the client failed to show up for work for a week.

Judy also complained about her three friends at work. One friend had suggested that the client may have over-reacted and advised her to drop the harassment charges and to get back on speaking terms with her boss in the interest of keeping her job. The client interpreted this as "siding with the enemy," rather than as an attempt to be helpful. In an outburst of temper, she accused her friend of being a hypocrite, stopped speaking to her, and advised her other two friends to do the same out of loyalty to her. She bombarded her friends constantly with her side of the story until they began to avoid her and failed to return her phone calls. She eventually approached her boss in an attempt to improve the situation, but this initiative soon deteriorated into demands to be told what she did wrong and repetitive attempts to justify her behavior, thereby alienating the boss even more.

Standard CBT techniques included conflict management, emotion-regulation, and stress-inoculation skill-training to soften the client's aggressive style. These were supplemented by cognitive techniques to challenge distorted automatic thoughts about the meaning of upsetting events and to address mistrust/abuse schemas. Attempts were then made to persuade the client to experiment with the more-appropriate responses. However, the client continually challenged and countered these initiatives, blaming the therapist for not understanding or caring about her, just like her boss, friends, and family members throughout her life. This deadlock persisted until the Developmental Phase was initiated.

The Developmental Phase   Developmental CBT assessment tools were first used to obtain a developmental history of the client's family and social experiences over the years. They revealed the following additional information:

Judy was born out of wedlock to a teenage mother who subsequently abandoned her to be raised by a reluctant grandmother. The grandmother was abusive and rejecting and complained of having been left with the burden of raising another child. Judy spent her childhood hoping to be rescued some day by her mother, but these hopes were never realized because her mother had moved on to another relationship with more children and had no interest in reuniting with her daughter. With no knowledge of her father, a mother who wanted nothing to do with her, and a grandmother who showed no sympathy for Judy's pain at being abandoned, Judy felt she had never had anyone who really cared about her or understood her suffering. She spent years plagued by angry ruminations about the unfairness of her abusive family situation and the absence of loving parents. In spite of this, she managed to cope with schoolwork and to eventually establish an adequate career path. Judy adopted many of her grandmother's aggressive patterns and relied on obnoxious behavior to gain attention. As a teenager, Judy resorted to a combination of temper tantrums to dramatize her pain and threats and guilt trips to manipulate her grandmother. These aggressive techniques helped her survive her miserable home situation but were less successful with peers. As a child, she had responded aggressively to perceived peer harassment and became known as the class bully. As a teenager, she associated with similar aggressive peers and consequently was ostracized by more socially skilled classmates, thereby depriving herself of the opportunity to learn more adaptive interpersonal skills. As an adult, she was still relying on her aggressive adolescent patterns and inappropriate demands for loyalty but never managed to find people who cared enough or were sufficiently loyal.

Developmental CBT strategies were used to increase client insight and motivation for change through identification of various components of her self-defeating aggressive pattern and exploration of the origins of these components. She was also educated about the adaptive interpersonal patterns that she had failed to develop over the years. Finally, the developmental strategies increased Judy's understanding of the way in which her angry–aggressive style had been curtailing successful performance of major adult tasks and roles in several areas over the years. She realized that it had interfered not only with her ability to develop satisfying adult friendships, but also with her ability to develop successful romantic partner relationships, as well as work relationships, and had significantly curtailed her chances for career advancement.

The Developmental Task Block Analysis strategy increased the client's insight into the early roots of her unsuccessful lifelong struggle to achieve a sense of personal worth, peer acceptance, and satisfying friendships. She was helped to view her aggressive style within a developmental context, and labeled it her "childish confrontational pathway." She concluded that she learned her provocative interpersonal style from her grandmother and from early peer relationships and that her aggressive patterns were maintained over the years by her anger at being abandoned, coupled with a core belief that a person has to fight to survive. Although her aggressive pattern had helped her as a child to cope with her difficult home and peer situations, it subsequently got in the way of desired friendships with normal peers. She realized that reliance on emotional outbursts, repetitive self-justifications, and demands for loyalty had always been counter-productive, precluding the deep satisfying friendships she craved. During early adulthood, her childish confrontational pathway had further prevented her from sustaining satisfying romantic relationships and had led to difficulties with work colleagues. Currently, that same aggressive style was jeopardizing both her career and her friendships.

Using Table 5.1 as a reference, the therapist educated Judy about normal childhood development in areas of social cognition and emotional and behavioral skills. Judy became more open to the challenge of learning and experimenting with new nonaggressive patterns at this stage of her life that most people acquire effortlessly as children growing up in a normal family environment. She was also helped to view her negative work performance evaluation in a larger context, as part of the normal ups and downs of a career that spans several years, rather than as a catastrophe. She was encouraged to view management's negative evaluation as a temporary setback that was a useful learning experience and was asked to consider the possibility that successful people have periodic setbacks but have developed the capacity to cope with disappointments and move on.

The Adaptive Versus Obsolete Coping Style strategy was used to help Judy isolate components of her childish confrontational pathway.

She was first asked for several examples and detailed descriptions of stressful interactions with her boss and friends. She identified several components of her residual obsolete childish interpersonal style, including her emotional outbursts, repeated self-justifications in attempts to prove she was right, repeated demands to know what she did wrong, and heightened sensitivity to slight or perceived hostility. She identified her penchant for provocative challenges, angry accusations, threats, moralizing, and name calling. The client was then asked to observe people at work who used a more gentle, courteous approach and was intrigued by the notion of adopting some of their techniques even though they didn't feel natural. On the basis of her observations, she was able to work with the therapist to outline an adaptive style that consisted of the following: (1) inhibiting the urge to jump to conclusions about the other person's malevolent intentions, (2) avoidance of no-win debates, (3) decreasing the frequency of emotional outbursts by increasing self-awareness of the common triggers precipitating emotional outbursts in the past, (4) distancing herself from potentially explosive situations, (5) using humor, and (6) reminding herself to stay calm, use a neutral tone of voice, and keep explanations short. She labeled this a "mature nonconfrontational pathway."

The Developmental Deficit Skill-Building strategy was used to teach the client pro-social components of the new gentler mature nonconfrontational pathway. She was also asked to recall families she had observed at some time in her life who seemed not to rely on aggressive interactions. She recalled having spent some time at a neighbor's house as a teenager, where mutual parent–child problem solving seemed to be the favored approach. She was again asked to observe more socially effective colleagues who did not become involved in confrontational exchanges and to pay particular attention to their listening skills. She had the opportunity to observe her friend handling an angry client and noted the following patterns: listening without interrupting and acknowledging and validating the other person's statements and feelings in a soft nurturing manner (e.g., "I can understand your dilemma, that's an interesting view, that's one way of looking at it," or silent nonverbal acknowledgment). The therapist enlisted standard CBT techniques for increasing client empathy, reflection, and sensitivity to other people's needs. The client was also taught to use neutral responses to replace angry explosive responses and tearful outbursts in reaction to perceived hostility.

Once the client was educated about normal developmental acquisition of conflict negotiation skills and other nonaggressive approaches to interpersonal stress, she had a better understanding of her skill deficits that were curtailing her capacity to cope with anger-provoking situations in a nonconfrontational manner. She was again asked to observe more socially effective colleagues who did not become involved in confrontational exchanges and to pay particular attention to their listening skills. Judy then practiced the following skills in preparation for forthcoming meetings with her boss and friends: reflecting back the other's view, identifying areas of agreement, admitting her own mistakes, and using a neutral tone of voice and neutral responses to provocative statements. In this way, she was helped to begin to gradually shift to a mature nonconfrontational pathway.

Finally, the Negative Life Review strategy was used to address the client's angry ruminations about past injustices from childhood and adolescence stemming from the absence of loving parents, a punitive grandmother, and her early feelings of inferiority in the company of peers from normal families. She realized that these factors had led her to associate with aggressive peers with similar abusive or neglecting parents who would be able to understand her situation. She labeled this her "inferior–bitter pathway" and was then helped to challenge angry ruminations confined to maintain this pathway. These included her preoccupation with the irreparable damage caused by her unhappy childhood and bitterness at the fact that people never understood her pain, had always been against her, had never been there to help, and had never really cared about her. She was helped to challenge her assumption that she had been so damaged that she could never have normal friendships and a second assumption that it was the responsibility of her friends to intuitively understand her point of view and be supportive. The client was also helped to realize that one positive side effect of her early family situation was that it shaped a strong young woman determined to succeed. She had become an excellent student, and her career performance to date had been outstanding, given her early circumstances. She decided to capitalize on her capacity for survival in the face of adversity and utilize these strengths in response to current interpersonal challenges. She began to refer to a new "resilient social pathway" extending to relationships at work.

Judy's immediate goals were to repair her relationships with her boss and with her friends and thereby improve her sense of self-worth. She decided to publicly adopt a pleasant cooperative attitude in keeping with her mature nonconfrontational pathway and to write a letter to her boss stating that she was prepared to sign the evaluation and to drop the harassment charges, without attempting to justify her previous behavior. Although this approach felt unnatural, and she was still grappling with residual anger, Judy managed to use her new social skills and her determination to embrace her resilient social pathway to diffuse her explosive work situation and repair her relationships with colleagues and administration.

THE SUPERIOR–ENTITLED SOCIAL STYLE

The superior–entitled social style is characterized by exaggeration of one's own abilities (self-aggrandizement) and an expectation to be granted special privileges and status. The *superior* component often involves bragging, showing off, and core beliefs about one's obligation to expose the inferiority of others and to educate less-enlightened people, often without the realization that this self-righteous and judgmental stance alienates others. Clients in this category believe they must continually prove their own superiority, which may be defined by morals, intellect, class, wealth, or other criteria. These clients tend to be intolerant of views and lifestyles that differ from theirs and often dominate social gatherings with their views. In fact, self-aggrandizement often masks an exaggerated need for approval and feelings of inferiority stemming from any number of causes such as an impoverished background, family stigma, or inadequate educational or occupational attainments. They may fear that if they fail to demonstrate their superiority, they will be labeled inferior.

The *entitled* component involves a belief in one's right to special treatment from others, owing to one's superiority or as compensation for hardships endured, such as a difficult childhood or other personal misfortunes. These clients often have a long history of successfully using and manipulating people and getting their way, but ultimately their selfishness and thoughtlessness get in the way of friendship. Typical entitlement themes include beliefs about the right to inconvenience others, expectations that others will somehow anticipate and fulfill one's needs, and expectations that others should be making a bigger effort, followed by disappointment when they fail to do so. Excessive demands on other people's time and inappropriate loyalty demands are also common. The superior–entitled style is often seen in combination with the angry–aggressive style discussed in the previous section.

A good illustration of the superior–entitled social style is Martha, the client described in Chapter 4 who was helped to understand how her entitlement pathway had been responsible for her insufficient self-discipline and poor career performance over the years. In spite of this, Martha was still mystified by her lack of friends. She was unaware of the extent to which her long-standing superior–entitled pattern and underlying beliefs had extended to her interpersonal relationships and had precluded formation of the satisfying friendships she craved.

Client Example

Martha complained about her lack of friends and the fact that people often sought her friendship when they first met her, but after a few meetings they quickly drifted away and avoided her. She complained that "people should be there for me when I need them since *I'm* always there for them." She gave two recent examples of "friendly debates" with work colleagues that gradually escalated to shouting and insults. Following each of these incidents the other person avoided future contacts with her, leaving Martha with feelings of anger and self-condemnation for allowing herself to be drawn into these arguments and to lose control. Martha explained that she felt it was her duty to educate others when they were wrong. She felt compelled to always make her point in order to keep up the appearance of being as good as her colleagues who had the university credentials she lacked. Otherwise, she would be judged a failure. She said that she had always depended on "out-talking: the other person and "talking a good line" and realized that this was a means of covering up her own insecurities.

The Developmental Phase   Recall that in the previous chapter the Developmental Task-Block Identification and Analysis strategies had helped Martha understand how her superior–entitled pattern had enabled her to justify her poor self-discipline and occupational failure over the years. However, she was still not fully aware of the degree to which this pattern was undermining her social relationships. This time, the Developmental Task-Block Analysis was used to help Martha understand the consequences of her long-standing tendency to debate, challenge, confront, and assert her superiority.

During childhood Martha had sought to cover up her embarrassment about her working-class background and her father's decision to desert the family. She resorted to bragging about her toys and her nonexistent "rich grandfather," and to buying candy and trinkets for friends. Her mother insisted that Martha was blessed with superior intelligence and demanded that she be placed in an enriched class at school. Given Martha's poor self-discipline, this turned out to be a disaster. Martha's superior–entitled pattern was further developed during adolescence when she began to show off her superior knowledge of almost any topic. Later, during early adulthood, she continued to pose as an "intellectual" to hide the fact that she had never been to university. In recent years she had begun referring to her nonexistent "university days."

The developmental analysis helped Martha identify her "superior social pathway" and trace its origins and various manifestations over the years. She realized that during childhood and adolescence, her need to show off functioned to neutralize her feelings of inferiority with respect to her humble family background and her poor academic results. Later, her intellectual "superiority" functioned to neutralize negative feelings stemming from her failure to attend university. Currently, it was Martha's way of handling her embarrassment about her inferior job status. Unfortunately, her adopted superior social pathway had continued to sabotage her chances for real friendships. Martha was helped to gain a clearer understanding of her underlying core beliefs, skill deficits, and developmental influences. She admitted that she always knew deep down that her IQ was no more than average, but she went along with her mother's exaggerated claims anyway.

The Developmental Task-Resolution Planning strategy was used to help the client find ways to build enduring friendships for the first time in her life. Her current goals were to develop at least one deep mutually satisfying friendship; to inhibit her tendency to show off, initiate debates, and allow them to escalate; and to break the pattern of winning the debate but losing the friendship. She decided to adopt what she termed a "modest–sincere pathway" and a more accommodating interpersonal style that would enable her to lose the argument in order to win the friend.

Using the Adaptive Versus Obsolete Coping Styles strategy, the client made a deliberate attempt to learn new skills that would enable her to experiment with losing the argument and preserving the friendship. The client identified the following components of her ongoing problem with social relationships: beliefs that it was her duty to educate others, that her fellow colleagues were not as smart, that it was necessary for her to make her point each time in order to conceal her impoverished background and inadequate educational attainments, and a belief that if she conceded an argument, she would be seen as a failure.

This obsolete coping style was also characterized by poor listening skills, poor negotiation skills, bragging, attempts to educate the other person, pointing out other people's flaws "for their own good," exaggerating, lying, asserting her moral superiority, and a pattern of out-talking the other person. Developmental patterns from adolescence through adulthood included attempts to get out of mundane school or work tasks by "talking a good line," attempts to hide her lack of formal education by pretending to be intellectually superior, educating the person about the "truth," and trying to impress others in order to feel that she was as good as her colleagues.

She was then helped by means of the Developmental Deficit Skill-Building strategy to develop and evaluate a new adaptive coping style consisting of the following: active listening, encouraging the other person to talk, reflecting back others' views, expressing areas of agreement, self-deprecation, and admitting her own vulnerabilities and mistakes. This new style also consisted of inhibiting the urge to brag and to challenge everything and the urge to be "honest" by pointing out others people's weaknesses. In addition, she was taught conflict de-escalation skills to use when she found herself slipping back into her old pattern.

Martha began experimenting with her new modest–sincere pathway. Although she complained that it did not feel right, within weeks she began to reap the benefits. Social stress at work was significantly reduced, and she developed one close friend in her evening class with whom she felt she could be completely honest. At this late stage, Martha began to master a formula for handling work colleagues, in addition to a means of building friendships for the first time in her life.

THE ANXIOUS–AWKWARD SOCIAL STYLE

The anxious–awkward social style is characterized by personal inadequacy schemas, social anxiety, and deficits in social interaction skills. These clients are often depressed about their lack of social life but are too anxious or lacking in basic social skills to do anything about it. They are reluctant to make friendly initiatives and may unrealistically expect other people to initiate contacts with them. They may have inflexible beliefs about how people should act. They may spend an excessive amount of time each day engaged in solitary pursuits such as TV or the Internet, thereby decreasing the likelihood of experiencing positive social feedback, learning social skills, and forming friendships. Feelings of inferiority are common, and social isolation may be a means of avoiding peer criticism, scrutiny, or rejection. Physically, they may present with poor eye contact, poor hygiene and grooming, or inappropriate dress.

Anticipatory anxiety underlying avoidance of social situations may be accompanied by physical symptoms such as heart palpitations and breathlessness. Sometimes the social fear is so intense that the person avoids talking to people altogether or repeatedly finds it necessary to escape from intolerable social situations. Escape may provide temporary relief, but afterwards clients are likely to condemn themselves for being abnormal. They may engage in prolonged periods of social withdrawal when the person decides not to answer phone calls, spends long hours in bed, or indulges in self-soothing behaviors such as over-eating or substance abuse. There may be inappropriate attempts to initiate friendships with disinterested or unavailable peers or failure to respond to friendly initiatives from appropriate peers. Some resort to inappropriate tactics to win approval or attempts to buy friendship.

Social anxiety and awkwardness may be secondary to depression or anxiety disorders. Typical anxiety disorders include agoraphobia, panic attacks, phobias, or obsessive–compulsive disorder with idiosyncratic preoccupations or time-consuming compulsive rituals that leave very little time for socializing. Clients may insist that they do not want to attempt to form friendships, and that their preference is to be alone. They may report that they find most people disgusting. These clients are often extremely self-absorbed, and superior–entitled patterns may coexist with social inferiority schemas. Although these clients may continue to complain of being friendless and abnormal, they are usually very resistant to therapist attempts to facilitate interpersonal contacts.

Deficits may be observed in social information processing, so that clients frequently misinterpret social cues, exaggerating other people's criticism of them. Deficits in social judgment are also common, resulting in inappropriate social behaviors when they do mix with others, such as too much self-disclosure too soon after meeting someone, raising inappropriate topics, going on too long and boring others, resorting to excessive flattery, apologizing too profusely, volunteering to do too much for people, or giving in to others' unreasonable requests for money, possessions, help, or time.

Characteristic themes associated with the anxious–awkward social style taken from case histories are shown in Table 5.2.

Early Patterns and Influences

Early child adolescent patterns of socially anxious clients include childhood depression or anxiety disorders, extreme shyness, embarrassment about physical defects, social isolation, decreased social contact with peers, and absence of childhood friends. Typical family of origin patterns include: (1) various forms of parent psychopathology; (2) dysfunctional child-rearing styles such as parental rejection, abuse, neglect, and over-involved or over-protective parenting; and (3) inappropriate parental restrictions on the child's involvement in normal peer activities. Frequently, parental role models are also socially anxious,

Table 5.2 Typical Themes Associated with the Anxious–Awkward Social Style

Defectiveness themes: Nobody would want me as a friend; I'm abnormal, damaged, fat, too stupid to mix with people; people don't like me; I don't deserve friendships

Fear of scrutiny, or discovery of shame: People will probe, ask embarrassing questions about my sickness, my career, my broken relationship, why I'm not married, etc.; if they knew my problems they would never want to be my friend

Fear of embarrassing situations: I never know what to say to people; I might have a panic attack and disgrace myself

Hypersensitive to perceived criticism: People are always making fun of me behind my back

Alienation themes: I don't fit in, I'm different from all other people; nobody can really understand me; people can never give me the support I need; I'm alone; no one cares about me

Abandonment themes: It's only a matter of time before people drop me; people use me and then leave me behind; people don't call, they're not available, they don't want to be with me

Superior disinterest: I have no interest in people; nobody could measure up as a friend; I can't enjoy wasting time with people; people always disappoint me; people are ugly, their habits disgust me; people tire me, they interfere with my work

Unrealistic expectations: Friends should contact me and find out if I'm o.k.

Idiosyncratic beliefs blocking socialization: I must divulge my defects to a person before we can be friends

awkward, or isolated, and there is an absence of socially effective role models in the family. Early school and peer influences include frequent absences from school or school phobia, peer rejection, and exclusion from normal peer group activities.

Client Example

Jeffrey presented with complaints of loneliness dating back to childhood, when embarrassment about his family history of mental illness made him reluctant to associate with peers. Publicly he came across as self-absorbed, superior, and detached, while privately he was hurt by the harsh reality that people did not want to spend time with him. After years of trying to get people to like him, he concluded that his stressful childhood had made him unacceptable to others. In spite of the absence of friends at school and later at university, he devoted himself to his studies and managed to achieve respectable grades and a bachelor's degree. However, after graduation his social anxiety had restricted his job options to those requiring minimal social interaction, so that his current job as a computer data-entry technician was far below his potential. He worked alone in his office all day and felt self-conscious eating alone in the cafeteria, believing that colleagues were making fun of him. He lived alone and spent evenings and weekends pursuing his fascination with the criminal mind, watching TV crime programs, reading biographies of criminals, and searching the Internet for new developments in forensic science. On rare occasions when he found himself in a group situation, he was either afraid to speak or would launch into a monologue on unsavory details of criminal cases or a diatribe on the inadequacy of the current justice system. This was usually met with an awkward silence. At the same time, he had little knowledge of common pursuits of colleagues his age or topics of interest of other young adults.

Several standard CBT techniques were initially tried with limited success. These included anxiety-control techniques, cognitive-change techniques for defectiveness schemas, and activity scheduling and graded task assignments to increase the client's time in social (versus solitary) activities. However, the client's participation in these interventions was compromised by his overriding belief that he would never be able to act normally in social situations and that people would never be able to relate to him.

The Developmental Phase   Developmental CBT assessment instruments were then used to obtain more information about early influences and pathways leading to his current social predicament.

Jeffrey's father suffered from severe mental illness that seriously disrupted the whole family. His father's emotional outbursts were never discussed in the family. His mother was detached and helpless, unable to provide responsible parenting. There was little communication between the client and his parents or his sister. The client never brought other children home and avoided peers at school because of a belief that children from normal families would never want to befriend someone from such a sad, horrible home situation. He harbored an idiosyncratic belief over the years that he was obligated to reveal his father's mental illness and details of his violent home situation to people he met before he could become friends, which had the effect of turning people off or inhibiting him from pursuing friendships at all. From early on, the client spent long periods of time on his own as a means of avoiding social situations, fearing that people may be curious about his family. He felt excluded and anxious every day at school and never managed to develop a close friend. He once overheard a classmate refer to him as "weird," and this confirmed his increasing conviction that he had inherited the family "sickness."

The Developmental Task-Block Identification and Analysis strategies helped provide the client with an alternative interpretation of underlying reasons for his long-standing social anxiety and awkwardness. Therapist and client identified the following developmental components of the client's social discomfort and isolation: (1) excessive time spent in solitary pursuits, curtailing exposure to potential friends, (2) social cognition skill deficits linked to inappropriate social behaviors such as raising distasteful topics and inappropriate self-disclosure of father's mental illness, (3) inadequate familiarity with typical interests and views of age mates, (4) conversation skills deficit, (5) defectiveness and alienation schemas contributing to avoidance of social situations, and (6) the client's conviction that he had an obligation to divulge his family history of mental illness to people before they could become friends. These strategies also helped increase the client's awareness of the part he himself had played in limiting his own potential for developing friendships by restricting his own exposure to peers. He realized that he had repeatedly discouraged friendship initiatives from peers over the years, fearing exposure of his abnormal family situation. In addition, his failure to participate in normal day-to-day activities with peers in the neighborhood and at school deprived him of the opportunity to master crucial social skills and acquire sufficient knowledge of typical interests and views of peers his age.

He also realized that his failure to develop an affectionate relationship with either of his parents had likely contributed to his awkwardness when expressions of affection and warmth were called for in social relationships. He was able to see how his failure to master basic relationship skills had perpetuated past and present social discomfort. The client's new understanding of his developmental deficits helped weaken his conviction that he was inherently abnormal and sick like his father and his self-imposed obligation to disclose his family history of mental illness to prospective friends. Finally, Jeffrey became painfully aware that his ongoing social anxiety continued to preclude establishment of what he considered to be a viable career, further contributing to his feelings of inferiority.

Using the Developmental Deficit Skill-Building strategy, the therapist first sought to educate the client about patterns of normal development with respect to acquisition of crucial social perception and judgment skills during the early years, using Table 5.1 as a reference.

The client was then helped to conceptualize the causes of his social awkwardness and lack of friends in terms of unresolved tasks in his early social development rather than abnormalities inherited from his father. The client labeled these gaps in his early socialization his "social deprivation pathway" and listed the following components:

- Emotionally distant parents responsible for the client's failure to develop skills for expressing warmth and interest in others, necessary for deep friendships
- Lack of socially skilled family role models
- Inadequate interaction in routine social situations with peers during childhood and adolescence restricting opportunity to observe, learn, practice, and master effective conversation skills and appropriate perceptual and behavioral social skills

With his increased understanding, the client became more optimistic about his prognosis for change. He became more receptive to taking part in CBT social-skill training interventions over the next several sessions, selected and adapted by the therapist to address his particular developmental gaps. Initial sessions were concerned with training in social perception and judgment to improve the accuracy of the client's attributions about colleagues' judgments and motives. He was helped to interpret daily interpersonal situations and to differentiate between colleagues who would be most (or least) likely to respond positively to friendship initiatives.

Later sessions were devoted to training in behavioral social skills such as initiating, maintaining, and terminating casual conversations. He practiced using effective opening lines, initiating new topics, elaborating on answers, asking appropriate direct questions, asking for advice, introducing topics of general interest and using open-ended questions. The client was also taught several techniques for deepening relationships: appropriate self-disclosure and strategies for demonstrating an interest in the other person (e.g., active listening, reflection, giving compliments, encouraging other people to talk about themselves).

The client was asked to observe the interactions of more socially successful colleagues and to note appropriate expression of affection and caring, as well as popular topics of casual conversation such as current movies, books, and TV programs, so that he was then able to educate himself about these topics and participate in future conversations. He also learned to identify and avoid inappropriate topics in his own attempts at conversation and to attend to feedback from others. At the same time, he avoided his monologs on forensic science and unsavory details of criminal cases.

Over the next few weeks the client managed to spend time each day in casual social activities with work colleagues, first as an observer and later as a participant using his new skills. He gradually reported some improvements in his social situation at work and got to a point where he managed to initiate a short social interaction with a work colleague each day. He gradually progressed to initiating occasional activities outside of the work setting and became part of a regular Friday evening dinner group.

As Jeffrey's social skills improved and he was able to increase time spent in social situations, he was in a better position to address his second major developmental block: failure to develop what he considered to be a more acceptable career path. By means of the then and now strategy, the client was helped to identify a more successful period in his life in terms of a career path. He recalled a more positive view of his future during his university years when he started an internship for a publishing company as part of a final-year co-op program. However, he subsequently found dealing with criticism from management and colleagues at meetings too stressful and quit the internship. He retreated into his shell, once again the victim of his "social deprivation pathway." He realized that his inability to deal with social aspects of work had forced him to resort to an inferior job to minimize social demands.

By means of the Alternative Pathways strategy, Jeffrey imagined what his life would be like today if he had somehow deviated from his social deprivation pathway and acquired sufficient skills to allow him to tolerate social discomfort at work. This would have enabled him to pursue his original career plan. He hypothesized that he would have continued in his job in publishing and would have been an editor today, a far more satisfying career worthy of his educational level. He now realized that he need only improve his social skills to a level that enabled him to cope with periodic meetings and the challenges of coping with routine criticism from colleagues. He was well on his way to mastering these elementary social-interaction techniques and labeled his new pathway his rudimentary social coping pathway. He was able to reconsider his career goals and pursue his original career path, adapting it in such a way that the social demands would not be too overwhelming. He felt much better about himself when he realized that he would be able to meet the middle-adulthood challenges of occupational growth and an acceptable midlife career. He also concluded that although he would never become a "social butterfly," he now had a method for observing more socially skilled colleagues and could thereby learn and practice new skills that would enable him to maintain effective interpersonal relationships in the work setting.

SUMMARY OF MALADAPTIVE DEVELOPMENTAL SOCIAL PATHWAYS

Developmental CBT practitioners are encouraged to compile examples of characteristic client developmental pathways associated with various social interaction problems. These would be helpful for future reference and would include not only the dysfunctional developmental pathways identified, but also names and components of corresponding adaptive pathways generated by clients. A summary of pathways from case studies reviewed in this chapter appears in Table 5.3.

Table 5.3 Summary of Client Pathways Linked to Problematic Social Styles

Social Style	Maladaptive Pathways	Adaptive Pathways	Developmental Strategies
Angry–aggressive	Childish–confrontational pathway Inferior–bitter pathway	Mature–nonconfrontational pathway Resilient social pathway	Adaptive versus Obsolete Coping Style Developmental Deficit Skill Building Negative Life Review
Superior–entitled	Superior social pathway	Modest–sincere pathway	Adaptive versus Obsolete Coping Styles Developmental Deficit Skill Building
Anxious–awkward	Social deprivation pathway	Rudimentary social coping pathway	Developmental Deficit Skill Building Then and Now Alternative Pathways

6

MALADAPTIVE DEVELOPMENTAL PATTERNS AFFECTING INTIMATE PARTNER AND FAMILY FUNCTIONING

This chapter will demonstrate the Developmental CBT approach with typical client problems in the interrelated areas of intimate partner relationships and parenting roles. The emphasis will be on the relationship between a client's difficulties in resolving previous developmental tasks and current difficulties in partner and family functioning. Marital and family dysfunction often overlap since a strong marriage is a valuable buffer against various forms of family distress, especially with respect to child rearing.

NORMAL PARTNER AND FAMILY CHALLENGES ACROSS THE LIFE SPAN

Normative partner and family tasks and challenges have been the subject of numerous publications in the life span developmental literature (e.g., Cicirelli, 1998; Cross & Markus, 1991; Levinson, 1978, 1996; McGoldrick & Carter, 1989; Turner, 1980). Partner-relationship challenges today reflect changes in family patterns in recent decades. Young adults are becoming sexually active at a younger age but marrying later. A larger percentage of young adults live with one or several partners before deciding to marry, so many clients who seek therapy present with a history of one or more failed common-law relationships. Double-income families are now the norm, catalyzing a major redefinition of marital roles. Up to 10% of American women are choosing not to marry. There is also a growing tendency for couples to postpone childbearing for a number of years after marriage and for a percentage of women to choose to remain childless.

Dating, courting, partner selection, marriage, and starting a family are common tasks of early adulthood but may occur later for some people. Initial beliefs and expectations about intimate-partner relationships are formed during childhood and adolescence as children observe the marital interactions of their parents and relatives. Under normal circumstances, a person develops a capacity for affection, emotional intimacy, sexuality, nurturing, companionship, commitment, and respect for a partner's independent individual growth. During adolescence, social interactions in the school setting and community provide the opportunity to form ideas about what various peers of the opposite sex might have to offer in terms of potential for a satisfying long-term relationship. Exposure to a variety of heterosexual interactions and partner options through group activities and dating is an important step in the process of developing one's own criteria for preferred qualities in a partner. One of the most important adult tasks involves the selection of a spouse with potential for a satisfying enduring marital relationship and for responsible parenting some time in the future. Dating is invaluable for dispelling romantic fantasies and for developing sufficient judgment and insight to choose a suitable spouse. Courting, and subsequent cohabitation in some cases, provides the opportunity for the young adult to get to know a potential spouse's strengths and weaknesses well before making a final commitment to marriage.

When things do not work out, a person must have sufficient resources to terminate the relationship or to adjust to a partner's decision to leave, usually a very painful challenge. Most people will have to cope with the termination of an intimate relationship at some time in life, given that separation, divorce, and multiple common-law relationships are more prevalent today than in past decades.

Clients presenting with relationship dissatisfaction may be dating, cohabiting, newly married, or married for several years. They may be concerned about a partner's disturbing behavior patterns, ongoing marital conflict, an empty relationship, or their own inability to function effectively in the partnership. Some will have decided to remain in the relationship, at least for the present time, but describe the union as stressful or intolerable and may report feeling trapped or depressed. Often the positive aspects that initially sustained the relationship are no longer present. Reevaluation of the relationship after many years of marriage may prompt the couple to seek therapy. Frequently, clients express unrealistic expectations that the partner will change, and many clients with complaints of marital dissatisfaction have little insight into their own contribution to the breakdown of the relationship.

Most couples will be faced with the challenging task of raising children in addition to maintaining a satisfying marital relationship. Parents must work together in assuming child-rearing, financial, and household responsibilities and mastering the art of effective parenting. Over the life span, a couple will move through the various stages of child rearing, from parenting small children, to parenting adolescents, to launching grown children, to the late-life challenge of maintaining healthy relationships with adult children. Some couples will have to cope with the decreasing likelihood of pregnancy as the wife approaches menopause. Other couples may be deeply affected by the departure of their children.

The term *empty nest syndrome* is generally used to refer to the process of adapting to the loss of one's central maternal or paternal role after the last child leaves home. For some who have defined themselves primarily in terms of their role as a parent, the departure of the children may be accompanied by an overwhelming sense of loss and will necessitate decisions as to how to fill the psychological void and the extra time and freedom created by the children's departure. At the same time, the couple is reminded that with the children grown, they have now entered the later stages of life and are faced with the process of coming to terms with their own mortality.

As children grow up and leave home, spouses may need to shift gears from a mutual concern with child care to concerns about improving their own relationship. If children's needs have been functioning as an outlet for the couple to divert attention from themselves in a strained marital relationship, that relationship may now become more problematic. If the relationship has been strong, this new phase may allow spouses more time to rediscover and enjoy one another.

Severe marital tensions, the end of a serious love affair, divorce, and parenting challenges are some of the partner and family events that precipitate midlife crises. Anger or guilt may resurface, associated with betrayal by others, or with unwise decisions made in the past that have negatively affected the lives of loved ones. The term *midlife crisis* has generally been used to refer to the task of reappraising the past and modifying one's current life structure. People begin to review their current lives, to reappraise how they have lived life thus far, to modify negative elements of the present structure, and to plan for the next phase. Doubting and searching are common during midlife transitions, as is the agony associated with challenging the illusions and vested interests that have formed the basis of one's early-adult life structure. The midlife reassessment process is painful because it involves making choices and establishing priorities, and this necessarily involves retaining some aspects of the status quo and rejecting others. Men and women who successfully resolve midlife crises will be those who will find some meaning in their loss and accompanying emotional upheaval and who will then move on to consideration of future possibilities for a more satisfying mature adulthood. In the area of family functioning, some people break out of an unbearable life structure by leaving a spouse. Others, who are overwhelmed by competing demands of home and job, may decide to invest less time in career pursuits and more time with family.

CHALLENGES OF SINGLE ADULTS

Many adults spend a considerable part of their lives without a spouse as a result of personal choice, career demands, lack of opportunity, divorce, or widowhood. Some struggle with acceptance of what appears to be a permanent single status. The single woman who chooses to make her career her top priority in life to the exclusion of husband and children is a relatively recent development.

Single people who never marry face a different set of family-related tasks and challenges across the life span. As men and women approach their fortieth birthdays without having found a hoped-for spouse, they may experience a growing sadness about the increasing likelihood of remaining unmarried and childless for the rest of their lives. If they have entertained hopes for the traditional marriage and family, they may perceive their lives as disappointing or meaningless or they may be perpetually "on hold," waiting for a partner to materialize. Traditionally, societies have viewed spinsters and bachelors as somewhat tragic. Those who continue to have difficulties with their single status will be those who believe they cannot achieve a satisfying or meaningful life without a partner or without children. Those who adapt best to a disappointing single status are those who build supportive social or family networks and those who chose to invest in their career, hobbies, or other pursuits. Many childless people fill the void by developing close relationships with nieces, nephews, or other relatives or with a surrogate family. Attempts to deal with these disappointments may precipitate a turning point and a redirection of energy from preoccupation with one's permanent single or childless status to career, hobbies, or other leisure pursuits.

An exhaustive discussion of the numerous types of intimate relationship and family presenting problems with developmental features is beyond the scope of this book. Instead, this chapter will be limited to a demonstration of the Developmental CBT approach with client examples from the following categories of intimate partner and family relationship difficulties frequently encountered by therapists:

- Problems forming intimate partner relationships
- Problems selecting appropriate intimate partners
- Problems sustaining adaptive intimate partner relationships
- Problems terminating intimate partner relationships
- Parenting role problems

There will be considerable overlap between these categories in terms of personality patterns and early negative influences.

INTIMATE PARTNER RELATIONSHIP PROBLEMS

This section will focus on developmental dysfunction affecting formation and maintenance of satisfying heterosexual relationships. Although gay and lesbian relationships will not be addressed in this book, some of the recommended developmental interventions for heterosexual relationship problems will also be useful in work with homosexual clients.

Intimate partner problems may involve difficulties with establishing, maintaining, or terminating a relationship. Difficulties may arise in dating, mate selection, long-term commitment, or maintenance of a healthy long-term relationship. Some clients may have difficulty leaving an incompatible partner or adjusting to a spouse's unilateral decision to end the marriage. Some clients lack the basic intimacy skills for establishing affectionate, mutually satisfying heterosexual relationships. Clients may be anxious about dating or have insufficient exposure to potential partners. Some clients present with a history of several failed relationships and lack sufficient judgment and insight to select a stable, loving partner. Other clients are unable to make a commitment to marry or cohabit. Some clients marry but are unable to achieve a mutually supportive partnership and child-rearing team strong enough to survive difficult times. Mental health problems such as depression or anxiety may be contributing factors.

Early Developmental Influences Linked to Intimate Partner Relationship Problems

Dysfunctional interaction styles learned in the family of origin often preclude satisfying, enduring partner relationships. Ample evidence supports a link between negative or traumatic childhood experiences and partner relationship problems in adulthood. Common examples cited in the literature include childhood sexual abuse and exposure to marital violence during the early years (Andrews & Brewin, 1990; Gold, 1986). Difficulties with intimacy may date back to early family experiences where there was little affection shown or little communication between family members. Family systems theorists were among the first to note that unresolved family of origin issues may lead people to become self-protective, closed off, or fearful about making themselves vulnerable to further hurt, thereby creating significant barriers to intimacy. People have unrealistic expectations for potential partners, such as expecting a partner to make up for past trauma, injustices, or an unhappy childhood. Self-defeating interaction patterns and family rules affecting adult relationships may be learned in the childhood home through persistent exposure to dysfunctional parental models, marital conflict, or damaging childrearing styles such as physical or sexual abuse, rejection, or neglect. These negative parental influences increase the likelihood that the young adult will adopt similar maladaptive styles in his or her own intimate partner relationships. Children exposed to severe marital conflict or domestic violence are more likely to have difficulty committing to a long-term partner relationship, fearing an unhappy situation similar to that of their parents. Children who have not had the opportunity to observe healthy marital role models will be unfamiliar with effective partner-interaction patterns, which are necessary for satisfying intimate relationships.

Beliefs about relationships learned in the family of origin also set the stage for healthy or unhealthy relationships in adulthood. Family rules clarify interpersonal boundaries, govern communication, and regulate intimacy in a family. In normal families these rules facilitate communication and understanding among family members, in contrast to the situation in dysfunctional families, where rules tend to hinder the growth of family members by discouraging genuineness and denying free expression of thoughts, feelings, wishes, and needs.

Negative family influences may jeopardize adult relationships in a variety of ways. For example, parental neglect or absence owing to death, divorce, or maladaptive child rearing may deprive the child of crucial parent–child bonds, reducing his or her potential for giving and accepting affection in adult relationships. Deprivation of love may lead to a pattern of excessive demands for proof of love or a pattern of testing the limits and sabotaging potentially good adult relationships. Physical or sexual abuse diminishes the child's sense of self-worth and may be linked to subsequent victimization and tolerance of partner abuse. Exposure to punitive, aggressive, or narcissistic parental role models may shape a similar dysfunctional partner-interaction style in adulthood.

Insufficient parental discipline, expectations, or control may be equally harmful, fostering a sense of entitlement in the child and shaping a self-centered, demanding style in future partner relationships.

Early deprivation of routine peer experiences may also be linked to adult problems with intimate partner relationships. Some parents disapprove of mixed-group events and refuse to allow their children to participate in what would be considered normal heterosexual activities. Anxious, over-protective parents may also curtail their children's social development because of exaggerated fears of potential harm. There may be expectations that teenagers should choose to spend time with family rather than peers. Finally, peer ridicule or rejection in childhood and adolescence may deprive the youngster of friends and inclusion in normal heterosexual activities. Restricted involvement in normal mixed-peer-group activities curtails the youngster's opportunity to progress gradually from mixed-peer-group activities, to pairing off from the group, dating, and eventually sexual intimacy.

The Developmental CBT Approach to Intimate Partner Relationship Problems

The Developmental CBT approach is similar for all categories of intimate partner relationship problems, whether they be difficulties in forming, maintaining, or terminating relationships:

- Obtain a developmental history of early experiences in the family of origin (e.g., separation, divorce, and other family hardships; family conflict; parent–child interaction patterns; sibling relationships).
- Obtain a developmental history of peer relationships (e.g., friendships or absence of friendships, dating history, sexual development).
- Obtain a history of past intimate partner relationships and identify former maladaptive couple-interaction styles that may still be operating with the current partner.
- Identify task blocks from previous developmental periods that have an impact on current partner relationship problems.
- Assess the client's partner-interaction style and identify gaps in effective partner coping skills that the client failed to acquire.
- Use new developmental strategies to address unresolved tasks and long-standing dysfunctional pathways leading to current intimate partner relationship problems. Evaluate therapy effectiveness on the basis of the client's progress in altering

maladaptive pathways and blocks to mastering normative partner-relationship tasks.

Problems Forming Intimate Partner Relationships

Clients in this category express a strong desire for an intimate partner relationship, marriage, and family but are uncomfortable and unable to function effectively in heterosexual situations. (They differ from those who express little desire for intimate relationships.) Many of these clients have never experienced an intimate relationship, whether young, middle-aged, or mature adults. They have never dated, never been sexually intimate, and some have never experienced friendships with peers of either sex. Some may have experienced feelings of love and sexual attraction but have not acted on these feelings. Negative perceptions of one's body, sexuality, or appearance are common. Other frequent features are social anxiety, avoidance of social situations, and extreme shyness. Social anxiety may be specific to peers of the opposite sex or generalized to include same-sex peers as well. Many of these clients have had little exposure to members of the opposite sex during childhood and adolescence and have failed to acquire basic heterosexual skills such as appropriate self-disclosure, flirtation, expression of affection, or communication of interest or empathy. There may be comorbid anxiety disorders such as obsessive–compulsive disorder, panic disorders, or phobias. Common sexual issues blocking heterosexual relationships include sexual fears or disgust, impotence, or sexual-orientation factors. Examples of typical themes from case histories of clients with problems forming intimate heterosexual relationships are shown in Table 6.1.

Client Example

Tom, the client who was used in Chapter 3 to illustrate the Developmental Deficit Skill-Building strategy, experienced ongoing difficulties initiating a romantic partner relationship. Recall that he was helped to conceptualize the basis of his unsuccessful approach with women in terms of a social isolation pathway and was then helped by means of standard CBT techniques to acquire appropriate conversation skills for heterosexual situations. However, although he learned to converse more easily, he still failed to realize that his strategies for finding a partner were inappropriate and self-defeating.

Tom stated that his goal was to find a beautiful woman who would agree to marry him and start a family as soon as possible since he

Table 6.1 Typical Themes Associated with Problems Forming Intimate Partner Relationships

Defectiveness/shame: Nobody would want me; I'm unworthy, damaged, sexually abused, undesirable, shameful, fat, ugly; I hate men looking at me, judging me; women find me repulsive, ugly; nobody would want me with my mental problems; nobody would want to date someone with my pathetic job

Social isolation/alienation: I'm different from other people; I don't fit in with the opposite sex; people don't really want to be with me; I'm more comfortable being alone

No time: I'm too busy to date right now; I can't give up my routine; I can't give up my Saturdays; I have to jog two hours every day before I can do other things

Procrastination themes: I can't join a group until I get my apartment renovated

Stubborn refusal to change: So I'm a slob, I want someone to like me as I am

Unrealistic standards for self: I can't try to meet anyone until I lose 50 pounds, get a job with more status, learn to cook gourmet meals

Unrealistic standards for prospective partner: He would have to be a successful professional or a businessman; she would have to lose at least 20 pounds

Sexual issues: I could never really enjoy sex; I'll be ridiculed; I've had no experience with women; I don't know where to start; I can never be sexually normal due to my past; I'm sexually damaged

It's too late: I've lost my chances forever; I'm too old for marriage and children; I've wasted my fertile years

Magical thinking: Mr. Right will find me some day

was approaching his fortieth birthday. Tom's understanding about the way in which romantic relationships develop was based on television relationships in which instant mutual attraction was quickly followed by sexual intimacy, cohabitation, and marriage. His few initiatives with women drew negative reactions. On one occasion he impulsively went up to a complete stranger on the street and asked her for a date. On another occasion he alienated a woman he met through a dating agency by inappropriate sexual innuendo and by raising the topic of marriage on the first date.

Tom lacked a clear understanding of why his abortive attempts with women had been so unsuccessful. The Developmental Assessment provided additional information.

Tom's early history revealed a lack of normal social experiences with members of either sex. He had been socially isolated from the start, discouraged by his anxious over-protective mother from participating in peer activities as a child and excluded from mixed-peer activities during adolescence. Consequently, he had never achieved acceptance in a supportive peer group, never developed close male bonds, and never developed platonic friendships with girls. As an adult he took a job as a mail sorter because it required minimal social interaction. He spent most weekends and evenings at home alone, engaged in solitary pursuits such as watching TV, sketching, or surfing the Internet.

Tom's "social-isolation pathway" contrasted sharply with the normal sequence of developmental experiences as a youngster progresses from casual mixed-group activities, to platonic relationships with girls, to pairing off, dating, and intimacy. Not only did Tom fail to develop friendships with members of either sex, but his exclusion from normal peer activities left him insufficient opportunity to observe men and women interacting in normal every-day situations. Years of social isolation had left huge gaps in his knowledge of how love relationships generally evolve and the normal sequence of events leading up to an intimate relationship.

Through the Developmental Task-Block Identification and Analysis strategies, Tom gained further insight into his ongoing failure to develop an intimate relationship. He identified the following unresolved developmental tasks in his childhood, adolescence, and early adulthood, components of his social-isolation pathway: (1) insufficient childhood involvement in activities with casual friends because of parental prohibitions, shyness, and embarrassment about physical appearance, (2) failure to develop close bonds with same-sex peers, (3) inadequate teenage involvement in mixed-peer group activities, curtailing the opportunity to learn basic heterosexual relationship skills, (4) lack of normal dating experience, (5) early adult choice of a safe job as a mail sorter with minimal social demands and interaction, and (6) leisure activities restricted to solitary pursuits at home, further decreasing opportunities for meeting women. At this time Tom spoke of a desire to disrupt his social-isolation pathway in favor of a new "socially experienced pathway."

Utilizing the Developmental Deficit Skill-Building strategy, the first step was to educate Tom about the way in which lasting partner relationships normally evolve and to contrast this with his distorted understanding of the process based on TV programs. He was helped to understand that, unlike the proverbial one-night stand, lasting partnerships usually develop gradually and that the normal sequence of events in the development of an intimate relationship generally consists of the following components spanning several weeks, months, or even years: first getting to know a person through casual contacts, becoming friends, dating, experiencing increasing admiration for the person, wanting to spend more and more time together, falling in love, desiring an exclusive intimate relationship with the person, and sexual intimacy. The declaration of a wish to spend one's life with that person comes much later, after feeling confident that the person shares this same desire.

After this introduction, the therapist helped Tom analyze his own approach to women and identify inappropriate components of his current style that resulted in negative reactions from women. Tom began to gain insight into the consequences of specific developmental gaps in his own heterosexual development, such as the absence of platonic relationships with girls and women and inadequate opportunities to observe normal heterosexual interactions in mixed peer groups. These developmental gaps prevented him from learning skills that children with adequate exposure to mixed-peer-group activities acquire effortlessly over the years through observation and practice. For example, Tom's lack of normal experiences with girls and women over the years left him with poorly developed social-perception skills. As a result, he tended to misread signals and social cues, which led him to approach women who were unavailable to him as potential partners.

Table 6.2 shows examples of typical areas of heterosexual skill deficits based on case histories. A number of these areas applied to Tom, and the table provided a valuable reference for the therapist in helping the client to pinpoint specific skill deficits.

Gradually, therapist and client began to identify problematic areas of skill deficits affecting Tom's life. Both agreed that Tom would need

Table 6.2 Common Areas of Client Deficits in Heterosexual Interaction Skills

Active and empathetic listening

Demonstration of interest in the other person (e.g., ask questions, reflect back, etc.)

Communication of sexuality (verbal and nonverbal)

Appropriate self-disclosure

Conversation skills (ability to initiate and maintain conversation, knowledge of popular age-appropriate interests and pursuits)

Appropriate use of flattery

Flirtation: verbal and nonverbal (e.g., smiling, eye contact, etc.)

Accurate perceptions and attributions about the meaning of the other person's words and actions

Accurate social judgment and appropriate response

Use of feedback from others to monitor own behavior

Appropriate emotional response (e.g., suitable emotional range, affect regulation, etc.)

Communication of trust

Expression of affection: verbal and nonverbal

to fine-tune his newly learned conversation skills, as well as social perception, judgment, and social-performance skills. He also needed to address his difficulties experiencing and expressing affection.

Tom had also failed to develop a capacity for intimacy and had little understanding of what intimacy entailed. He was helped to identify specific aspects of intimacy such as the ability to discuss thoughts, views, and feelings with a partner. Tom was helped to understand that intimate relationships in adulthood can be profoundly influenced by the level of intimacy observed by children in their own parents' marital relationship, including implicit rules about intimacy that parental models provide. He realized that his family situation precluded the opportunity to learn basic intimacy skills from parental models during his childhood but that he could take steps during current therapy sessions to address these deficits.

A behavioral approach was then utilized to help Tom acquire these skills through a combination of didactic teaching, therapist modeling, and role-playing. He was taught to express affection and caring. He was also taught how to discuss his thoughts and feelings. He practiced these new skills during therapy sessions, and this increased Tom's confidence that he would know how to proceed with a partner when the opportunity arose. Behavioral components of sexual intimacy and expression in a developing relationship were also discussed, and Tom's difficulties with accurate perceptions and attributions about the meaning of the other person's words and actions were also addressed. Therapists may need to expand their repertoires of standard CBT social-interaction techniques for teaching these skills. When standard strategies are lacking, they will have to use their ingenuity in devising ways to teach appropriate skills to fill gaps from earlier developmental stages.

The therapist sought to expose Tom to experiences that would help compensate for early developmental deficits. He was also helped to devise a plan for progressing through a sequence of experiences that would simulate normal steps in heterosexual development, namely, a progression from casual mixed-group activities, to platonic relationships, to dating and sexual intimacy. Tom was advised to proceed slowly, to provide time to learn and practice new skills for heterosexual interactions, both during and between therapy sessions. For example, Tom was instructed in techniques for using his newly learned conversation skills to get to know a prospective partner. He was taught techniques for encouraging a woman to talk about herself and to disclose her interests and hobbies by asking leading questions, and he was coached in techniques for demonstrating a sincere interest in what the woman was saying. He was also encouraged to educate himself about a potential friend or partner's interests and to consider pursuing similar interests as a way of deepening the friendship.

Tom was encouraged to seek out opportunities to practice his conversation skills and opportunities for observational learning in mixed social groups at work or in other social settings. This would give him a chance to observe various ways in which other men interacted with women and the types of responses that various approaches elicit. In this way he would gradually become more comfortable in mixed company and would gain a better understanding of women in general. Tom was also encouraged to seek out opportunities to develop platonic friendships with women as a preliminary step to pursuing an intimate relationship. He understood that casual relationships with several women would help him form more realistic expectations about what various women have to offer as potential long-term partners.

In addition, Tom was encouraged to spend less time in solitary pursuits and more time in social situations at work and in the community, where he would be most likely to develop friendships and to meet potential partners. Suggestions included casual gatherings with work colleagues, general-interest lectures or courses, and volunteer work. Since this would involve major changes in his current daily routine, the current life structure reorganization strategy was used to facilitate these changes.

Tom generated the following plan for increasing his exposure to the types of experiences he missed growing up and lacked throughout his life. He decided to go to the cafeteria for lunch every day. He also joined a Saturday-morning art class at a local recreation center. His goal was to develop at least one platonic friendship with a woman over the next two months. Tom gradually became friends with a woman in his art class who was much older than him. He found her to be nonthreatening and a good listener, and he was able to chat with her for short periods each week about their shared interest in art. He found himself enjoying her company. This was a new experience for Tom, who would never have made the effort to get to know a woman who was older than him or physically unattractive. Through her, Tom was introduced to others in the class, and over the next few months he joined his new friends for lunch after the class or for occasional Sunday sketching trips. Consequently, Tom was part of a mixed social group for the first time in his life. He felt less driven to find a wife and was content for the time being with his new friends. He also began to appreciate the role of shared values and interests in a friendship and in a future partner relationship.

Problems Selecting Appropriate Intimate Partners

Choosing a partner with potential for a stable, satisfying long-term relationship is one of the most important adult challenges. It involves the ability to go beyond infatuation and one's own vulnerabilities to realistically assess a partner's strengths and weaknesses in terms of a lifetime companion. Many clients present with a series of poor choices and failed relationships with incompatible or dysfunctional partners.

Clients may have a penchant for partners who are physically or psychologically abusive, emotionally unstable, unfaithful, prone to substance abuse, or chronically unemployed. They fail to recognize, or choose to ignore, warning signals in potential partners. Some repeatedly choose partners who are already married or otherwise unavailable, partners who have a history of mental illness, or partners who are cold and remote and unable to provide adequate affection, caring, or communication. Some allow undesirable partners to choose them, frequently because of underlying dependency problems, fear of abandonment, or beliefs in their own defectiveness.

Decisions to marry or cohabit with unsuitable partners are frequently based on reasons other than love, admiration, or shared values and interests. Reservations about marrying an undesirable partner may be overruled by pregnancy, overwhelming sexual attraction, the opportunity to escape an intolerable living situation, or fears that the undesirable partner may be the last chance for marriage. Some clients ignore their strong, realistic reservations about a potential partner when the person provides a temporary solution to their own difficulties in negotiating other psychosocial tasks and challenges, such as finding employment, financial security, forming adult friendships, or negotiating the leaving-home transition. The partner may be the first person who showed interest in a client who never managed to make friends. For clients who failed to bond with their own parents, the major attraction might be the partner's family if family members are able to provide some of the nurturing missed in childhood

Clients with a history of failed relationships often select undesirable partners who will be able to compensate for the client's vulnerabilities, such as dependency needs, a penchant for risk taking, or poor self-discipline. They have a pattern of choosing dysfunctional partners who enable them to continue to reenact their early Maladaptive Schemas and self-defeating behavioral patterns (Young & Klosko, 1994). These authors suggest that early maladaptive schemes formed in childhood can significantly influence a person's choice of intimate partners because people are most strongly attracted to partners who trigger and maintain their negative schemas.

Typical core schemas of clients with a pattern of selecting dysfunctional partners include abandonment, emotional deprivation, defectiveness, shame, dependence, incompetence, vulnerability, subjugation, and self-sacrifice. For example, a person with a strong fear of abandonment shaped by neglectful or absent parents will be more likely to be attracted to partners who show insufficient commitment. Ironically, lack of commitment feels familiar and more comfortable because it is what the person has always known. This ensures reenactment of childhood abandonment schemas and client expectations of being abandoned once again. Similarly, clients who were abused as children tend to be attracted to abusive partners in adulthood. People who were subjected to excessive parental control during childhood may be drawn to partners who are aggressive or dominant and who force them into a pattern of submission or self-sacrifice. People who were made to feel defective by abusive parents or peers may be dawn to partners who are also physically or emotionally abusive, or they may avoid intimate relationships altogether for fear of further hurt. Some abused clients gravitate toward anyone willing to accept their "shameful" past. They are prepared to settle for less and end up with partners who are undesirable, unavailable, or needy. People who were emotionally deprived of affection as a child may be uncomfortable with expressions of love and may protect themselves from closeness by selecting partners who are cold and unavailable, or they may break off relationships when they become too close.

Depression, anxiety, or early trauma may be linked to a chronic pattern of relationships with undesirable partners. Depression may predispose clients to choose undesirable partners who are willing to put up with them. Clients suffering from debilitating anxiety disorders will be drawn to partners who are willing to protect them from perceived danger. They will choose partners mainly on the basis of that person's availability to accompany or rescue them. Finally, clients who were overly dependent on parents during childhood tend to be drawn to partners who foster their dependency by taking charge of most aspects of their daily lives.

Clients in middle and mature adulthood may present with a long history of selecting dysfunctional partners over the years. They are usually aware of their past mistakes but still fear they will be unable to resist further involvement with similar undesirable partners. For example, one victim of childhood sexual abuse had married two alcoholics, and prior to that she had been involved in serious relationships with partners who were already married. She felt it wasn't really her fault because she did not choose these partners — they chose her. She stated that losers always seemed to sense that she would look after them and that she had concluded that she was not capable of anything better. The following is a similar example of early developmental influences linked to a pattern of involvement in relationships with a series of undesirable partners.

Client Example

Melissa was a 31-year-old day-care assistant who had been living for the past year with a jealous controlling partner she did not love. He prohibited her from spending time with girlfriends, and she lost her one and only friend and confident. She said she remained in her current abusive situation because was afraid to live alone and admitted that her worst fear was that her boyfriend would leave her. Over the past decade she had lived with a succession of four abusive or unstable boyfriends because it was better than having no boyfriend at all. She also believed on some level that she deserved what she got. All of her previous boyfriends had ended the relationship, and in each case Melissa felt she had no alternative but to move back in with her parents, waiting for the next opportunity to find another partner who could help her escape from the oppressive family home. Melissa said she hated herself for lacking the courage to live alone in her own apartment and for acquiescing to her parents' guilt trips and pressure to return home.

Schema therapy techniques were first used to identify and address dependence, defectiveness, and subjugation schemas underlying her current inability to leave her partner (Young & Klosko, 1994; Young, Klosko, & Weishaar, 2003). The client learned that these schemas were responsible for her chronic pattern of impulsive decisions to move in with unsuitable partners and her subsequent failure to establish an independent living situation after each relationship ended. Although the client clearly benefited from her deeper understanding of the impact of these schemas, she still continued to remain with her boyfriend.

The Developmental Phase   Further information about the origins of Melissa's pattern of rebellion and dependency was obtained from the stress coping-style history, family of origin patterns, parent–offspring interaction styles, and intimate partner relationship history questionnaires.

Melissa was the only child of eastern European immigrants. When Melissa was young, her mother frequently kept her home from school on a variety of pretexts. Her mother was afraid of her aggressive husband, had no friends, and relied on her daughter for company. Melissa developed a pattern of missing several days of school at a time due to supposed illness, after which she would feel panicky when she attempted to return to school, dreading the nasty comments of classmates about her being a "skipper." This led to more absences and intermittent episodes of school phobia. As Melissa approached adolescence, her father became increasing abusive and controlling, forbidding her to spend time in mixed company where boys would get her in trouble. He called her cheap for wanting to attend school dances and for talking to boys at school. Melissa became convinced that she was bad and undeserving of good things in life.

As Melissa approached her eighteenth birthday, she began to rebel by skipping school to spend time at a cafe during the day and by regular attendance at all-night drinking parties, claiming to be sleeping at a girlfriend's house. Surprisingly, her parents failed to keep track of their daughter's whereabouts, deluding themselves into believing that everything was all right. At this time Melissa's social contacts were primarily with other rebellious, promiscuous girls from similar abusive home situations and older boys she met at parties. In spite of her promiscuity and new social life, she failed to develop any deep, lasting friendships. Eventually, the school informed the parents that Melissa had been suspended for truancy. The father's violent response prompted Melissa to leave home the next day and move in with one of her current boyfriends. She believed this to be her only option, in spite of her concerns that the boyfriend had many of her father's undesirable aggressive traits.

By means of the Task-Block Identification and Analysis strategies, the client was able to see how her family situation was connected to her failure to resolve earlier tasks and challenges involving independence and development of healthy peer relationships and deep friendships. In spite of her anger at her father's aggressive treatment, Melissa still sought his approval and was still unable to break free and create an independent life for herself. She had failed over the years to achieve true psychological independence from either parent and had failed to develop friends who could help her through difficult times. Although she had a secure job and potential for financial independence, her unreasonable dread of ever being alone prevented her from establishing an independent residence.

Melissa labeled the deviant pathway leading to her present predicament her "defective–dependent–defiant pathway." This dated back to her childhood when she would reluctantly stay home from school to be with her mother. Her parents made her feel guilty, first when she complained of being trapped and smothered and later when she demanded to be allowed to date boys and live a normal teenage life. Her defiant self-destructive phase began with her truancy and promiscuity and developed into her subsequent pattern of moving in with abusive boyfriends to avoid living under her parents' roof.

Melissa was helped to understand the residual negative effects of her abusive, guilt-engendering father and her helpless demanding mother, assisted by the parent–offspring interaction styles instrument. She realized that the combination of parental abuse, guilt, and inconsistent limits had been instrumental in shaping a daughter who was dependent, angry, defiant, and ultimately self-destructive, manifested over the years in her promiscuity and relationships with abusive partners. This understanding helped Melissa challenge her persistent belief that she was inherently bad and unworthy and incapable of happy relationships. She now began to view her shame, dependency, and self-destructive rebelliousness as a method of coping with the effects of highly dysfunctional parenting. Melissa's new goal was to disrupt her defective–dependent–defiant pathway and establish a new adaptive "independent–confident pathway."

The Future Developmental Stage Planning strategy was utilized next to help the client visualize a lifestyle over the next two years that did not involve moving in with a new partner. She imagined herself leaving her boyfriend and sharing an apartment with another woman to reduce her anxiety at the thought of being alone. She visualized herself making career and friends her main priorities, rather than devoting all her energy to finding a new boyfriend.

The Developmental Task Resolution Planning strategy was initiated next. Melissa stated that her goal was to break off her current relationship and live with friends, thereby achieving both physical and emotional independence from both her parents and her boyfriend. Client and therapist then generated the plan shown in Table 6.3 to finally address unresolved tasks and challenges dating back to childhood.

The next six months were devoted to helping Melissa negotiate the difficult challenges of terminating her abusive relationship and implementing the move to her new apartment that she would be sharing with a girlfriend from work. She managed this by the end of the six-month

Table 6.3 Client's Developmental Task Resolution Plan

Targeted Task Difficulties	Interventions
Task #1 Complete the leaving-home transition and establish an independent adult life structure	• Devise a step-by-step plan for finding a roommate and apartment, and implementing the move
Task #2 Terminate current destructive relationship; establish a happy, successful intimate relationship in the future	• Devise and implement step-by-step plan for leaving partner • Avoid new intimate relationship for at least one year • Intimate relationship skill training • Get to know several men before becoming involved in another serious relationship
Task #3 Build and maintain supportive friendships	• Social-skills training • Spend more time with work colleagues
Task #4 Maintain independence from parents and adaptive adult relationship	• Family therapy to address childhood abuse issues • Decrease time spent with parents • Assertiveness training

period. During that time Melissa had also worked hard to build a social support group of work colleagues, which helped her deepen her resolve and resist pressure from her boyfriend to resume the relationship.

Following the move, the Resiliency Training Strategy was used to help Melissa cope with the daily challenges of her transition from dependent to independent living situation. Melissa gradually began to develop a more positive view of herself. In spite of ongoing anxiety, she felt good about finally succeeding in living an independent adult life, rather than regressing to a life with her parents that would be more appropriate for a teenager. Melissa became more and more comfortable with her single status as time went by, and although she began dating, she was still living independently two years after moving to her new apartment. This provided her with ample time to increase her understanding of the way in which her Maladaptive Schemas had gotten in the way of choosing a desirable partner with potential for a satisfying long-term relationship.

Problems Sustaining Adaptive Intimate Partner Relationships

Clients present with a variety of reasons for difficulties sustaining successful intimate partner relationships. Some clients present with unrealistic marital role expectations. Others lack the capacity for trust, commitment, communication, and cooperative problem solving.

Most are involved in relationships in which the day-to-day interaction patterns between the partners are maladaptive. Therefore, the first step of the assessment process is a behavioral analysis of partner-interaction patterns that the client finds stressful. This is usually based on client descriptions of typical daily situations involving the partner. If the therapist has the opportunity to meet with the couple, he or she will be able to observe couple-interaction patterns firsthand. In either case, therapists should also pay attention to beliefs and attributions that spouses make for negative relationship events and unrealistic beliefs that spouses hold about intimate relationships and marriage.

When assessing couple relationships, Bradbury (1995) recommends that therapists focus on the following four key domains of marriage suggested by longitudinal literature on marital outcomes: (1) marital quality in terms of commitment and satisfaction, (2) adaptive processes with respect to partner interaction patterns, (3) relevant life events and circumstances (e.g., health problems, unemployment, cultural differences, problems with in-laws), and (4) enduring personal vulnerabilities that spouses bring to their relationship. Young and Gluhoski (1997) also provide a useful framework for conceptualizing couple-conflict problems. They delineate the following five spectrums of behavior with maladaptive poles or coping stances that partners engage in as they relate to each other. Marital dissatisfaction frequently results from a couple's difficulties in resolving conflicts along one or more of these spectrums:

- **Connection:** Smother versus isolate
- **Power:** Submit versus dominate
- **Feeling:** Over-dramatize versus intellectualization
- **Mutuality:** Self-sacrificing versus self-absorbed
- **Valuing:** Over valuate partner versus under-value partner

Table 6.4, based on case histories, provides another useful tool for targeting maladaptive partner-interaction styles.

In addition to assessment of couple-interaction patterns, a Developmental CBT assessment approach focuses on client histories tapping previous family of origin and peer experiences, sexual development, occupational attainments, and previous intimate relationships. This will be demonstrated in the following case example of a client who had ongoing difficulties with commitment.

Previous developmental blocks are frequently linked to relationship commitment problems. Some clients have failed to achieve sufficient independence from family of origin to make a long-term commitment to a partner, especially when parents disapprove of the partnership or when needy parents inappropriately monopolize adult children.

Table 6.4 Examples of Dysfunctional Partner Interaction Styles

Angry–aggressive–controlling pattern: Abusive (physically or psychologically); easily upset, hurt, offended, blaming; unrealistic demands and expectations for partner; jealousy; temper tantrums; dominating; discomfort with partner's individual development or independence; silent treatment

Dependent pattern: Clinging; demands for accompaniment; anxiety symptoms; constant demands for reassurance of love or loyalty

Entitled pattern: Infidelity; unrealistic demands on partner; sulky

Psychologically unstable: Alcohol or drug abuse; depression, anxiety disorder, or other mental health problems

Labile manipulative pattern: Emotional excess, tests the limits; dramatic behaviors; suicidal threats or gestures to gain partner's sympathy or compliance

Cold–detached pattern: Poor communication; withdrawn, introverted; unemotional, nonreactive; unsympathetic; unaffectionate; inadequate nurturing, intimacy, or sexual expression; silent treatment

Self-sacrifice pattern: Take undue responsibility for partner's problems or happiness; blame self, rescue partner

Incompetent pattern: Abdicate responsibility for basic tasks such as sound financial management, parenting, housekeeping

Other clients have failed to secure sufficient occupational and financial stability to make a commitment. There may also be a previous history of failed relationships, or a belief that successful marital relationships are impossible in light of childhood exposure to marital conflict at home. Other blocks to commitment may involve unresolved sexual orientation issues, promiscuity, mental health problems, addictions, or unrealistically high expectations for a partner or for oneself in a relationship.

Examples of cognitive blocks to commitment from case histories are listed in Table 6.5.

Client Example

The following client was nearing 50 when he sought therapy for depression following what appeared to be the inevitable end of his relationship with his girlfriend of three years. He admitted that he had been ultimately responsible for the failure of the relationship and that he did not deserve a good partner. He said that he always preferred to end relationships before his partners had the chance to break up with him.

John admitted that his girlfriend was too good for him, and although he wanted a traditional marriage, he had never been able to bring himself to propose marriage. Susan had introduced a measure of financial stability and order to his life, and her willingness to subjugate her own needs to his was a major attraction

Table 6.5 Examples of Themes Associated with Relationship Commitment Problems

Mistrust/abuse: Women can't be trusted; it's a matter of time before she'll be unfaithful; I've been hurt once too often

Vulnerability: I need to be in full control of my life before I can think of marriage

Entitlement and self-aggrandizement: Nobody can be good enough; women are stupid; I'm not prepared to compromise

Unrealistic standards: The person for me would have to be in perfect shape; I'm waiting for Mr. Right; most girls are not good looking enough; I would only consider a professional or business man

Family of origin issues: After what I saw of my parents' marriage I would never want to get involved with anyone; Mother found all my boyfriends unacceptable; any partner of mine would have to allow my mom to live with us; I can't leave mom alone after all she sacrificed for me

Procrastination: I must resolve all my problems before I can marry

Defectiveness: I'm always depressed, so I can never be a suitable partner; I'm a flop sexually; I've never been able to be demonstrative; I don't deserve anyone but losers

from the start. In spite of this, he admitted that he could not prevent himself from being mean to her. A subsequent session with the client's girlfriend revealed that John was a demanding, angry man given to temper outbursts and occasional physical abuse. Although she was willing to try couple therapy to save the relationship, John felt that this would be futile because he had always had a temper and there was nothing he could do about it. He felt that he could not commit to a permanent relationship because he had been cursed with a volatile disposition.

Relevant information about John's early family experiences was obtained by means of the Parent–Offspring Interaction Styles, Family of Origin Patterns, and Stress Coping-Style instruments.

John's father had been an abusive controlling husband until his wife took the children and left him when John was 12 years old. After this John never saw his father again. Following the divorce his mother became depressed and was unable to cope adequately with her four children and with John's temper tantrums. John blamed his mother for breaking up the family, and when he did not get his way, he retaliated by breaking dishes. His mother took him to psychiatrists who diagnosed oppositional–defiant disorder, and on their recommendation John was enrolled in a special-education class for difficult children that was meant to provide the discipline he required. However, his mother later learned that John had been bullied by classmates and had been subjected to sexual abuse.

She withdrew him from the class but blamed herself for her son's misfortune and consequently put up with his temper outbursts and capitulated to his demands to an even greater degree.

Information about John's previous romantic relationships was obtained using the Intimate Partner Relationship History questionnaire. A history of failed relationships emerged, with similar patterns.

John was blessed with good looks and had no difficulty attracting women. On two previous occasions 5 and 10 years ago, he had lived with stable loving partners but in each case was unable to make a commitment to marriage. His pattern in each of these relationships was similar to that of his current relationship with Susan. At first things went well but would begin to deteriorate after a few months when the question of marriage was raised. John would suddenly allow his temper outbursts to take over, precipitating the end of the relationship. Underlying this pattern was a belief that he was damaged and not deserving of happiness and his conclusion that he was destined for women who were "losers."

John began to gain more insight into the origins of his history of sabotaging potentially healthy relationships. He was aware that his aggressive style was responsible for his failed relationships and that he purposely allowed his aggressive patterns to destroy everything he had built up. However, he felt helpless to change, believing he had been cursed with a violent temper he could never control. Because of John's early history of abuse and the lingering impact of his traumatic experiences at school, interventions for posttraumatic stress disorder were initiated at this time before introducing further Developmental CBT strategies (Meichenbaum, 1994). Several sessions were devoted to helping John reframe the traumatic events and identify coping strengths to help him move forward.

After he had made sufficient progress, Developmental CBT strategies were introduced to further increase the client's understanding of his own role in the failure of his relationships and how this might be rectified.

The Task-Block Identification and Analysis strategies helped John identify several unresolved tasks linked to his intimate-relationship skill deficits and commitment problems. During childhood and adolescence, he had failed to achieve a sense of self-worth, owing in large part to his father's early departure and subsequent failure to initiate contact with John. He was also deprived of the opportunity to observe effective interpersonal skills or adaptive intimate relationship skills through exposure to parents with a loving marital relationship. Instead, John seemed to have learned his aggressive style and poor self-control from his father — traits that alienated everyone over the years. They had affected his school performance and, subsequently, his job potential and chances for a comfortable financial situation, as well as his chances for a happy marriage.

John had been successful from early on in making his mother feel guilty for depriving him of a father and for the abuse he suffered at school, and he used this guilt trip to force her to capitulate to his wishes. The result was a spoiled, demanding child who still expected others to cater to him. His mother was still at his beck-and-call and was still putting up with his childlike demands and behaviors. John admitted that his aggressive style was self-defeating, but he did not know what to do about it. He began to realize that his lifelong patterns of manipulative temper outbursts and inappropriate expectations for special treatment stemmed from a belief that this was due to him because he had suffered a harsh childhood. He began to understand how this pattern of entitlement had impeded his development with respect to mastering school, work, and relationship tasks and roles and that it was currently affecting his relationship with Susan. He labeled this his "explosive–entitlement pathway," initially shaped by a guilty mother manipulated by her son's anger about the loss of his father. This in turn shaped the son's "oppositional–defiant" style, leading to difficulties at school and subsequent placement in a special behavioral class where he suffered peer harassment and abuse. His mother's guilt about the abuse maintained her pattern of submission to her son's tantrums and manipulations, and this strengthened John's belief that his mother and others should tolerate his aggression in light of the suffering he had endured. He was able to see how his explosive style and entitlement beliefs later generalized to his relationships with women.

John labeled a second pathway his "damaged–undeserving pathway." He realized that this was shaped by his early sorrow at the absence and indifference of a father who failed to maintain contact with his son and later by peer abuse. He saw himself as a victim of an ongoing curse: no father, peer abuse, failed intimate relationships. Later this was manifested in John's belief that he did not deserve loving, stable partners and his pattern of sabotaging potentially healthy relationships when issues of commitment and marriage were raised.

The client reiterated his goal of saving his current relationship and making a firm long-term commitment to marriage, and the Adaptive Versus Obsolete Coping Styles strategy was used to help him achieve this goal. He labeled his self-defeating tantrums and pattern of sabotaging good relationships his "Obsolete Coping Style." Obsolete childhood beliefs that were still fueling his damaged–undeserving pathway included the belief that he was irretrievably damaged psychologically by his misfortunes and family genes. Another childhood belief was that his temper outbursts were beyond his control and that he was unable to affect what happened to him (e.g., I'm damaged, cursed, abnormal; my mother and her mother were depressed, so it's in my body chemistry, a curse on my life; I'm destined to mess up good relationships; my girl-friend is too normal for me, and I don't deserve her; she can't endure my tantrums, and I can't change). He also labeled his tantrums as childish and therefore obsolete.

In order to develop an Adaptive Coping Style, John was encouraged by the therapist to identify someone he knew who was involved in a successful relationship who he might observe and emulate. John identi-fied a cousin who was raised in a stable, happy family who appeared to be happily married. John began spending more time with his cousin and his wife and made a conscious effort to adopt more adaptive meth-ods he learned from them, such as making and accepting apologies and various courtship techniques.

This intervention was supplemented by the Developmental Deficit Skill-Building strategy, which was used next to teach the client more appropriate partner-interaction patterns. First, the therapist sought to educate John about normal families and some of the intimate relation-ship skills that children learn naturally by observing and imitating parents with a healthy marriage. John found it easier to acknowledge his part in the breakdown of his relationship with Susan when his destructive explosive behaviors were reframed in the context of deficits in relationship-enhancing skills as a consequence of his lack of expo-sure to a successful marital relationship as a boy. He realized that he needed to be taught basic partner-relationship skills. Several sessions were devoted to identification of cognitive and behavioral components of John's destructive patterns in the relationship. These included his low frustration tolerance, poor impulse control, and aggressive style, and his self-centered belief that he was entitled to explode whenever he felt frustrated. Other patterns included his moodiness and his habit of making unreasonable demands followed by disappointment, anger, and silent treatment for days.

Next John was taught adaptive partner-interaction skills to be used as alternatives to his explosive style. He was taught to discuss thoughts and feelings with Susan. He was also taught techniques for stress toler-ance, for de-escalating uncomfortable emotions, and for diffusing con-tentious topics rather than insisting on the last word. John's expectation that Susan should be prepared to tolerate his outbursts was then challenged in attempts to weaken his entitlement schemas. Realistic partner expectations were discussed that were more in keeping with a give and take pattern.

Standard CBT interventions at this point included distress-tolerance and affect-regulation skill training (Linehan, 1993). Techniques adapted from CBT couple-therapy approaches were also used (e.g., Beck, 1988; Baucom & Epstein, 1990). Underlying defectiveness and entitlement schemas were also addressed with cognitive- and schema-therapy interventions.

At this point in the therapy, John began to fall back into his old habits of blaming Susan for making him feel small and minimizing the negative effects of his own demands and tantrums on the relationship. Consequently, he was less motivated to practice new relationship-enhancing skills. The therapist decided to change direction and utilize further developmental strategies to increase John's motivation to persist with his new adaptive coping style.

The Fast Forward and the Future Developmental Stage Planning strategies were initiated. John predicted that if he allowed his aggressive pattern to take over and failed to make a commitment to Susan, he would find himself in the same unenviable situation he was in five years ago — living alone, unable to afford a comfortable apartment, and suffering from depression after another failed relationship. Although he admitted that Susan was not the woman of his dreams, he was grateful for the financial and emotional stability she brought to his life. He saw in her his last hope for what he considered to be a desirable situation for the later years of his life leading up to retirement, namely a comfortable home, companionship, the opportunity for friendships with other couples, and sufficient financial stability to ensure a yearly holiday. He realized that his salvation lay in altering his problematic aggressive style by taking advantage of the opportunity to learn basic relationship-enhancing skills at this point in his life. His goal was to use these new skills to interrupt his self-defeating explosive–entitled pathway and to initiate what he termed a "compatible-partner pathway" and thereby gain the confidence he needed to make a long-term commitment to Susan.

Problems Terminating Intimate Partner Relationships

The emotional and physical upheaval of terminating a romantic, common-law or marital relationship may take place at any stage of the adult lifecycle. Young couples who have been dating for several weeks may find they have little in common, or middle-aged couples whose marriages have worked for several decades may become vulnerable when children leave home and are no longer the major focus.

Because divorce affects over one-third of married couples in North America, most people will experience the break-up of at least one romantic relationship in their lifetime. Termination of an intimate relationship is therefore a common adult transition. Divorce can be especially devastating for the noninitiator spouse who must adjust to the pain of abandonment as well as unwanted single status and the void left by the spouse's departure. Couples with children may have to contend with a child's depression or intense anger at one or both parents for breaking up the family. The transition from couple to single status will affect several areas of the person's life. There will be changes in the person's social network and economic status. For women who have never worked outside the home, new financial burdens may necessitate entering the work force in a competitive job market where advanced age and lack of experience are serious handicaps.

Whether it involves the end of a relatively short romantic liaison or the dissolution of a lengthy common-law or marital partnership, process of terminating a relationship follows predictable stages similar to those outlined by Turner (1980):

- Relationship disenchantment
- Decisional conflict often characterized by ambivalence
- Decision to separate
- Sociological transition after separation
- Restabilization and growth
- Postdivorce adjustments involving children, in-laws, economic and legal factors, and social relationships

When clients are stuck at one of these stages for an inordinate amount of time, underlying developmental task blocks may be involved, warranting a developmental approach. For example, the developmental roots of various factors keeping a client in an unhappy relationship may need to be explored and unresolved tasks addressed before the situation can be remedied.

Decisional Conflict   Many clients present with a stated wish to separate or divorce but manifest various degrees of ambivalence about such a major decision. They may state that they are deeply unhappy but are unable to make a firm decision to either stay in the relationship and take steps to improve it or to begin the separation process. Typical themes from case histories linked to difficulties terminating dysfunctional relationships are shown in Table 6.6.

Table 6.6 Examples of Themes Associated with Relationship Termination Problems

Unrealistic hopes for reconciliation: I'm waiting for him to start feeling guilty and sorry he lost me

Unrealistic hopes for partner change: If I love her enough she'll stop drinking

Ambivalence: I hate the way he treats me, but I still care for him; I can't be faithful, but I want my family; I know he loves me

Dependent: I can't live alone due to my panic attacks; he supports me, there when I break down, what if I get sick?

Pity/guilt: I'm all she has, her lifeline; she's been hurt so much, I can't hurt her more by leaving

Fear of partner revenge: She'll kill herself if I leave; he has threatened to hurt me and the children

Punishment: I'll never free her up to marry someone else

Rigid beliefs about family: The parents must stay together no matter what the cost

Grief about losing the children: I can't imagine not putting them to bed every night

Self-sacrifice/duty: I have to keep him calm, steady; I have to watch him to make sure he doesn't drink; he can't survive without me

Subjugation: A woman has to accept her lot in life

Make excuses: It's not his fault, it's the alcohol; he doesn't love the other women (it's just for sex)

Various personality disorders are often at the core of a client's ongoing failure to implement a stated wish to leave an undesirable partner, such as dependent partners who are terrified of living alone or self-sacrificing partners who are "programmed" to tolerate abuse. Substance abuse, depression, anxiety disorders, or somatoform problems may also be factors. Both partners may be equally dysfunctional and consequently unable to either separate or problem solve within the partnership.

Frequently, clients who are unable to terminate a dysfunctional relationship are victims of partner abuse, both physical and psychological. Female victims of spousal abuse often have a history of childhood physical or sexual abuse and a tendency to blame themselves on some level for the poor treatment they receive (Andrews & Brewin, 1990). Clients who tolerate ongoing partner abuse often have early family histories of domestic violence. Typical families of origin are detached, explosive, and unpredictable. Many victims of partner abuse have been exposed to critical, rejecting, neglectful, or punitive parents, so that the client's current treatment is similar to that experienced as a child. Marital role models in the family of origin frequently fit the abusive–submissive pattern. Themes of abandonment, instability, abuse, mistrust, and emotional deprivation are typical, accompanied by an expectation that one's needs for stability, nurturance, and empathy will not be met. A characteristic expectation is that one's partner will humiliate, cheat, lie, manipulate, or behave in an aggressive manner when angry. The person expects aggressive treatment from a partner, considers it to be inevitable, and therefore tolerates a level of abuse that would be unacceptable to most people (Young, 1990).

Client Example

The Developmental CBT approach will be demonstrated with the following client, who had wanted to leave her abusive alcoholic husband for years but was unable to do so. She worried that she would be unable to survive on her own and that her children would be traumatized by a divorce.

> Victoria was 26 years old and married to an alcoholic husband who was routinely abusive not only toward his wife, but also toward his children. Victoria feared the negative long-term effects on her son and daughter. She worked as a waitress but had no friends or support group because she was determined to keep her husband's drinking a secret. She had attempted to leave her husband three times over the past five years, but each time she changed her mind when her husband warned her that he would win custody of the children on the basis of her past history of mental illness. Victoria felt totally helpless, and she continued to put up with her hateful domestic situation.

The Developmental Assessment provided more insight into the link between patterns in the client's family of origin and her ongoing inability to leave her husband.

> Victoria endured a difficult childhood and adolescence with a father who was an alcoholic and a mother who was financially dependent on her husband and could not leave. The mother had simply tolerated her husband's abuse, insisting that a wife should pray for help and stand by her man no matter what. Victoria and her sister had few friends over the years since their situation precluded bringing peers home. Although the sister rebelled by getting involved in drugs, Victoria's role evolved into that of a caregiver for her parents, striving to ensure that her father did not harm himself or his wife on one of his binges. The stress of functioning as a buffer between her mother and father took its toll, and at age 16 Victoria was helped through a serious bout of agitated depression by her school counselor.

School had always been Victoria's refuge. She dreamed of becoming a high school teacher, in addition to having a normal happy family of her own. In spite of her stressful home situation, she was a good student and was successful in earning a university scholarship. Victoria entered university with high hopes, grateful for the opportunity to live in a dormitory and be free from the embarrassment of her family situation. For the first time she found herself in a position to cultivate friendships and a boyfriend. She coped quite well until the pressure of Christmas exams increased her anxiety to the extent that she feared that she was headed for another breakdown. Her solution was to leave university and marry her boyfriend. Victoria's major priority now became that of creating a happy normal family life, and within weeks she became pregnant. Ironically, around this time she gradually began to realize that her husband had a drinking problem, and her safe little world began to fall apart. She went on to have a second child but found herself socially isolated and dependent, keeping the secret of her husband's drinking problem.

Victoria identified her primary problem as that of decision paralysis. She admitted that she frequently found herself wishing that her husband would disappear or die and leave them alone. The therapist first carried out a behavioral analysis of stressful interaction patterns between the couple and between the husband and children. This provided the therapist with more information and also heightened the client's awareness of the damaging long-term consequences of her husband's drinking patterns on the children. Following this, the therapist and client worked together to identify relevant beliefs, attitudes, and other factors that were preventing Victoria from leaving her husband, such as pity, unrealistic expectations for change, duty, and intermittent positive reinforcement when her husband chose to be nice. Victoria said that although her husband's drinking was ruining her children, she felt sorry for him, especially when he would beg her not to break up the family and take his children from him. Once again, she would put her own feelings on hold and renew her efforts to make the marriage work. She said that deep down she believed that keeping the family together was more important than her misery and that if she were to leave her husband, she would be depriving her children of a normal two-parent family. She admitted that she still had hopes that one day he would stop drinking. When discussing leaving him, she said her immediate fears were financial insecurity if she were to attempt to establish a separate residence with her children and the anticipation of her husband's angry reaction to her departure, which would undoubtedly involve his threat to cite her breakdown at age 16 as proof that she was not fit to raise children.

Victoria began to see the influence of her mother as a role model and the similarities between their family situations in terms of underlying themes of defectiveness, self-sacrifice, subordination, and unrealistic hopes for partner change. These schemas were first addressed with standard cognitive therapy techniques. This was supplemented by therapist education and information from articles on family law that the client was asked to read to address the client's conviction that she would be deemed an unsuitable mother and denied custody of the children on the basis of one episode of depression 10 years ago.

The Developmental Task-Block Identification and Analysis strategies were used to help the client identify unresolved tasks of childhood and adolescence linked to her ongoing difficulty in carrying out her wish to leave her husband. Victoria realized that her relationship with her parents precluded sufficient autonomy to pursue normal teenage activities or friendships or to develop positive feelings about her own accomplishments. Instead, she felt responsible for ensuring that her parents were safe and subordinated her own needs to theirs. Victoria had also failed to attain sufficient educational credentials to ensure financial stability and to realize her dream of becoming a teacher.

Currently Victoria was experiencing difficulties with several important adult tasks: (1) termination of a destructive partner relationship, (2) establishment of a healthy home environment for her children, (3) development of supportive adult friendships, which was curtailed by embarrassment about her husband's drinking, and (4) effective parenting. The latter was currently impossible because her husband's binges were sabotaging her own efforts to provide consistent order, discipline, and routine.

Victoria concluded that her indecision about leaving her husband was just another manifestation of a "self-sacrificing victim pathway" that she had been stuck in since childhood when she felt personally responsible for her parents well-being. At that time she had sacrificed normal teenage pursuits to protect her mother from her father and her father from himself. She realized that her current predicament was just another chapter in her self-sacrificing-victim pathway, only now she was not only sacrificing her own happiness, but also her children's opportunity for a normal family life. Underlying the whole process were her misguided beliefs about a wife's spousal duty, unrealistic hopes for her husband's sudden rehabilitation, and a sentimental belief instilled in her by her mother about the inherent sanctity of a two-parent family unit and the necessity of preserving this at all costs. The family of origin analysis helped the client gain insight into the role played by her mother's toleration of her father's abuse in shaping long-standing beliefs maintaining Victoria's victim role, such as the absence of expectations for fair treatment, the passive acceptance of abuse, and unrealistic hopes that her husband would stop drinking. Her mother had been a victim of spousal abuse who had failed to establish a healthy independent life for herself and her children, and Victoria realized that she would have to take a different path to avoid repetition of her mother's mistakes.

The client was now prepared to consider advantages and disadvantages of different options for resolving her predicament. Victoria generated the following alternatives: maintaining the status quo, seeking out couple therapy in a further attempt to save the relationship, an informal trial separation, or a legal separation leading to divorce.

Using the Fast Forward strategy, the client was asked to imagine life in five years if she chose to remain in the relationship. This was supplemented by the use of the Parent–Offspring Interaction Styles instrument to help the client contrast the probable long-term consequences of divorce on her children's mental health with the consequences of daily life in a home dominated by an abusive alcoholic father. Victoria came to the conclusion that the negative effects on the children would be greater if they remained in the abusive environment. She concluded that the children would be increasingly traumatized and that she would likely suffer another breakdown. She pictured her children as teenagers, increasingly angry about sacrificing their childhood years to the whims of an alcoholic father, similar to the anger Victoria and her sister had experienced. She imagined them resorting to self-destructive forms of rebellion like her sister did. She was then asked to imagine the best possible future, and she pictured herself providing a healthier independent home for her children and living a more serene life, still in regular contact with her husband, but without the daily tension surrounding his drinking. It would not be the ideal life she pictured for herself all those years, but it would be an improvement over the current situation. At this point she decided that anything would be better than the status quo five years from now, and she was now firmly determined to leave her husband and create a new healthy home environment for herself and her children. She labeled her new path her "healthy single-parent pathway."

The Future Developmental Stage Planning strategy was next used to help Victoria prepare for the separation process and for negotiating the move to an independent residence. The client was helped to list issues that would have to be addressed over the next few weeks as she prepared to leave. She was helped to formulate steps in a plan for implementing this decision, such as informing her husband, financial planning, and child custody and visitation arrangements.

In many instances, therapists must first educate themselves about various aspects of a process or stage that the client will be facing. This may take the form of consultation with other professionals, a literature search, or Internet investigation. This is an extremely important part of the Future Developmental Stage Planning strategy because logistics are frequently a major stumbling block impeding healthy transitions. In this case the therapist educated herself about components of the separation process through her own reading, consultation with various agencies, and advice from a divorce lawyer. She was then in a position to guide Victoria through various steps in the separation process. The therapist also found a Women-in-Transition support group for the client, and Victoria began to attend sessions. She was also encouraged to make use of a women's self-help resource center and a free legal advice telephone line.

Over the next few sessions, Victoria was asked to anticipate various tasks in the separation process and make concrete plans and preparations for coping with each. With the therapist's help, Victoria listed the following:

- **Preliminary legal fact finding:** Consult a lawyer to find out about child custody and visitation laws, financial support and monthly payments, division of property and other assets, etc.
- **Housing issues:** Find an apartment.
- **Financial issues:** Make a preliminary budget, determine children's financial needs, and estimate amount of support payments.
- **Inform husband about the decision to separate and divorce:** First inform husband's brother and sister and request that they be present for purposes of safety and support when husband is informed of the separation.
- **Joint meeting with lawyer:** Husband and wife meet with lawyer to work out financial, child custody, and visitation agreements.
- **Inform others:** Inform the children. Inform the school and extended family.
- **Maintain normal home environment:** Stick to daily routines during the separation process.
- **Implement the move:** Formulate logistics and concrete plans for the move (e.g., create timeline, request assistance from others).

- **Ensuring children's mental health:** Find out about helping children cope with separation and divorce (e.g., consult with school psychologist, read literature about children's emotional reactions to divorce).

A preliminary discussion with a lawyer helped increase Victoria's understanding of family law and address her unrealistic fear that she would be deemed an unsuitable mother and denied custody of the children. The lawyer reassured her that her husband's long history of abusive treatment of the children would be deemed more damaging to the children's welfare than Victoria's history of one episode of depression 10 years ago. He also reassured her that, given her children's young ages and her own record as a steady loving parent, she would almost certainly prevail in her quest for custody of the children. This gave her the courage to proceed, and she continued to implement the various tasks she had listed. She was helped to anticipate problems arising at each step and to plan for each. She convinced her husband's brother and sister to be present when she informed her husband, and, luckily, her worst fears did not materialize. With their help, she managed to negotiate the move to her own apartment within two weeks.

In the days leading up to the move, Victoria found herself continually overwhelmed by the enormity of her decision. The Future Developmental Stage Planning strategy was again utilized to help allay some of her fears by helping her plan for the postseparation, single-parent stage of her life. She was asked to visualize her life as a divorced single parent and to anticipate new tasks and challenges. The client generated the following list:

- Maintain children's school and social routines.
- Maintain normal household routines.
- Maintain spousal boundaries; consult a lawyer if necessary.
- Establish an effective postseparation relationship with husband and ensure cooperative parenting; arrange for joint sessions with a counselor if necessary.
- Fine-tune financial and visitation agreements.
- Develop friends and community support network.
- Find recreational diversions.
- Once settled, explore possibility of university night school courses to improve long-term job potential and financial situation.

In the process of ending the destructive relationship with her husband, Victoria managed to divert herself from her long-standing self-sacrificing victim pathway to her new "healthy single-parent" pathway. She now had adequate autonomy and energy to accomplish the crucial tasks of providing a healthy home environment and effective parenting for her children. In the process she also achieved a new degree of autonomy from her own parents and was in a position to develop supportive friendships that had eluded her in the past.

PARENTING ROLE PROBLEMS

The final section will demonstrate the Developmental CBT approach for clients who are experiencing difficulties with parenting. Child rearing is one of the most demanding tasks of adulthood, even in terms of normal every-day challenges of parenting across the adult life span.

Couples move through various stages of child rearing, each with its characteristic tasks and demands. The transition to parenthood following the birth of a first child involves a major adjustment with its new responsibilities and the willingness on the part of the parents to subjugate their own needs to those of the new child. This is followed by a decade or more of unrelenting demands on the parents' time and energy as they strive to meet the daily needs of small children. As parents enter their middle adulthood years, they are faced with children who have entered puberty and are in the process of becoming physically mature, socially active, and psychologically independent. Parents may find caring for adolescents less satisfying and more stressful than caring for small children. Difficulties may arise when adolescents challenge parental authority. As children reach late adolescence and prepare for higher education, parents must also cope with added financial burdens. This may coincide with other changes in the family. For example, a wife who is no longer parenting small children may be investigating new career opportunities outside the house. The couple may be coping with the demands of their own aging parents at this time, and there may be changes in the occupational sphere, where options are becoming more limited with age.

The mature years of child rearing introduce further challenges to parents as they prepare to *launch* adult children. *Launching* refers to the process of physical, financial, and psychological separation from grown children who have entered college, university, or the work force. Although the launched child may still be in need of parental support, the parent is no longer able to arrange optimal conditions in the home and community environment to shield the child from potential hardships. At this point the parents must learn to step back and acknowledge that launched children are now responsible for the consequences of their own behavior. Parents may provide psychological support but must resist rescuing adult children. Instead, they must facilitate the launched child's new financial and physical independence and, frequently, the child's decision to live and work elsewhere.

Parents need to renegotiate relationships with launched children and to interact with grown children on an adult-to-adult basis. They also need to adjust to relationships with new extended family members and to master their new roles as in-laws and grandparents as adult offspring marry and begin families of their own. A major challenge will be coming to terms with the way in which adult children have turned out in terms of the child's personal and social adjustment, educational and occupational attainments, and performance as a spouse and parent. A major challenge for mature parents of adult offspring is accepting the grown child's life decisions even when these are viewed as mistakes.

The quality of the marital relationship will have a significant effect on the quality of parenting provided by the couple (although a successful marriage does not automatically guarantee successful parenting). Spousal cooperation is an important factor in the division of financial, child-care, and household responsibilities. It is also important that spouses share a similar child-rearing philosophy, ensuring a united approach to raising the children.

Traditionally, the father was the primary wage earner, while the mother assumed the majority of child-care and household responsibilities. Currently, this division is less clear cut, with the increase in two-income families and increased reliance on outsiders who are hired to assist with child-care responsibilities. Parents need to find a way to balance competing family and career demands, and each parent must spend sufficient time with the child to develop strong emotional bonds.

Effective child rearing depends on the parent's ability to provide adequate love, nurturance, supervision, and discipline. This ensures sufficient parental influence over the child when difficulties arise in years to come. A parent's family experiences as a child affect his or her parenting style and effectiveness. A parent who grew up in a happy well-adjusted family will have been provided with models of effective parenting.

Common presenting problems of clients who seek therapy for child-rearing difficulties include concerns about the disturbing behavior of a child, stressful parent–child interaction styles, ineffective disciplinary practices, and marital conflict jeopardizing parent effectiveness. A parent's mental health problems often underlie child-rearing difficulties. Anxiety disorders, anger problems, chronic depression, alcoholism, and various personality disorders are frequent components of a client's parenting difficulties. Some parents are unable to establish a home environment with sufficient order and routine. Others are simply unable to put children and family needs before their own. Client mental health problems may be manifested in a variety of dysfunctional child-rearing patterns, such as punitive, over-coercive, over-protective, neglecting, or over-submissive parenting styles. Each of these may have negative effects on the child's development for different reasons.

Anxious over-protective parents are common therapy clients. They frequently suffer from anxiety disorders, such as panic attacks, OCD, or phobias that restrict their daily activities. Those with unreasonable fears about a child's school experience or peer relationships have often experienced school failure or peer rejection themselves. Many have suffered from anxiety disorders since childhood and were raised by family members who also suffered from anxiety disorders or other forms of mental illness. Anxious parents are often preoccupied with finding ways to keep their children nearby to ensure safety or to shield the child from routine disappointments, thereby depriving them of normal experiences. In the process, they may unintentionally curtail the child's peer activities and acquisition of social skills or stifle the child's independence. Parents with exaggerated worries about their child's safety may resort to excessive structure or elaborate rituals for checking on their children as they go about routine peer and school activities. Anxious parents often doubt their own competence. They serve as poor role models, shaping similar anxiety behaviors and beliefs in their children so that their children gradually begin to feel anxious in the school environment or during peer activities outside of the home. The children may begin to develop avoidance strategies or copy the parents by resorting to somatoform complaints to get out of uncomfortable situations. These disturbing symptoms in the child then prompt the parent to seek therapy.

Perfectionist standards may also be part of the picture. Anxious parents not only impose unrealistic expectations on themselves as parents, but may also impose perfectionist standards on their children or on their children's caregivers or teachers.

Over-submissive parents who provide lax or inconsistent discipline are also frequent therapy clients. They tend to defer to their child's aggression, guilt trips, and manipulations. They often resort to excessive threats or restrictions and then fail to follow through. Frequently, their homes are disorganized, with few healthy family routines. Neglect may be a component owing to parental alcoholism or psychopathology. In some cases over-submissive parents have strong beliefs about letting children develop on their own with minimal parental interference, and often they were raised by parents with similar childrearing philosophies. Guilt may be a factor, with the parent adopting a permissive stance to make up for past injustices in the child's life.

Over-submissive parents usually seek therapy when their children are out of control. Frequent themes include anger at the unfair treatment, abdication of responsibility, failure as a parent, excuses for the child's unreasonable behavior, and fears about how the child will end up. Marilyn, the client with the difficult 11-year-old daughter described in Chapter 3, was an over-submissive parent who was motivated by the Future Developmental Stage Planning strategy to take control of the situation.

Client Example: Over-Submissive Parent

Marilyn was a single mother who sought therapy when her 11-year old daughter, Colleen, began ignoring her curfew and staying out late with her friends. Colleen was also skipping school and experimenting with alcohol. Marilyn's marriage broke up before Colleen was born, and Marilyn worried endlessly that her daughter would suffer psychological damage similar to the sense of deprivation she herself had experienced as a child. Marilyn felt so guilty about her failed marriage that she went overboard in her attempts to prove her love for her daughter by complete and utter devotion. At first she exhausted herself with unsuccessful attempts to breast feed her daughter and then fired a succession of eight nannies in the space of two years for failure to carry out her elaborate instructions for meeting Colleen's every need. Over the years she indulged and spoiled Colleen. Marilyn had no time for friends and broke up with her boyfriend because Colleen disapproved of him. Instead, she spent all of her free time with Colleen and monopolized Colleen's time to such an extent that it precluded opportunities for her daughter to play with peers after school or to participate in extra-curricular activities. Consequently Colleen had no friends and felt alone and alienated at school. As she approached puberty, she became more and more resentful of having to spend so much time with her mother.

At age eleven Colleen was defiant, aggressive, and rebellious. She befriended classmates who flaunted the rules, skipped school, and were allowed to stay out late. At this point, Marilyn lost control of Colleen. In desperate attempts to regain her daughter's approval she capitulated to Colleen's escalating demands for money and inappropriate privileges and tolerated Colleen's foul language. On a couple of occasions Colleen demanded that she be allowed to stay out until midnight. Marilyn went along with this, afraid to investigate further, for fear of what she would discover.

Standard CBT parent-training interventions were met with a great deal of resistance. Marilyn insisted that she was not a conventional boring mom and that prohibiting her daughter from going out in the evening with undesirable peers would not work because she would get together with them after school instead. She said that it would alienate Colleen more, and when the possibility of drugs was raised, Marilyn said that her only hope was to allow Colleen to experiment with "soft drugs" but convince her not to touch "hard drugs." Because of this impasse, the therapist initiated the Developmental Phase in an attempt to identify and address developmental patterns underlying Marilyn's inability to set limits.

The Developmental Phase   The developmental assessment revealed the following:

> Marilyn's father died when she was five, and her mother had a series of live-in boyfriends, with little time left to spend with Marilyn. Throughout her childhood and adolescence, Marilyn worried constantly about her mother. She was unable to fall asleep until her mother was safely home in the early hours of the morning, and she worried about her mother's mental health each time she broke up with a boyfriend. Marilyn longed for a normal family with parents who cared, and consequently vowed that *her* children would grow up in a normal family with devoted parents.
>
> Marilyn was left to do as she pleased, with no curfew or restrictions as a teenager. At one point she found herself skipping school but got herself back on track and managed to finish high school. Marilyn reacted to her mother's disinterest over the years with constant unsuccessful attempts to get her mother to pay attention to her. She tried taking over most of the household chores, but her mother seemed not to notice. Her quest for approval and acceptance was similar with peers. She resorted to buying friendships with gifts and eventually to promiscuity to please boyfriends. One of these relationships led to pregnancy and Marilyn's short-lived marriage.

The Developmental Task-Block Identification and Analysis strategies revealed several unresolved child and adolescent tasks. For example, Marilyn failed to achieve a secure bond with her mother and failed to develop a positive self-concept or sense of self-worth, manifested in deprivation and defectiveness schemas. She also failed to develop supportive friendships. Unresolved adult tasks were in the areas of intimate partner selection and interaction skills, adult friendships, and parenting skills. Marilyn also failed to develop interests and hobbies of her own since all of her energy went into meeting her daughter's needs.

The client labeled her maladaptive developmental pathway culminating in her current ineffective childrearing approach her "defective–subordination pathway." It was shaped by a neglectful mother who left her daughter feeling deprived and inferior. Throughout her childhood, Marilyn tried to cope with the neglect by subordinating her own needs to those of her mother and striving unsuccessfully to secure attention and approval by being the perfect daughter. This generalized to her subsequent attempts to be the perfect friend and perfect girlfriend. For the past 11 years she had sacrificed her own chances for a normal life, friends, and remarriage while striving unsuccessfully to be a supermom. Underlying this current manifestation of her defective–subordination pathway, was a fear that she would lose her daughter's love if she did not give her what she wanted or if she tried to curtail her daughter's reckless lifestyle. All of her years of sacrifice backfired, and Marilyn felt defective as a parent.

The Developmental Task-Block Analysis helped Marilyn realize that she had been deprived of role models for effective parenting. Consequently, she found herself adopting a lax and inconsistent disciplinary approach similar to her mother's, but in her case it was not for lack of caring but because of caring too much. She was desperately trying to be both parent and best friend to her daughter, neither of which she had experienced with her own mother.

By means of the Fast Forward strategy, the client was encouraged to speculate about additional challenges of parenting a teenager in two years time in light of her lax discipline and pattern of capitulating to her daughter's demands. Since Marilyn currently allowed her daughter to stay out until midnight at age 11, she was asked how she would respond to her daughter staying out all night at age 14. She was also asked to speculate about the type of peers she would be with and Colleen's school performance if she habitually stayed out all night. This helped Marilyn see the degree to which her daughter was already out of her control and her responsibility as a parent to regain control before it was too late. This strategy, and the Future Developmental Stage Planning strategy described in Chapter 3, increased Marilyn's motivation to participate fully in parenting-training interventions.

Recall that the Future Developmental Stage Planning strategy helped familiarize Marilyn with new tasks and challenges she would be faced with in the next stage of her childrearing endeavor — parenting a teen-ager. She realized she would have to provide increasing supervision to ensure that her daughter not become involved in the drug culture. This necessitated changing her work hours so that she would be home in the evenings with Colleen. She would also need to ensure that Colleen associated with friends with desirable qualities who would help her internalize pro-social values. Another major responsibility was that of guaranteeing that Colleen's educational attainments were sufficient for graduation from high school or college acceptance.

The Adaptive Versus Obsolete Coping Styles strategy was useful in helping Marilyn formulate goals for her daughter's development in years to come. She stated that she wanted Colleen to be responsible, considerate of others, disciplined about her school work, and associate with serious students who were not interested in drugs. She also wanted a daughter who respected her mother and was willing to spend time with her. Marilyn labeled her long-standing lax and inconsistent disci-plinary approach her "obsolete parenting style," since it was instrumen-tal in shaping an entitled, undisciplined, pleasure-seeing child used to getting her own way. She wanted to replace it with an "adaptive parent-ing style" that would increase the likelihood of fostering the qualities she had hoped for in a daughter but admitted that she was at a loss as to what that would be and how to achieve it. The Parent–Offspring Interaction Styles instrument was helpful in educating the client about the probable effects of various components of maladaptive childrearing styles, many of which Marilyn had been relying on for years. She was surprised to learn that her head-in-the-sand stance and her failure to provide and enforce clear rules and regulations were forms of parental neglect that encouraged a child to become undisciplined and to drift. Once Marilyn had gained sufficient insight into the origins of her dif-ficulties with the parenting role in terms of her long-standing defec-tive–subordination pathway, she was motivated to participate in the following strategy designed to introduce Marilyn to adaptive parenting techniques that would achieve the results she wanted.

The Developmental Deficit Skill-Building strategy was used to edu-cate the client about adaptive parenting techniques that she had never observed in her own family during her childhood and youth. These included: (1) setting and enforcing age-appropriate expectations and limitations, (2) appropriate curfews, (3) ensuring regular school atten-dance by working with school personnel, (4) enlisting the help of other mothers in structuring regular activities with pro-social peers, and (5) keeping abreast of her daughter's daily activities so that she would be able to provide adequate supervision. She was taught assertive parenting techniques for establishing routines, for resisting her daughter's demands and attempts to control her, and for establishing curfews, rules, and regulations, with clearly stated consequences for breaking the rules spelled out beforehand. Marilyn also consented to joining a parent support group to increase her knowledge of effective techniques and to strengthen her resolve to stick with her new pathway that she labeled her "effective–assertive parent pathway." This included a shift from her former preoccupation with being her daughter's best friend and subordination of her own needs to Colleen's whims to a new preoccupation with being a skillful parent capable of raising a responsible daughter.

Once Marilyn began to see some positive effects of her new parenting strategies and to feel less defective, she was ready to make changes in her lifestyle to further deflect herself from her subordinate role. The Current Life-Structure Reorganization strategy helped her reevaluate her current practice of spending endless hours at home, making herself available to a daughter who never sought her company. Instead, she planned one specific event per week that simulated mother-daughter quality time. The only event that Colleen would tolerate at first was a weekly dinner date joined by a cousin and aunt who Colleen enjoyed. Marilyn had already changed her work hours to be available during weekday evenings to provide adequate supervision and to ensure that Colleen stayed at home and devoted some time to school work. Marilyn also resolved to spend time with people her own age and to begin dating again as part of her new assertive versus subordination stance. She began by attending social events with a new friend from her parent support group. Although Colleen remained defiant and difficult, Marilyn was successful in keeping her in school and at home during the evenings. Consequently, Colleen was no longer able to spend much time with her old acquaintances and began spending more time with her cousin's friends, which gradually led to more desirable friendships. At the same time, she raised no objections to her mother's new independent life.

SUMMARY OF MALADAPTIVE DEVELOPMENTAL PARTNER RELATIONSHIP AND PARENTING PATHWAYS

Table 6.7 presents a summary of maladaptive developmental pathways and corresponding adaptive pathways generated by the preceding clients in the areas of intimate partner relationships and parenting difficulties. In each case the Developmental Task-Block Identification and Analysis strategies were utilized first to help the clients define their dysfunctional

Table 6.7 Summary of Client Pathways Linked to Intimate Partner and Family Problems

Task Difficulty	Maladaptive Pathway	Adaptive Pathway	Developmental Strategies
Problems forming intimate partner relationships	Social-isolation pathway	Socially experienced pathway	Developmental Deficit Skill-Building Current Life Structure Reorganization
Problems selecting appropriate intimate partners	Defective–dependent–defiant pathway	Independent–confident–pathway	Developmental Task Resolution Planning Future Developmental Stage Planning Resiliency Training
Problems sustaining adaptive intimate partner relationships	Explosive–entitlement pathway Damaged–undeserving pathway	Compatible partner pathway	Adaptive Versus Obsolete Coping Styles Developmental Deficit Skill-Building Fast Forward Future Developmental Stage Planning
Problems terminating intimate partner relationships	Self-sacrificing–victim pathway	Healthy single-parent pathway	Fast Forward Future Developmental Stage Planning
Parenting role problems	Defective–subordination pathway	Effective–assertive parent pathway	Fast Forward Future Developmental Stage Planning Adaptive versus Obsolete Coping Styles Developmental Deficit Skill-Building Current Life Structure Reorganization

pathways, followed by additional Developmental CBT strategies for establishing more appropriate pathways, shown in column 4. Therapists are encouraged to keep similar records of developmental strategies found to be successful in deflecting particular types of clients from various maladaptive pathways. It provides a useful reference for designing future treatment plans for clients with similar developmental difficulties.

REFERENCES

Achenbach, T. (1990). What is "developmental" about developmental psychopathology? In J. Rolf, A. Masten, D. Cicchetti, K. Nuechtenlein, & S. Weintraub (Eds.), *Risk and protective factors in the development of psychopathology,* (pp. 29–48). New York: Cambridge University Press.

Alymer, R. (1989). The launching of the single adult. In B. Carter & M. McGoldrick (Eds.), *The changing family life cycle: A framework for family therapy* (2nd ed., pp. 191—208). Boston: Allyn & Bacon.

Andrews, B., & Brewin, C. R. (1990). Attributions of blame for marital violence: A study of antecedents and consequences. *Journal of Marriage and the Family, 52,* 757–767.

Bagwell, C. L., Newcomb, A. F., & Bukowski, W. M. (1998). Preadolescent friendship and peer rejection as predictors of adult adjustment. *Child Development, 69,* 140–153.

Baldry, A. C., & Farrington, D. P. (2000). Bullies and delinquents: Personal characteristics and parental styles. *Journal of Community and Applied Social Psychology, 10,* 17–31.

Basco, R. B., & Rush, J. (1996). *Cognitive behavioral therapy for bipolar disorder.* New York: Guilford Press.

Baucom, D., & Epstein, N. (1990). *Cognitive-behavioral marital therapy.* New York: Brunner/Mazel.

Beck, A. T. (1963). Thinking and depression. I. Idiosyncratic content and cognitive distortions. *Archives of General Psychiatry, 9,* 324–333.

Beck, A. T. (1964). Thinking and depression. II. Theory and therapy. *Archives of General Psychiatry, 10,* 461–471.

Beck, A. (1972). *Depression: Causes and treatment.* Philadelphia: University of Pennsylvania Press.

Beck, A. (1976). *Cognitive therapy and emotional disorders.* New York: International Universities Press.

Beck, A. T. (1988). *Love is never enough.* New York: Harper and Row.

Beck, A., & Emery, G. (1985). *Anxiety disorders and phobias.* New York: Guilford Press.

Beck, A., & Freeman, A. (1990). *Cognitive therapy of personality disorders.* New York: Guilford Press.

Beck, A., Freeman, A., & Davis, D. (Eds.) (2004). *Cognitive therapy of personality disorders.* New York: Guilford Press.

Beck, A., Rush, J., Shaw, B., & Emery, G. (1979). *Cognitive therapy of depression.* New York: Guilford Press.

Beck, J. (1995). *Cognitive therapy: Basics and beyond.* New York: Guilford Press.

Bedrosian, R., & Bozicas, G. (1994). *Treating family of origin problems. A cognitive approach.* New York: Guilford Press.

Bowlby, J. (1969). *Attachment and loss: Vol. 1. Attachment.* New York: Basic Books.

Bowlby, J. (1973). *Separation.* New York: Basic Books.

Bowlby, J. (1988). *A secure base: Parent-child attachment and healthy human development.* New York: Basic Books.

Bradbury, T. (1995). Assessing the four fundamental domains of marriage. *Family Relations, 44,* 459–468.

Brewin, D., Furnham, A., Firth-Cozens, J., & McManus, C. (1993). Self-criticism in adulthood and recalled childhood experience. *Journal of Abnormal Psychology, 101*(No. 3), 561–566.

Burback, D., & Borduin, C. (1986). Parent-child relations and the etiology of depression. A review of methods and findings. *Clinical Psychology Review, 6,* 133–153.

Carter, B., & McGoldrick, M. (1989). *The changing family life cycle: A framework for family therapy* (2nd ed.). Boston: Allyn & Bacon.

Cicchetti, D. (1984). The emergence of developmental psychopathology. *Child Development, 55,* 1–7.

Cichetti, D. (1990). An historical perspective on the discipline of developmental psychopathology. In J. Rolf, A. S. Masten, D. Cicchetti, K. H. Nuechterlein, & S. Weintraub (Eds.), *Risk and protective factors in the development of psychopathology* (pp. 2–28). New York: Cambridge University Press.

Cicchetti, D., & Cohen, D. (1995). Perspectives on developmental psychopathology. In D. Cicchetti & D. Cohen (Eds.), *Developmental psychopathology: Vol. I. Theory and methods* (pp. 320). New York: John Wiley & Sons.

Cicchetti, D., Toth, S., & Maughan, A. (2000). An ecological-transactional model of child maltreatment. In J. Sameroff, M. Lewis, & S. Miller (Eds.), *Handbook of developmental psychopathology* (2nd ed., pp. 689–722). New York: Kluwer Academic/Plenum.

Cicirelli, V. G. (1998). Intergenerational relationships in modern families. In L. L'Abate (Ed.), *Family psychopathology. The relational roots of dysfunctional behavior.* New York: Guilford Press.

Cohen, S., & Wills, T. A. (1985). Stress, social support, and the buffering hypothesis. *Psychological Bulletin, 98,* 310–357.

Cohler, B. (1991). Life-course perspectives on the study of adversity, stress, and coping: Discussion of papers from the West Virginia conference. In E. Cummings, A. Greene, & K. Karraker (Eds.), *Life span developmental psychology: Stress and coping* (pp. 297–326). Hillsdale, NJ: Lawrence Erlbaum.

Cohler, B., & Boxer, A. (1991). Middle adulthood: Settling into the world—person, time and context. In E. Cummings, A. Greene, & K. Karraker (Eds.), *Life span developmental psychology: Stress and coping* (pp. 145–203). Hillsdale, NJ: Lawrence Erlbaum.

Conger, J. (1977). *Adolescence and youth* (2nd ed.). New York: Harper and Row.

Cross, S., & Markus, H. (1991). Possible selves across the life span. *Human Development, 34,* 230–255.

Dattilio, F., & Freeman, A. (Eds.) (2000). *Cognitive–behavioral strategies in crisis intervention.* New York: Guilford Press.

Deater-Deckard, K. (2001). Annotation: Recent research examining the role of peer relationships in the development of psychopathology. *Journal of Child Psychology and Psychiatry 42*(No. 5), 565–579.

Deater-Deckard, K. (2001). Cognitive behavioral therapy for children and adolescents. *Journal of Cognitive Psychotherapy, 15* (No. 3), 183–194.

Dryden, W. (1990). *Dealing with anger problems: Rational-emotive therapeutic interventions.* Sarasota, FL: Essential Professional Resource Exchange.

Ellis, A., McInerny, A., DiGiuseppe, R., and Yeager, R. (1988). *Rational emotive therapy for alcoholics and substance abusers.* New York: Pergamon.

Epstein, N., Schlesinger, S. E., and Dryden, W. (Eds.) (1988). *Cognitive-behavioral therapy with families.* New York: Brunner/Mazel.

Erikson, E. (1982). *The life cycle completed.* New York: Norton.

Featherman, D., Lerner, R., & Perlmutter, M. (1994). *Life-span development and behavior. Vol. 12.* Hillsdale, NJ: Lawrence Erlbaum.

Fischer, K., Ayoub, C., Singh, I., Noam, G., Margaganore, A., & Raya, P. (1997). Psychopathology as adaptive development along distinctive pathways. *Development and Psychopathology, 9,* 749–779.

Franz, C. E., McClelland, D. C., & Weinberger, J. (1991). Childhood antecedents of conventional social accomplishment in mid-life adults: A 36 year prospective study. *Journal of Personality and Social Psychology, 60,* 586–595.

Freeman, A., & Simon, K. M. (1989). Cognitive therapy of anxiety. In A. Freeman, K. Simon, L. Beutler, & H. Arkowitz (Eds.) *Comprehensive Handbook of Cognitive Therapy.* New York: Plenum.

Freeman, A., Simon, K., Beutler, L., and Arkowitz, H. (Eds.) (1989). *Comprehensive handbook of cognitive therapy.* New York: Plenum Press.

Gergen, K., (1977). Stability, change, and chance in understanding human development. In N. Datan & H. Reese (Eds.), *Life-span developmental psychology: Dialectical perspectives on experimental research* (pp. 135–158). New York: Academic Press.

Gerlsma, C. (1994). Parental rearing styles and psychopathology: Notes on the validity of questionnaires for recalled parental behavior. In C. Perris, W.A. Arrindell, and M. Eisemann (Eds.), *Parenting and Psychopathology* (pp. 75–105). New York: John Wiley & Sons.

Gerlsma, C., Emmelkamp, P., Arrindell, W. (1990). Anxiety, depression, and perception of early parenting: A meta-analysis. *Annual Psychology Review, 10,* 251–277.

Gold, E. R. (1986). Long-term effects of sexual victimization in childhood: An attributional approach. *Journal of Consulting and Clinical Psychology, 54,* 471–475.

Greenberg, L., & Paivio, S. (1997). *Working with emotions in psychotherapy.* New York: Guilford Press.

Greenburger, D., & Padesky, C. (1995). *Mind over mood: A cognitive therapy treatment manual for clients.* New York: Guilford Press.

Guidano, V. F. (1987). *Complexity of the self: A developmental approach to psychopathology and therapy.* New York: Guilford Press.

Guidano, V. (1988). A systems process-oriented approach to cognitive therapy. In K. Dobson (Ed.), *Handbook of cognitive behavioral therapies.* New York: Guilford Press.

Guidano, V. F., & Liotti, G. (1983). *Cognitive processes and emotional disorders.* New York: Guilford Press.

Hanson, R. O., Jones, W. H., Carpenter, B. N., & Remondet, I. (1986). Loneliness and adjustment to old age. *International Journal of Aging and Human Development, 24,* 41–53.

Hartup, W. (1983). Peer relations. In E. M. Hetherington (Vol. Ed.) & P. H. Mussen (Series Ed.), *Handbook of child psychology: Vol. 4. Socialization, personality and social development* (pp. 103—198). New York: Wiley.

Havinghurst, R. J. (1972). *Developmental Tasks and Education* (3rd ed.). New York: David McKay.

Hussong, A., & Chassin, L. (2002). Parental alcoholism and the leaving home transition. *Development and Psychopathology, 14,* 139–157.

Johnson, J., Sher, K., & Rolf, J. (1991). Models of vulnerability to psychopathology in childhood of alcoholics: An overview. *Alcohol Health and Research World, 15*(No. 1), 33–42.

Levinson, D. (1978). *The seasons of a man's life.* New York: Knopf.

Levinson, D. (1996). *The seasons of a woman's life.* New York: Knopf.

Linehan, M. (1993). *Skills training manual for treating borderline personality disorder.* New York: Guilford Press.

Masten, A. S., & Coatsworth, J. D. (1995). Competence, resilience & psychopathology. In D. Cicchetti & D. Cohen (Eds.), *Developmental psychopathology: Vol. 2. Risk disorder and adaptation* (pp. 715–752). New York: Wiley.

Masten, A., & Curtis W. J. (2000). Integrating competence and psychopathology: Pathways toward a comprehensive science of adaptation in development. *Development and Psychopathology, 12,* 529–550.

McClelland, D., & Franz, C. (1992). Motivational and other sources of work accomplishments in mid-life: A longitudinal study. *Journal of Personality, 60*(No. 4), 679–707.

McGinn, L. K., & Young, J. E. (1996). Schema-focused therapy. In P. Salkovskis (Ed.), *Frontiers of cognitive therapy*. New York: Guilford Press.

McGoldrick, M. (1989). The joining of families through marriage: The new couple. In B. Carter and M. McGoldrick (Eds.), *The changing family life cycle: A framework for family therapy* (2nd ed., pp. 209–233). Boston: Allyn and Bacon.

McGoldrick, M., & Carter, B. (1989). Forming a remarried family. In B. Carter and M. McGoldrick (Eds.), *The changing family life cycle. A framework for family therapy* (2nd ed., pp. 399–429). Boston: Allyn and Bacon.

McMullin, R. (2000). *The new handbook of cognitive therapy techniques*. New York: W.W. Norton.

Meichenbaum, D. (1994). *A clinical handbook / practical therapist manual for assessing and treating adults with post-traumatic stress disorder (PTSD).* Waterloo Ontario: Institute Press.

Missildine, W. H. (1963). *Your inner child of the past*. New York: Simon and Schuster.

Moos, R., & Schaeffer, J. (1986). Life transitions and crises: A conceptual overview. In R.H. Moos (Ed.), *Coping with life crises: An integrated approach* (pp. 3–28). New York: Plenum Press.

Okun, B. (1984). *Working with adults: Individual, family and career development*. Monterey, CA: Brooks/Cole.

Padesky, C. (1994). Schema change processes in cognitive therapy. *Clinical psychology and psychotherapy, 1*(No. 5), 267–278.

Padesky, C. (1995). *Clinician's guide to mind over mood*. New York: Guilford Press.

Parker, G. (1988). Parental style and parental loss. In A. S. Henderson & G. D. Burrows (Eds.), *Handbook of social psychiatry* (pp. 15–25). Amsterdam: Elsevier.

Perlman, D. (1987). Further reflections on the present state of loneliness research. In M. Hojat & R. Crandall (Eds.), Loneliness: Theory, research, and applications. *Journal of Social Behavior and Personality, 2*, 89–104.

Perris, C. (1988). A theoretical framework for linking the experience of dysfunctional parental rearing attitudes with manifest psychopathology. *Acta Psychiatrica Scandinavica, 78*(Supplement No. 344), 93–110.

Perris, C., Arrindell, W.A., & Eisemann, M. (1994). *Parenting and psychopathology*. New York: John Wiley & Sons.

Peterson, C., & Seligman, M. (1984) Causal explanations as a risk factor for depression: Theory and evidence. *Psychological Review, 91*, 347–374.

Putallaz, M., & Dunn, S. E. (1990). The importance of peer relations. In M. Lewis & S. Miller (Eds.), *Handbook of developmental psychopathology*, (pp. 227—236). New York: Plenum Press.

Roeser, R., & Eccles, J. (2000). Schooling and mental health. In A. Sameroff, M. Lewis, & S. Miller (Eds.), *Handbook of developmental psychopathology* (2nd ed., pp. 135—156). New York: Kluwer Academic/Plenum.

Rokach, A. (1989). Antecedents of loneliness: A factorial analysis. *Journal of Psychology, 123*(4), 369–384.

Ruble, D., & Seedman, E. (1996). Social transitions: Windows into social psychological processes. In E. T. Higgins & A. Kruglanski (Eds.), *Social psychology: Handbook of basic principles* (pp. 830–856). New York: Guilford Press.

Russell, M., Henderson, C., & Blume, S. (1985). *Children of alcoholics: A review of the literature.* New York: Children of Alcoholics Foundation, Inc.

Rutter, M. (1985). Resilience in the face of adversity: Protective factors and resistance to psychiatric disorder. *British Journal of Psychiatry, 147,* 598–611.

Rutter, M., & Sroufe, L. A. (2000). Developmental psychopathology: Concepts and challenges. *Developmental Psychopathology, 12,* 265–296.

Skinner, E., & Wellborn, J. (1994). Coping during childhood and adolescence: A motivational perspective. In D. Featherman, R. Lerner, & M. Perlmutter (Eds.), *Life-span development and behavior: Vol. 12* (pp. 91–133). Hillsdale, NJ: Lawrence Erlbaum.

Sroufe, L. A. (1989). Pathways to adaptation and maladaptation: Psychopathology as developmental deviation. In D. Cicchetti (Ed.), *Rochester symposium on developmental psychopathology: Vol. 1* (pp. 13–40). Hillsdale, NJ: Lawrence Erlbaum.

Sroufe, L. A. (1997). Psychopathology as an outcome of development. *Development and Psychopathology, 9,* 251–268.

Suls, J., & Mullen, B. (1982). From the cradle to the grave: Comparison and self evaluation across the life span. In J. Suls (Ed.), *Psychological perspectives on the self* (pp. 97–128). Hillsdale, NJ: Lawrence Erlbaum.

Tamir, L. (1986). Men at middle age: Developmental transitions. In R. Moos (Ed.), *Coping with life crises: An integrated approach* (pp. 185–194). New York: Plenum Press.

Turner, N. W. (1980). Divorce in mid-life: Clinical implications and applications. In W. Norman & T. Scaramella (Eds.), *Mid-life: Developmental and clinical issues* (pp. 149–177). New York: Brunner/Mazel.

Vandenbos, G. R. (1998). Life-span developmental perspective on aging: An introductory overview. In I. Nordhus, G. Vandenbos, S. Berg, & P. Fromholt (Eds.), *Clinical Geropsychology* (pp. 3–14). Washington, DC: American Psychological Association.

White, L. (1994). Co-residence and leaving home: Young adults and their parents. *Annual Review of Sociology, 20,* 81–102.

Young, J. (1982). Loneliness, depression, and cognitive therapy: Theory and application. In L. A. Peplau & D. Perlman (Eds.), *Loneliness: A sourcebook of current theory, research, and therapy* (pp. 379—405). New York: Wiley Interscience.

Young, J. and Stein, D. (Eds.) (1992). *Cognitive science and clinical disorders.* New York: Academic Press.

Young, J. E. (1990). *Cognitive therapy for personality disorders: A schema-focused approach* (3rd ed.). Sarasota, FL: Professional Resource Exchange.

Young, J. E., Beck, A. T., & Weinberger, A. (1993). Depression. In D. H. Barlow (Ed.), *Clinical handbook of psychological disorders,* (2nd ed., pp. 240–277). New York: Guilford Press.

Young, J. E., and First, M. (1996). *Schema mode listing.* Cognitive Therapy Center of New York.

Young, J. E. & Gluhoski, V. L. (1996). Schema-focused diagnosis for personality disorders. In F. Kaslow (Ed.), *Handbook of relational diagnosis and dysfunctional family patterns* (pp. 300–321). New York: John Wiley & Sons.

Young, J. E. & Klosko, J. S. (1994). *Reinventing your life. How to break free from negative life patterns.* New York: Plume Books.

Young, J., Klosko, J., & Weishaar, M. (2003). *Schema therapy: A practitioner's guide.* New York: Guilford Press.

Zarb, J. (1992). *Cognitive behavioral assessment and therapy with adolescents.* New York: Brunner/Mazel, Inc.

INDEX